SWORDFISH

Also by David Wragg

Airlift: a History of Military Air Transport
Boats of the Air
Bombers: from the First World War to Kosovo
Carrier Combat
A Dictionary of Aviation
The Fleet Air Arm Handbook, 1939–45
Flight Before Flying
Flight with Power: the First Ten Years
Helicopters at War
Jane's Airforces of the World
The Last Great Siege 1940–43
The Offensive Weapon: the Strategy of Bombing
Snatching Defeat from the Jaws of Victory
Speed in the Air
Wings over the Sea
The World's Major Airlines and their Aircraft

SWORDFISH

THE STORY OF
THE TARANTO RAID

David Wragg

9010979550
940.542

Weidenfeld & Nicolson

LONDON

Weidenfeld & Nicolson

The Orion Publishing Group Ltd
Orion House
5 Upper Saint Martin's Lane
London WC2H 9EA

Copyright © David Wragg 2003
First published 2003

British Library Cataloguing-in-Publication Data

A catalogue record for this book is available
from the British Library

ISBN 0-297-84667-1

Distributed in the United States by
Sterling Publishing Co. Inc.
387 Park Avenue South
New York, NY 10016-8810

Printed and bound in Great Britain by
Butler & Tanner Ltd, Frome and London

Contents

Acknowledgements

In any book of this kind the author is always indebted to those whose help has been invaluable in researching photographs, maps, and the personal details of the many characters in his narrative. In particular, I am very grateful to Jerry Shore and his enthusiastic team at the Fleet Air Arm Museum (FAAM) at RNAS Yeovilton, and for the help provided by the Photographic Archive at the Imperial War Museum (IWM) in London, as well as for the help of their Sound Archive, notably with the material for Richard Janvrin.

Introduction

The year 1940 was probably the bleakest of the entire Second World War for Britain. In 1939, she had threatened to confront Germany in an attempt to save Poland, but failed to dent Germany's ambitions and together with the French found herself at war. After a period of relative calm, Germany had struck first at Denmark and Norway; Denmark had been overrun, and despite British and French intervention, Norway had also fallen. Then it was the turn of the Netherlands and Belgium, followed by France, after which Britain stood alone, facing not just Germany, but also Italy which had declared war shortly before the fall of France. The United States was yet to enter the war, the Soviet Union was still, if not a true ally of Nazi Germany, a collaborator in the subjection of Poland. Italy's intervention threatened the Maltese islands and the Balkans. British and Italian forces confronted each other in North Africa, the prize for the Italians being the Suez Canal. The collapse of France was followed by the Battle of Britain, and then came the blitz on British towns and cities. Meanwhile submarine warfare built up steadily, threatening to starve the country into submission.

The RAF's bombing raids during the first two years of war saw losses which often meant that as many as half of the aircraft never returned.

Amidst this gloomy outlook, the Royal Navy launched a daring raid against the Italian fleet. The original plan was to use the Mediterranean Fleet's two aircraft carriers, *Illustrious* and *Eagle*, but it was left to *Illustrious* alone, and twenty-one obsolete biplanes, to launch the Fleet Air Arm's attack on the Italian Fleet at Taranto in 1940. In the event, this weak force caused as much damage to the enemy as the entire Grand Fleet managed at the Battle of Jutland, yet for the loss of only two aircraft. The audacious raid on Taranto is sometimes credited with having given the Japanese the idea of a surprise attack on the United States Navy's Pacific Fleet at Pearl Harbor, although in reality this operation had been war-gamed before the outbreak of war. Nevertheless, the Imperial Japanese Navy was aware of the success of the operation – which forced Italy to base her major fleet units elsewhere for the duration of hostilities.

This book tells the story of this daring operation. It begins with a history of naval aviation and of the aircraft carrier, revealing the attitudes towards both that shaped naval strategy between the wars. Yet, amidst this refusal to recognise the potential of maritime aviation, others were considering the opportunities. The idea of a raid on Taranto was not borne out of the desperation of the dark days of 1940, but instead had been considered as a response to the Italian invasion of Abyssinia during the late 1930s. Had the League of Nations taken more robust action against Italy, it might have been a precursor of today's UN peacekeeping efforts.

The book starts with a look at the ships and aircraft intended for this great operation. The ships included the modern HMS *Illustrious*, but the aircraft were none other than the obsolete and lumbering Fairey Swordfish, yet much loved by its crews and nicknamed the 'Stringbag', an affectionate reference to the complex of wire rigging and wooden struts that kept the biplane together. Then there was the British naval commander in the Mediterranean, whose attitude was such that when summoned to a meeting the CO of *Illustrious*, Captain Denis Boyd, feared that he was to be told to take his ship from the Mediterranean. The circumstances leading to HMS *Eagle*'s withdrawal and the delay of the operation are also covered in the planning of the attack.

Personalities and the part they played are important to the narrative, including the anxious days before the raid, when problems of reliability affected the aircraft. The operation itself is of course central to the book, with the reactions of those involved. Just two of the twenty-one aircraft were shot down, and the crew of one of these survived to become PoWs.

The book considers the impact of Taranto, both on the strategic situation in the Mediterranean and on future naval operations, as well as on the outcome of the Second World War. It also covers the revenge taken on *Illustrious* by the Luftwaffe and the Regia Aeronautica early the following year, and records the fate of the ship and those involved.

HMS Illustrious, 1940

Starboard side view

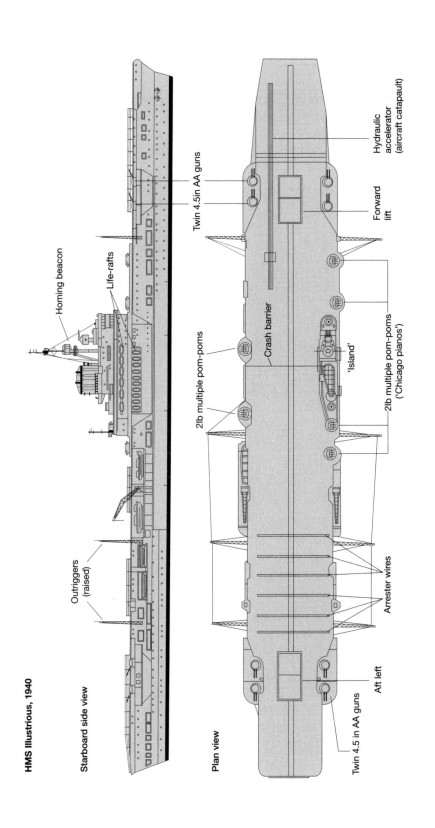

Homing beacon

Life-rafts

Outriggers (raised)

Twin 4.5in AA guns

2lb multiple pom-poms

Crash barrier

'Island'

2lb multiple pom-poms ('Chicago pianos')

Hydraulic accelerator (aircraft catapault)

Forward lift

Arrester wires

Plan view

Aft left

Twin 4.5 in AA guns

Map of the Mediterranean

SWITZ.

AUSTRIA

FRANCE

Venice

Trieste

Genoa

G. of
Genoa

ITALY

ADRIATIC

CORSICA

SPAIN

BALEARIC
IS.

SARDINIA

Naples

TYRRHENIAN
SEA

Cagliari

Palermo   Messina

Gibraltar

Algiers

Bone

Tunis

C. Bon

Reggio

SICILY

Oran

Syracuse

Pantellaria

MALTA

ALGERIA

Lampedusa

Kerkenah Is.

MOROCCO

TUNISIA

Tripoli

⊗ Flying-off position,
   HMS Illustrious. 11 November 1940

×════× The battle of Matapan

TRIPOLITANIA

0   100   200   300   400   500 miles

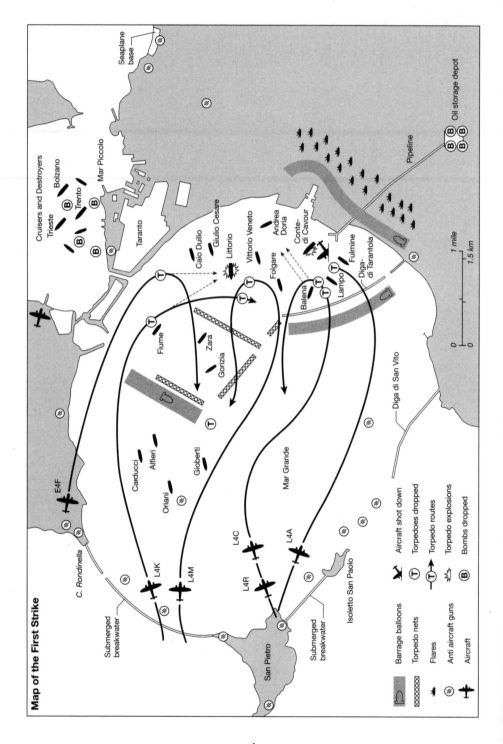

Map of the First Strike

Seaplane base

Oil storage depot

Pipeline

Cruisers and Destroyers

Trieste
Bolzano
Trento

Mar Piccolo

Taranto

Caio Duilio
Giulio Cesare
Littorio
Vittorio Veneto
Andrea Doria
Conte di Cavour

Folgare
Fulmine
Diga di Tarantola
Lampo
Balena

Fiume
Zara
Gorizia

E4F

Carducci
Alfieri
Oriani
Gioberti

Diga di San Vito

C. Rondinella

L4K
L4M
L4C
L4R
L4A

Mar Grande

Submerged breakwater

Submerged breakwater

Isoletto San Paolo

San Pietro

1 mile
1.5 km
0
0

Barrage balloons
Torpedo nets
Flares
Anti aircraft guns
Aircraft

Aircraft shot down
Torpedoes dropped
Torpedo routes
Torpedo explosions
Bombs dropped

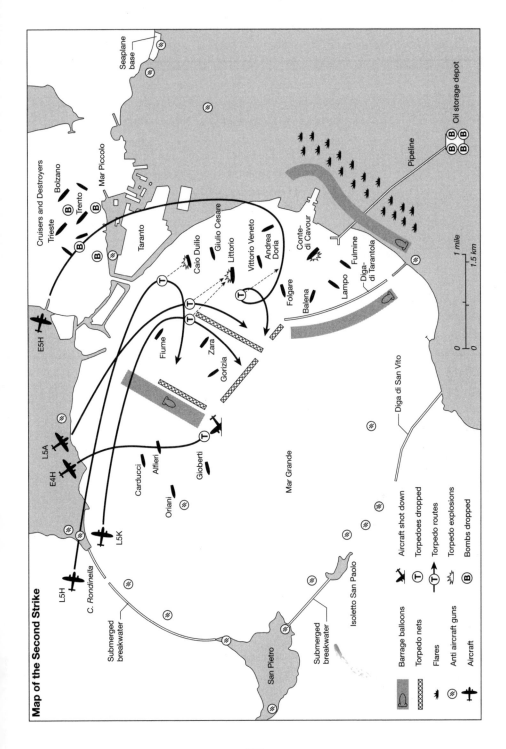

Map of the Second Strike

Cruisers and Destroyers
Trieste
Bolzano
Mar Piccolo
Seaplane base
Oil storage depot
Pipeline
Trento
Taranto
Caio Duilio
Giulio Cesare
Littorio
Vittorio Veneto
Andrea Doria
Conte di Cavour
Folgare
Balena
Fulmine
Lampo
Diga di Tarantola
Fiume
Zara
Gorizia
E5H
L5A
E4H
Carducci
Alfieri
Oriani
Gioberti
L5K
C. Rondinella
L5H
Submerged breakwater
San Pietro
Submerged breakwater
Isoletto San Paolo
Mar Grande
Diga di San Vito

Barrage balloons
Torpedo nets
Flares
Anti aircraft guns
Aircraft
Aircraft shot down
Torpedoes dropped
Torpedo routes
Torpedo explosions
Bombs dropped

0   1 mile
0   1.5 km

XV

CHAPTER ONE

A New Dimension to Naval Warfare

The American naval officer stared in disbelief at the aircraft, a biplane of obsolete appearance with wings folded back to allow it to be struck down on the lift into a carrier's hangar deck, its struts and wires giving a built-in headwind. With its three cockpits, all open to the elements, it looked as if it belonged to an earlier conflict.

'Where did that come from?' he asked.

'Fairey's', came the reply from a British naval officer standing near by.

He stroked his chin thoughtfully.

'That figures,' he replied.

The American knew little or nothing of Sir Richard Fairey's small company that had been in naval aviation almost from the start, building the World War One Campania floatplane. Later, it had also provided the Royal Air Force with the elegant Fox day bomber. He certainly could not be expected to know that in little more than a decade hence this same company was to provide a sleek world air speed record-breaking aircraft, the Delta 2, followed by the first feasible vertical-take-off transport, the Rotodyne, abandoned after the company was taken over by Westland, even though at the start of the twenty-first century others are still struggling to make this concept a reality.

If the Americans, with their powerful and robust naval fighters and attack aircraft, could afford to be dismissive of British naval aircraft, they were much kinder about the ships, and not simply because they were a welcome change from the alcohol-free ships of the USN. They were even envious, learning the hard way, as the war raged across the Pacific and the Japanese flung their Kamikaze suicide bombers at the allied fleets, of the virtues of the fast armoured aircraft carrier, the Illustrious-class with their armoured flight decks and hangar decks. One US liaison officer serving with the British Pacific Fleet was to comment: 'When a Kamikaze hits a US

1

carrier, it's six months repair at Pearl. In a Limey carrier, it's a case of "Sweepers, man your brooms!"'

It was not as if the Royal Navy was new to aviation at the beginning of World War Two. Both the British and American navies had been involved with naval aviation from the start, and by 1940, the Royal Navy should have been able to reap the benefit of continuous experience of naval aviation for thirty years. It hadn't. First it had to allow the Army control of all aviation between 1912 and 1914, with the Royal Flying Corps maintaining a Naval Wing, but control of naval aviation returned to the Royal Navy in July 1914, with the formation of the Royal Naval Air Service. Yet, even before the so-called Great War ended in November 1918, appropriately enough on 1 April, 'All Fools' Day', it had to hand over 2,500 of its aircraft to the newly formed Royal Air Force, and no less than 55,000 experienced personnel followed them. The RAF then controlled naval aviation for the next twenty-one years. The state of the ships and of the aircraft in 1940 told the story.

A SEA CHANGE FOR NAVAL WARFARE

Traditionally, naval warfare had always involved ships engaging one another, often at extremely close quarters. The great British naval hero, Horatio Nelson, had, after all, been killed at Trafalgar in 1805 by the musket of a marksman rather than by a cannon ball. The effective distance of a cannon ball was itself very limited, less than half-a-mile. The advent of breech-loading heavy naval artillery changed this only by degree, allowing ships with heavy calibre weapons such as the 15in guns of battleships and battlecruisers to strike at one another at distances of more than twenty miles. These circumstances created a mindset that encouraged the early aeroplane to be seen simply as a means of scouting for enemy warships, and then reporting the fall of fire. Many of the traditionalists took a dim view of the aeroplane, yet even before the outbreak of World War One, naval officers in the United Kingdom and the United States had experimented flying from warships, and had dropped a torpedo from an aircraft. Ships had been converted to carry seaplanes in both these countries as well as in France.

There were those in the armed forces who saw the aeroplane as being unsporting, with one army officer even complaining that the presence of aircraft on manoeuvres quite spoiled the event! He had his naval counter-parts. Even between the two world wars, one naval officer thought that having an aircraft aboard could be useful if attending functions ashore while the ship was anchored some way off.

Fortunately, there were many air-minded people both inside and outside the Royal Navy with an interest in helping the service realise the vast potential of the aeroplane. In 1910, the Royal Aero Club put two Short biplanes at the disposal of Royal Navy officers wishing to learn to fly. Those who were interested needed more than the nerve to get airborne in flimsy machines with unreliable engines; they also had to face opposition from their senior officers. Many a commanding officer felt it was his duty to discourage a promising young officer from learning to fly rather than, for example, specialising in gunnery. Those eager to fly often did so at their own cost. One officer, Sub-Lieutenant F. E. T. Hewlett, was even taught to fly by his mother, a woman of some character who flew in poor weather wearing sabots and smoking a pipe. Nevertheless, the die-hard traditionalists of the 'big gun' navy were soon to find that not everyone at high level shared their outlook: that official interest in aviation did exist may be gathered from the decision by the Admiralty as early as 1911 that in wartime the role of the naval aeroplane would be:

- Reconnaissance of enemy ports.
- Reconnaissance of the area surrounding the fleet at sea.
- Location of submarines.
- Detection of enemy minefields.
- Spotting, and no doubt correcting, the fall of shot from the fleet.

Flying an aeroplane in the midst of a naval battle was not an easy option, needing to keep away from the AA defences of increasingly heavily-armed capital ships and cruisers.

This somewhat restricted role envisaged for the aeroplane took account of its obvious limitations. Using aircraft to carry the battle to the enemy beyond the range of the guns of the fleet did not enter the equation at this stage and, of course, no one really considered that aircraft should defend the fleet from attacks by enemy planes. It would be wrong to blame traditional naval attitudes for this. The aircraft of the day were frail contraptions, quite likely to be blown backwards by a strong headwind. Much was to change over the next three years.

Nevertheless, progress was also being made ashore. So much so that as the German aerial threat to Britain began to materialise, the First Lord of the Admiralty, the ambitious Winston Churchill, was able to volunteer the Royal Naval Air Service for the aerial defence of the British Isles. The foe was not so much the aeroplane as the airship.

Given these circumstances, it comes as a surprise to find that the first effective use of naval aircraft came as early as Christmas Day 1914, when seven seaplanes from the seaplane tenders HMS *Engadine*, *Express* and *Riviera* bombed German airship hangars at Nordholz, near Cuxhaven. This was impressive, coming so early in the war and only four years after British naval officers had started experimenting with aircraft. Yet the seaplane was pitifully inadequate for all that the more air-minded officers expected of it. To the still poor performance of the early aircraft engines had to be added the extra weight and drag of the floats. Seaplanes, as bombers, could not carry a truly effective load, and as fighters, they had great difficulty in reaching, let alone out-climbing, an airship. Taking-off could be a problem, since hydro-aeroplanes – the term for seaplanes, flying boats and amphibians – were notoriously reluctant to 'unstick' in calm water, and liable to be damaged in rough water.

Many solutions were tried. One of the most promising was to launch aircraft from lighters towed behind destroyers at high speed; this got landplane fighters into the air over the fleet or any escorted merchant vessels, but sacrificed the aircraft as the pilot had to ditch when the sortie ended. The use of destroyers was significant. The seaplane carriers, many of them converted Channel and Irish Sea packets (those from the Isle of Man seemed to have been favourites) could not keep up with the fleet. Even if aircraft could be launched from the ship itself, this involved turning into the wind, which could mean leaving the formation of the fleet, and then struggling to catch up afterwards.

Converting warships to act as seaplane tenders was frowned upon. Even the light cruiser HMS *Hermes*, grudgingly converted to carry a seaplane for the 1913 Naval Review, was quickly converted back again. Such ships were too valuable in wartime and, moreover, the extent of any conversion would be costly and take too long. Merchant vessels were easier to convert, having both deck and hold space. The replacement for *Hermes* was a humble collier, given the grand title of HMS *Ark Royal*. In addition to the conversion of English Channel and Irish Sea packets, the decision was taken to convert the 18,000 ton Cunard liner *Campania*, an ambitious project for the time as she was larger and faster than anything used earlier. The conversion was also the most extensive – virtually producing a hybrid seaplane carrier and aircraft carrier with a 200ft wooden platform built over her forecastle, so that the new Fairey Campania seaplane could take off on wheeled trolleys placed under the floats. The aircraft could be recovered, landing in the sea, after each sortie. HMS *Campania* joined the fleet in 1915, and the following year, the ship's fore-funnel was divided to allow the rudimentary flight deck to be extended further aft. All this, and yet the Fairey Campania cruised at just 80mph, and had a service ceiling of 2,000 feet. By comparison, a Sopwith Camel flown off a lighter towed from a destroyer had a maximum speed of 120mph.

The aeroplane had shown that it could provide both the means of attack and of defence at sea, while it had served on reconnaissance in the lead-up to the Battle of Jutland. The challenge facing naval aircraft, whether based ashore or afloat, was that they had a more demanding role than those intended to attack land targets. Many land targets were 'soft', including barracks and railway junctions. Major warships, which then included battleships, were heavily armoured, so that bombs could, and did, bounce off; and even cruisers and destroyers had a good turn of speed and were often highly manoeuvrable. Lifting the warload that could inflict real damage was almost impossible. This was only part of the problem. Aircraft attacking warships had to face a very high rate of anti-aircraft fire from a highly concentrated armament fed by mechanised ammunition-handling systems, seldom available to shore-based artillery.

GOOD FORTUNE FROM MISFORTUNE

Just as it seemed that the Royal Navy was never to be offered ships that were large enough and fast enough to match the aspirations of the naval airmen, and meet the objectives of naval aviation, the situation changed with what was virtually the gift of a major warship. The battlecruiser HMS *Furious* was the last of three ships of what had became known in naval circles as the 'Outrageous'-class. The First Sea Lord, Admiral of the Fleet Lord Fisher, recalled from retirement to make the British fleet ready for war with Germany and her allies, pressed ahead with an ambitious plan to land British and Russian forces in Pomerania, on Germany's Baltic coastline, as close as possible to Berlin, and then advance inland. Central to this plan were three battlecruisers, with a heavy armament and a shallow draught making them ideal for operations off the coast. Two of the ships, *Glorious* and *Courageous*, had four 15in guns in two turrets, but *Furious* had two massive 18in guns. The direct attack on Germany was a non-starter. The British element of the invasion would have been easy targets sailing through the narrow straits between Denmark and the rest of Scandinavia, and could easily have been bottled up in the Baltic. And the Russian Army, it was soon clear, ill-equipped and infiltrated by revolutionary activists, was going nowhere other than home.

The three battlecruisers had an unhappy reception by the rest of the Fleet. To the wits on the lower deck, *Courageous* was known as *Outrageous*, *Glorious* as *Uproarious*, or alternatively the three ships were *Helpless*, *Hopeless* and *Useless*. These unfortunate nicknames soon proved well deserved, when on the night of 8 January 1917, in the undemanding weather conditions of a sea state 4, barely choppy water, *Courageous* – her stem lifting by 3ft – broke her back.

An embarrassed Admiralty was faced with making the best of a bad job, not wishing to scrap a major warship in the midst of hostilities. Certainly, no one wished to admit that they had got it wrong. Seeking a worthwhile role for the new ships, it was decided to convert *Furious*, still on the slipway, to launch aircraft. The fleet's misfortune was to be good fortune for the naval aviators. Her forward turret was replaced by an aircraft hangar with the flight deck running from the roof of the hangar to the bows, although the after turret was initially retained. This soon proved useless, as one of her officers later recorded that when the massive 18in gun fired, her lightly built hull rippled and rivets flew out of the plates across his cabin.

Landplane operation required that aircraft could land on the ship, and on 2 August 1917, Squadron Commander (the RNAS equivalent of Lieutenant-Commander) E. H. Dunning flew a Sopwith Camel fighter past the superstructure of the ship to land safely on the forward deck, just 228ft long, helped by his fellow officers who dragged the aircraft down on to the deck by grabbing hold of the toggles placed under the lower wing trailing edges. This was risky, since the deck really was only suitable for taking off. So it happened a few days later that a second attempt by Dunning resulted in his frail aircraft being blown over the side of the ship, and the unfortunate pilot drowned before he could escape from the cockpit.

The following year, *Furious* emerged from a further rebuild having lost her aft turret and gained a separate platform, 300ft long, for 'landing on', as naval terminology describes a deck landing. Aircraft could be man-handled on decking running on either side of the funnel and superstructure connecting the landing and take-off platforms. In this form, she could carry up to twenty aircraft, and had the high maximum speed of 32.5 knots. Landing was helped by arrester wires running fore and aft catching hooks under the undercarriage spreader bar, with a net to catch any aircraft missing the hooks. Alternatively, the landing platform could carry an airship.

In this form, *Furious* launched her aircraft in a successful air raid against the German airship sheds at Tondern in northern Germany on 19 July 1918, with her seven Sopwith Camels destroying the Zeppelins *L.54* and *L.60*. Naval aviation had indeed shown how it could add to the striking power of the fleet.

By this time, two further developments had taken place. First, the Royal Navy had gained a second aircraft carrier. An Italian liner still under construction was requisitioned and converted on the slipway to become HMS *Argus*, joining the fleet in September 1918, but too late to play a part in the war. Smaller and slower than *Furious*, at 15,775 tons and 20 knots, *Argus* nevertheless had the first through flight deck running from stem to stern, and no superstructure, since experience with *Furious* had already shown this to cause turbulence, which gave the still frail aircraft of the day many difficulties. A bridge, incorporating a small wheelhouse, was mounted on a lift, but this had to be put down during flying operations, causing difficulties since this proved to be the time when good all-round visibility was most needed by those running the ship. Ever keen to let his views on a new ship be heard, one wit of the lower deck called *Argus* the 'Flat Iron'.

The other development, and in the long run far more important, was that the Royal Naval Air Service no longer existed. The Admiralty had lost control of naval aviation on 1 April 1918, when both the RNAS and the Army's Royal Flying Corps had been merged to form the Royal Air Force. This move was on the recommendation of the Smuts Report, compiled by the South African general and statesman. The objective was to avoid duplication and overlap, since in the air defence of British cities and the air war in France, rivalry and replication between the RNAS and RFC had hindered operational effectiveness. It was to prove a clumsy solution. It was also strange, because the RNAS had been formed in 1914 from what had been the RFC's Naval Wing on the grounds that 'interchangeability' of pilots and observers between army and naval aviation was impractical. Most naval airmen became members of the RAF, with 55,000 transferring to the new service which also inherited 2,500 aircraft, but a few were allowed to remain in the Royal Navy, flying hydro-aeroplanes off battleships and cruisers. A partial transfer of shore-based naval fighter and bomber units into the new RAF would have been far more satisfactory in the long run, as indeed happened in France after the creation of the Armée de l'Air some time later.

The United States insisted on continuing the division of service aviation, resisting calls for an air force until 1948, although the United States Army Air Corps, later the United States Army Air Force, did develop primarily as a strategic air arm rather than as a tactical air arm for support of ground forces.

SEEKING THE IDEAL CARRIER

The ideal design for an aircraft carrier proved to be elusive, and the result was to be achieved by trial and error. While *Argus* was an improvement over *Furious*, she had faults of her own. Instead of a conventional smokestack, boiler-room smoke was vented through large ducts at the stern, making the landing approach difficult and unpleasant. The next stage was to convert the battleship *Almirante Cochrane*, under construction for the Chilean Navy and on which work had been suspended on the outbreak of war. Commissioning as HMS *Eagle* in 1924, the new carrier was the first to have the classic starboard island, albeit with two smokestacks, and in an effort to cut turbulence also introduced the cambered 'round down' that was to become a feature of British carriers, largely because British naval aircraft tended to be less robust than their US counterparts. At 22,600 tons, *Eagle* was a useful size, although somewhat slower than *Furious*, with a maximum speed of around 24 knots.

The choice of the starboard side for the island has puzzled many. One explanation could be that before the introduction of the rudder, ships were steered using a large oar on this side, with the term 'starboard' originating from 'steerboard'. As experience was gained, it also became apparent that in an emergency, most pilots tended to veer left. When the Japanese built two carriers with islands on the port side, to ease congestion over a carrier force when operating abeam of carriers with a starboard island, the number of serious accidents is reputed to have doubled. The design features introduced on *Eagle* were continued with the fourth British aircraft carrier, HMS *Hermes*, the first to be designed from the keel upwards as an aircraft carrier. Laid down in 1918, the construction of *Hermes* was delayed while the ideal layout for an aircraft carrier was finalised, and she was not completed until 1924. Her starboard island incorporated a single large funnel. At 10,850 tons, *Hermes* was the smallest fleet carrier ever operated by the Royal Navy, and not especially fast with a maximum speed of 25 knots. As aircraft sizes and take-off and landing speeds increased, she was to prove too small and too slow by the outbreak of World War Two.

The new ships offered a much longer flight deck. That of *Argus* was 550ft in length; *Eagle*'s was 652ft and *Hermes* had a 548ft-long flight deck. These lengths were academic, since in practice aircraft seldom, if ever, had the entire flight deck length in which to take off or land. Aircraft for an operation would be lined up on the flight deck, sometimes in an echelon formation on either side, ready for take-off, so only the last aircraft would have the entire flight deck length. The leader might have little more than half the length. As flight deck lengths increased, an additional advantage was that larger formations of aircraft could be put into the air.

The inter-war period is remembered by many as being the heyday of the hydro-aeroplane, the seaplane and the flying boat, which many saw as holding the key to the future of aviation. It was not altogether surprising that the Admiralty also hedged its bets, and continued to place seaplane carriers in service, with *Nairana*, *Pegasus* and *Vindictive*, the last-mentioned being a converted cruiser while the others were all converted merchantmen, entering service in 1917 and 1918. It also became standard for battleships and cruisers to carry amphibians for reconnaissance and communications duties, with up to three aircraft for a battleship and one or two for a cruiser, but the numbers varied according to the design of individual ships. Flying these aircraft remained the preserve of naval officers, not least because one of the tasks remained as plotting and correcting the fall of shot from the mother ships' guns.

INTO ACTION

While the carrier fleet was literally building, British naval aviation, even under RAF control, had not been idle. Whereas World War One is best remembered for the collapse of the Austro-Hungarian Empire, it also marked the final death throes of the Ottoman Empire, which had been allied with the Central Powers. Thus the immediate post-war period was far from peaceful following the collapse of the Central Powers with the break-up of that empire and the overthrow of the sultanate in Turkey, while Russia was already in revolution and civil war.

Allied intervention, originally designed to keep Russia in World War One, continued after the Armistice, and aircraft from the seaplane tender HMS *Vindictive* bombed the Red Fleet in Kronstadt Harbour on 18 August 1919. Fighting erupted between Turkish nationalists and occupying Greek forces in Thrace in 1920, after which British occupation forces in Istanbul, then known as Constantinople, and Chanak were confronted by Turkish forces. The seaplane carrier HMS *Ark Royal* brought five Fairey IIID sea-planes from Egypt to fly reconnaissance patrols, and also evacuated British forces from Chanak. Additional Fairey IIIDs and a number of Nieuport Nightjar fighters later arrived aboard HMS *Argus*.

British defence policy during the inter-war period was undermined by a number of difficulties. The new RAF was rapidly slimmed down to just twelve squadrons, ostensibly to eliminate rivalries between former RNAS and RFC members. Growth from this small size was seriously inhibited by financial constraints and by the adoption of the so-called Ten Year Rule, which postulated that the UK would have ten years in which to prepare for any emerging threat. Events were to prove this to be unrealistic. Anxious to prove that it had a role, and to ward off attempts by the Army to regain control of all service aviation as during 1912–14, the RAF for a while became heavily involved in the process known as air control in Mesopotamia, now Iraq. The needs of the fleet were largely neglected, partly due to a failure to appreciate their importance, but also because there was little enough money for the fighter and bomber elements. In an attempt to improve RAF/RN co-operation, the Fleet Air Arm of the Royal Air Force was formed following the recommendations of the Balfour Committee of 1923. Mean-while, the Washington Naval Treaty of 1922 had attempted to restrict the size of warships, setting an upper limit of 27,000 tons on new vessels of any category, and also restricting armament. Individual limits existed for every category of warship, with upper tonnage limits for type of ship, and overall total tonnages for each type. Cruisers, for example, were limited to an indi-vidual maximum of 10,000 tons. Both the Royal Navy and the United States Navy were given a maximum fleet tonnage of 525,000 tons, and within this the total tonnage of the carrier force was restricted in both cases to a total of 135,000 tons. The Treaty provisions were significant for the development of the carrier fleets, since, in the case of the Royal Navy and the United States Navy, total carrier tonnage amounted to more than a quarter of their total warship tonnage.

There were other restrictions as well, including a maximum gun size for aircraft carriers of 8 inches, but no British carrier ever had an armament of this calibre. Important distinctions were also made between types of warship; the difference between a heavy cruiser and a light cruiser, for example, was that the former was limited to 8in guns and the latter to 6in, tonnage having nothing to do with the classification.

The Washington Naval Treaty had the unexpected consequence of acting as a spur to aircraft carrier construction. This was partly due to the anxiety among the signatories that they should make full use of their total tonnage allowance, but also because the UK, USA and Japan all had battlecruisers in excess of their total allowance for these ships. The Royal Navy took the two unhappy sister ships of HMS *Furious*, *Courageous* and *Glorious*, and started a lengthy conversion to provide two additional carriers which joined the fleet in 1928 and 1930 respectively. Both ships reflected the now accepted thinking on carrier design, with starboard islands. They also incorporated a separate lower flight deck running from the hangar to the bows, intended to be a taking-off deck.

In the days before the concept of an angled flight deck had even been thought of, the separate deck for taking-off was an early attempt to ensure that aircraft could be landed and flown off at the same time; but it had a short life as aircraft sizes and speeds rose and the deck became too short, and eventually fell out of use, even though during one of her many conversions, *Furious* was also to gain this feature. Her two sisters, known as the Courageous-class, had flight decks of 530ft in length, as well as the short take-off deck from the upper hangar. To help take-offs, a slight incline was incorporated into the main flight deck at its forward end. Later, hydraulic accelerators were fitted to enable larger and heavier aircraft to be handled, especially in conditions with moderate winds. The Courageous-class have been described as the most satisfactory aircraft carriers in service with the Royal Navy during the early 1930s.

Eventually, after her modifications, *Furious* had a flight deck length of 576ft, plus another 200ft for the lower flying-off deck, about a quarter of it being in the upper of the two hangars with which she was now blessed.

The aeroplane had arrived in naval use somewhat later than the other significant new development in warfare at sea – the submarine. In two world wars, both were to show that they were to be the weapons of the future. It was perhaps not surprising that attempts were made to marry the two together with the aircraft-carrying submarine. As with so many of the early aircraft carriers, such a submarine was a conversion of an existing craft, in this case the British 'M'-class submarine. In their original form the three boats of this class were what the French described as 'corsair sub-marines' in that each carried a single 12in gun salvaged from a Majestic-class battleship. The idea was that the submarines would surface to destroy enemy merchant shipping. The Admiralty eventually decided that any target worthy of 12in shelling was worth a torpedo, at far less risk to the submarine and her crew.

The submarine *M2* was converted to carry an aircraft and recommissioned in 1927. A hangar was built forward of the conning tower, or fin, which also had a derrick fitted to lift seaplanes out of the water after landing. When the submarine surfaced, the hangar door would fold flat and a catapult launcher would be assembled over the door and the deck. The small Parnall concern built a floatplane, the Peto biplane, that could fit into the hangar. On landing beside the submarine, the Peto would be picked up out of the sea by the derrick, and returned to the catapult rail to have its wings folded and tucked back inside the hangar. The Peto was so small and weight-sensitive that its two-man crew had to wear plimsolls – legend has it that they received double danger money, flyers' pay and submariners'. Much was made of the safety precautions preventing both the outer and inner hangar doors from being open as the submarine dived, but on 26 January 1932, while diving off Portland, the submarine flooded and she disappeared with the loss of some sixty officers and men.

A further naval agreement came at London in 1930. Growing experience of the aircraft carrier and of developments in aviation meant that several of the participants wanted the maximum size of carrier raised from 27,000 tons. The UK took the contrary view, and actually wanted the upper limit reduced to 22,000 tons, less than the tonnage of all but two of the Royal Navy's existing six carriers, *Hermes* and *Argus*. This set a demanding task for the designers of the Royal Navy's next carrier, only the second British ship to be designed as a carrier from the keel up. The new ship, HMS *Ark*

Royal, saved weight by having minimal armour, except for some around the two hangar decks. The flight deck was not armoured, but she was unusual among British ships in having three lifts. *Ark Royal's* hull was plated up to flight deck level, while the flight deck was extended fore and aft beyond the stem and stern to provide the maximum possible length; at 78oft this was more than 20oft longer than any of her predecessors. At the time of her laying down, her capacity was put at seventy-two aircraft, but on operations sixty was more realistic. Her maximum speed was 32 knots.

Although many believe that the Illustrious-class were the first British warships to use the barrier landing system, adopted from the Americans, this had been installed in *Ark Royal* before *Illustrious* was completed. The new system ensured that aircraft missing the arrester wires were stopped before reaching the forward part of the flight deck, often used as an aircraft park or where aircraft just landed might be in the process of being 'struck down' into the hangar. In practice, the barrier system was little used aboard *Ark Royal,* and certainly at first she did not use a batsman to signal aircraft down on to the flight deck, although this was an idea that had been rapidly gaining favour in the Royal Navy as carrier aircraft became larger and faster. The concept had originated with the United States Navy, and strangely, until much later in the war, the Royal Navy used its own different system of batsman's signals.

By the time the '*Ark*' joined the fleet in 1938, the danger signs were clear. War was a certainty, it was only a question of when. Two new aircraft carriers had been ordered in 1936, originally as replacements for the first generation ships, *Furious, Argus, Eagle* and *Hermes*, whose limitations were by then all too apparent. Two more were ordered in 1937, and two more in 1938 as it soon became evident that, rather than replacing the earlier ships, some of which were already in reserve, the newcomers would be additional carriers. Indeed, so much was the Admiralty exercised by the need for more flight decks, that various conversions of merchant vessels were being considered, and at one stage it was even suggested that the two giant Cunard transatlantic liners, *Queen Mary* and the larger *Queen Elizabeth*, still under construction at the time – together the pride of the British merchant fleet – should be converted to aircraft carriers. It was the potential of these liners as fast troopships that saved them from conversion.

The new ships, the Illustrious-class, varied in several respects, but broke away from the constraints that had affected *Ark Royal*. They were heavily armoured, with the single hangar deck being in effect an armoured 'box', and were unusual for British warships in having three shafts. Despite being 23,000 tons – and the later ships were to be even larger – they carried fewer aircraft than the *Ark Royal* because of the armour plating and the single hangar. The flight deck was also slightly shorter, at 744ft. In addition to the strong armour, the ships also had a more effective anti-aircraft defence than their predecessors, each having eight turrets, two on each side, fore and aft, at the edges of the flight deck with two 4.5in AA guns apiece. A seventh ship, HMS *Unicorn*, was laid down with just two shafts and increased hangar headroom to act as a maintenance carrier; she was also to prove the fore-runner of the light fleet carriers of the future.

In laying down the specifications for the Illustrious-class, the Admiralty had already decided that a lightly-armoured carrier such as *Ark Royal* would be vulnerable during wartime, especially to air attack and to heavy shellfire. This proved to be the case. The author's father served aboard the ship at the beginning of the war, and recalled small 20lb practice bombs falling off an aircraft as it landed, and exploding, punching holes in the flight deck. The irony was that her fate was to sink as the result of being torpedoed by a U-boat, and then only after a prolonged period afloat during which efforts were made to save her.

The first three of the six ships, *Illustrious*, *Victorious* and *Formidable*, were much alike. Although nominally part of the same class, the later ships differed considerably, some having two hangar decks. Many prefer therefore to talk of the Illustrious- and Implacable-classes, with the latter comprising two decks. Of the original ships, the fourth, *Indomitable*, was something of a hybrid, incorporating a number of modifications later adopted for the two Implacable-class ships.

Illustrious herself was 744ft overall, with a 96ft beam and a draught of 25ft, and was powered by three turbines providing 110,000hp and a speed of 30 knots. Her standard displacement was 23,000 tons, but at full load, with fuel, supplies and aircraft, this rose to 28,000 tons. The freeboard (the height between the waterline and the flight deck) was 43ft compared with just over 60ft for the *Ark Royal*. The flight deck armour was 3in thick over the hangar, but just 1½in at the ends fore and aft, with 4½in thick armour to the sides of the hangar and at the bulkheads fore and aft, and a 3in hangar deck. Heavier armour plating might, in the light of subsequent events, have been useful, but in a ship there is a balance to be struck between armour and the risk of becoming too top heavy. The only breaks in the armoured hangar and flight-deck box were the two lifts. Further protection came in the form of armoured shutters or curtains to break the hangar up into three compartments in case of fire. Waterline armour plating was 4½in, and the steering compartment, or flat, was protected by 3in armour. The bridge had light armour to protect against shrapnel or strafing.

The number of aircraft that could be accommodated in the single hangar deck, with its 16ft headroom, was far less than in *Ark Royal's* two hangar decks, just thirty-six, with the emphasis on what today would be counted as strike aircraft, rather than fighters.

One naval officer with experience of the old converted battlecruiser carriers was later to remark that comparing *Illustrious* with *Courageous* was like comparing the new carrier with Noah's Ark!

Laid down in April 1937, *Illustrious* was launched in April 1939 and completed fitting out a year later. A shake-down cruise to Bermuda was followed by a refit during which some problems were rectified.

THE ROYAL NAVY TAKES OVER

These developments were to give the Royal Navy the best aircraft carriers of World War Two. Meanwhile, the argument over control of naval aviation had come to a head, with intense lobbying by the Admiralty. By this time, the belief that the aeroplane was here to stay and that any modern fleet worthy of the name needed its own organic air power had reached the top, for it was due largely to the determination of the First Sea Lord, Admiral Sir Ernle Chatfield (later Admiral of the Fleet Lord Chatfield) that the battle for control of naval aviation was won. On 30 July 1937 the Minister for the Coordination of Defence, Sir Thomas Inskip, recommended to the Government that the Admiralty be given sole control of naval aviation. The Admiralty formally took control on 24 May 1939, but before this Parliament gave the Admiralty permission to implement a fourfold increase in Fleet Air Arm personnel. In addition to recruiting pilots and observers, and telegraphist air gunners (TAGs), the fleet was trawled for volunteers to train as maintainers. In fact, many, including officers for training as observers, were 'pressed' into the Fleet Air Arm in addition to those volunteers who saw better opportunities for advancement in the new arm of the service, especially as they took over from members of the RAF who remained during the transitional period. Some 1,500 RAF personnel also volunteered to transfer to the Royal Navy.

Even so, in contrast to many other countries, prominent among them the United States and France, control of shore-based maritime reconnaissance remained with the RAF.

While still under RAF control, the Fleet Air Arm had already replaced the series of flights numbered in the 400 series, and had instead been assigned squadron numbers in the 700 and 800 range to distinguish them from standard RAF squadrons. This practice survived the transfer, with squadron numbers in the 700 range being reserved for 'second line' non-combat squadrons. These included units involved in training and operational conversion, in contrast to the RAF practice of having numbered operational training units (OTUs), and, of course, the essential fleet requirements units, towing target practice drogues, helping in radar calibration and many other less glamorous duties. Combat squadrons, whether fighter, torpedo bomber or bomber, used numbers in the 800 series.

Yet the Inskip Award could not of its own repair the damage of neglect over two decades. The problem lay in the aircraft available to the Fleet Air Arm. There was the Gloster Sea Gladiator, a flying museum piece and a cousin to the RAF's Gladiator fighter, the last biplane fighter, and entering service at a time when the future shape of aviation already lay with the monoplane. The Fairey Swordfish was the mainstay for offensive operations and for anti-submarine patrols, and this was even more of a museum piece with few concessions to modernity. Many naval aviators were to grow to love the 'Stringbag', appreciating its ruggedness and reliability, so that in due course it was to outlive its successors, the Albacore and Barracuda, the former being notoriously unreliable and the latter a maintenance nightmare.

First flown in April 1934, the first Swordfish did not enter service until July 1936, and the last one, 2,392 aircraft later, was not retired until July 1945. A single Bristol Pegasus III provided 690hp, although later MkII and MkIII Swordfish had the more powerful 750hp Pegasus XXX. The aircraft had a wingspan of 45ft 5in, and was 36ft 3in long, with an overall height of 12ft 10in – it was a fair size for the day, and had a maximum weight of 9,250lbs. There were usually three members in the crew, each with his own open cockpit; the pilot and observer were both usually commissioned, and the rear cockpit was occupied by the telegraphist air gunner, who was a naval rating. The range was 450nm, but this could be increased to 896nm with additional fuel tanks. Aircraft assigned to act as dive-bombers could have the extra tank mounted under the fuselage, but for the torpedo-droppers this was not possible, and the extra range was gained by placing a 93 gallon tank in the observer's cockpit, and relegating the observer, with his bulky Bigsworth chart board, to the confines of the TAG's cockpit. This provided cramped accommodation for the observer, who had the extra duty of having to handle any communications that might be needed and also had to contend with the real danger of being soaked in high-octane aviation fuel as the aircraft took off or climbed. His position was not enviable, especially with the risk of the flimsy cockpit being pierced by AA tracer shells, or 'flaming onions', as they became known. The maximum speed was 125 knots, and most Swordfish aircrew would maintain that even 100 knots was seldom, if ever, achieved, especially on operations.

Initially the aircraft was assigned to torpedo, spotter, reconnaissance and TSR duties, but by 1939, this had changed to torpedo, bomber, reconnaissance or TBR. The armament consisted of two 0.303 Vickers machine guns, one in the TAG's cockpit. A varied range of munitions could be carried, either a single 18in Mk XIIB 1,620lb torpedo, four 250lb depth charges, three 500lb bombs – the largest available to the Royal Navy in 1939 – or six 60lb rockets. A varied range of munitions was essential for an aircraft that seemed to be burdened with almost every task that the Fleet Air Arm could demand of it, except, of course, the fighter role.

By comparison with the best carrier aircraft available, from the United States, the performance of the Swordfish was hardly sparkling. The United States Navy had retained control of its own aviation, largely because aviation had remained with the two services despite lobbying for an autonomous air force by Brigadier-General William 'Billy' Mitchell and others, and despite the fact that the United States Army Air Corps, later the United States Army Air Force, behaved like an autonomous air force. The American Douglas TBD1 Devastator could manage 200 knots and a range of 985 miles carrying a 1,000lb torpedo. Better still, the Japanese Navy Air Force's Nakajima BSN2, known to the Allies as 'Kate', had a maximum speed of 235 knots, a range of 1,400 miles and could carry one of the Imperial Japanese Navy's excellent torpedoes of 1,764lbs.

Still not for the first time, and not for the last, the Fleet Air Arm had to make the best of what it had. Attitudes to their aircraft were soon to become part and parcel of the various ditties that comprised *The Fleet Air Arm Songbook*, one of which to the tune of 'My Bonny Lies Over the Ocean', ran thus:

> *The Swordfish fly over the ocean*
> *The Swordfish fly over the sea;*
> *If it were not for King George's Swordfish*
> *Where the 'ell would the Fleet Air Arm be?*

In defence of the Swordfish, its one advantage was that an aircraft of this type could loiter in a way that a more powerful aircraft could not. The ability to hang around, as it were, meant that the maximum effort could be extracted from each aircraft on reconnaissance and anti-submarine patrols. This was important as the numbers deployed aboard escort carriers were limited, and the situation was even worse with that predecessor of the escort carrier, the MAC-ship, or merchant aircraft carrier, each with only three or four aircraft. The venerable Swordfish could stay in the air longer, forcing U-boats to keep below periscope depth and enabling convoys to slip through safely. What is more, the Swordfish could cope with the short length of the MAC-ships' decks, and their slow speed, in a way that a higher performance aircraft could not. Small wonder then that the Swordfish survived the war, especially as later on they were often fitted with radar to help them detect submarines and surface vessels.

The monoplanes available were also short on performance. The Blackburn Roc was one of that breed that included a rear gunner in the cockpit behind the pilot, but the extra weight so affected performance that any advantage of being able to protect the fighter's tail was undone. The Blackburn Skua was described as a fighter/dive-bomber, reconnaissance, but as one wag put it, 'it was more dive-bomber than fighter.'

Even when the Fairey Fulmar became available, the two-man crew, pilot and observer, affected performance, despite use of the Rolls-Royce Merlin engine, as in the Hurricane and Spitfire. Nevertheless, the Fulmar was the best fighter the Fleet Air Arm had early in the war. It first flew in January 1937, and entered service in June 1940, with the last of 600 built not retiring until March 1945. The wingspan was 46ft, length 40ft 2in and height 11ft 6in, with a maximum weight of 10,350lbs. A single Rolls-Royce Merlin XXX provided 1,260hp, and with a two-man crew it could manage 231 knots, about 100 knots less than the early Spitfires. Range was 691nm. Armament consisted of eight 0.303 Browning machine guns – and at this stage, both RAF and RN fighters were usually fitted with machine guns rather than the heavier, and much more effective, cannon of later aircraft. As a fighter-bomber, two 250lb bombs could be carried.

Part of the problem was the belief of many naval officers that high-performance aircraft could not operate off aircraft carriers, and the insistence on carrying an observer even in fighters. By contrast, the Americans and Japanese favoured single-seat fighters, realising that on bomber escort duties they could rely on the bombers for navigation, while the true 'observer' element was not needed in a fighter. The other fighter role, that of providing combat air patrols (CAP) over the fleet, meant that an aircraft would very rarely be out of sight of the carrier, and the advent of the homing beacon was an added security for the pilot who had lost his bearings. Finally, the new generation of carriers were fitted with homing beacons to help stray aircraft return to the mother ship – an important consideration given a home base that could move at speeds of 30 knots or more.

The shame of it was that the Fulmar was also far more expensive than the Spitfire, at around £8,000 against £6,000 for superior performance, albeit with more than a degree of delicacy when landing on a carrier's flight deck. The naval version of the Spitfire was designated the Seafire. 'The Seafire was too genteel for the rough and tumble of a carrier's heaving flight deck,' recalled one naval aviator. In contrast with many other aircraft, including the Sea Hurricane, the Seafire was also more difficult to repair in a hurry, and in fact was one of the first aircraft for which specialised training was provided for maintainers, who hitherto had been given a handbook and told to get on with it.

On the outbreak of war, the Fleet Air Arm was still constrained by its almost complete dependence on the Royal Air Force for training both naval aviators and what would in RAF terms be described as 'ground crew'. This was to be a bottleneck in the rapid expansion of naval aviation. Indeed, many naval air squadrons were still heavily dependent on RAF personnel at the time, although around 1,500 transferred to the Royal Navy. During the first year or so of war, civilians who volunteered for the RAF and were accepted had to return home and wait, often several months, before being called forward for training. While the RAF has been criticised for its treatment of the needs of the Royal Navy, under the pressures of building up its own strength to meet wartime needs its systems came under considerable stress.

So it was that on the outbreak of war the Royal Navy was in the process of receiving excellent aircraft carriers, but aircraft that failed to do them justice.

CHAPTER TWO

Engaging the Enemy

The heavy armour plating of major warships soon showed that the torpedo had more potential as an effective anti-ship weapon than the bomb. On 28 July 1914 Lt Arthur Longmore dropped a standard naval torpedo from a Short Folder Seaplane for the first time, flying at Calshot, near Southampton. Longmore was later to become one of the many RNAS personnel who passed into the RAF, where, as we shall see, he served with distinction and achieved high rank.

There were two problems in using torpedoes rather than bombs. The first was that if a torpedo was dropped too high, it risked breaking up. The second was that actually catching the target could be extremely difficult. During the 'run' of the torpedo, the target had time to take evasive action, and naval officers who were good ship handlers soon acquired the skill of 'combing' the torpedo, turning the vessel so that torpedoes passed by harmlessly. Pilots launching a torpedo at a ship under way at sea also had to be capable of judging the speed of the ship, aiming their torpedo slightly ahead of the target, but just how far ahead depended on the speed of the ship. Catching a ship in port was obviously the ideal option, provided there was enough room for an aircraft to descend to torpedo-dropping height, that the anti-aircraft defences were not too intense and, most important of all having surmounted these obstacles, that the target ship was not protected by anti-torpedo nets. Another problem with attempting torpedo attacks in many harbours was that shallow water would often result in torpedoes being caught in the mud, failing to reach their target.

The air-dropped torpedo had proved itself early in World War One when, on 17 August 1915, Flight Commander (another RNAS equivalent of Lieutenant-Commander) C. H. K. Edmunds dropped a 14in torpedo from his Short 184 biplane, flying from the seaplane carrier *Ben-my-Chree*, to sink a 5,000 ton Turkish military transport in the Sea of Marmara. This was the first successful aerial torpedo attack.

FIRST BLOOD

Despite the problems, it soon became clear that the best chance of success when using a torpedo was to catch enemy warships in harbour or at anchor. The same could be claimed for bombing. The first sinking of an operational enemy warship came on 10 April 1940, during the Norwegian campaign. Twenty Blackburn Skuas of 800 and 803 squadrons, flying from their shore base at Hatston, on Orkney, bombed and sank the cruiser *Konigsberg*, lying alongside at Bergen. A cruiser was probably the largest warship that aircraft could bomb successfully at the time – lightly armoured in contrast to the larger battleships.

The first year of war saw the Royal Navy lose two of its precious aircraft carriers because of poor tactics. A fortnight after war broke out, *Courageous* was sunk by a submarine, torpedoed while on an anti-submarine sweep. Her escort of just two destroyers was below the size recommended for a major fleet unit, but even so, the real problem was that she was, as some have put it, 'trailing her cloak', hoping to catch a submarine. This was a poor strategy, akin to looking for a needle in a haystack; a far more effective role would have been as a convoy escort, with the convoy attracting the submarine packs, and the carrier's aircraft being used to force them to keep out of sight.

During the withdrawal from Norway, *Glorious* was sunk when she was caught unawares by the two German battlecruisers, *Scharnhorst* and *Gneisenau*. Much has been written about her steaming at low speed to conserve fuel, but others have cast doubt on the lack of fuel. More to the point, she lacked radar to give her advance warning of trouble, and did not even have a lookout stationed in the crow's nest. Worst of all, she was not flying air patrols that could have alerted her to trouble. Her aircraft had been disarmed and their torpedoes sent down to the magazines, so that mounting an offensive strike at short notice was impossible. Her commanding officer, when once asked what he would do when confronted by an enemy warship, had replied that he would steam towards them at full speed firing all of his guns. The thought of sailing away while aircraft were despatched on a strike did not occur to him. Not only was the ship lost, with most of her ship's company, many of whom are believed to have died from exposure after abandoning ship, but so too were many RAF personnel escaping from Norway. These included fighter pilots, who, despite their lack of deck landing experience, had managed to land sixteen of their eighteen Hurricanes, without arrester hooks, safely on the carrier, so that the scarce aircraft would be saved to fight another day. Lost too were her two escorts, the destroyers *Ardent* and *Acasta*, in a desperate attack on the German ships.

Given this record of incompetence, it is strange to learn that so much about carrier operations in wartime had already been considered between the wars. Many senior officers, not all of them airmen or even particularly air-minded, had a reasonable appreciation of the strengths and weaknesses of the carrier and of carrier-borne aircraft, and many knew the limitations of the carrier or of particular strategic situations.

Italy's invasion of Abyssinia, modern-day Ethiopia, starting in 1935, was to prove the spur for much serious thinking about naval warfare, and in particular, carrier warfare. Italy's ambitions for an African empire caused concern. Alarm bells rang, too, in the League of Nations, the international talking shop set up in the wake of World War One. The Geneva-based League had been one of the measures suggested by the American president, Woodrow Wilson, for ending the war, but the League was weakened by the subsequent absence of the United States as a member, and by the lack of any formula to enforce its decisions. Throughout the late 1930s, cinema audiences were shown newsreel footage of Italian forces, including armoured formations and fighter and bomber aircraft, engaged in an unequal battle with tribesmen on horseback. The public's inchoate sense that something must be done eventually spread to the statesmen of the day, and as the decade progressed, war with Italy became a strong possibility.

The main naval base in the Mediterranean at the time was at Malta, roughly halfway between Gibraltar and Alexandria, which were also used as naval bases by the British. Both Malta and Gibraltar were British colonies. Egypt was effectively run by the British, almost as a colony, defending the Suez Canal which provided a short-cut to India and the Gulf, and to a lesser extent, Australia. The Mediterranean Fleet included the aircraft carrier *Glorious*, which based her aircraft, when in Malta's famous Grand Harbour, at the Fleet Air Arm base at RAF Hal Far. Near by, there was a seaplane and flying boat station on the coast at Kalafrana.

Commander-in-Chief in the Mediterranean in 1935 was Admiral Sir William Wordsworth Fisher, who has been described simply as a very fearsome man. It was at his instigation that plans were prepared for aircraft from *Glorious* to attack the Italian fleet in its harbour at Taranto. When Italy invaded Abyssinia, Fisher expected his country to declare war on Italy immediately, and was prepared. Instead, he was told to apply peaceful sanctions, including checking Italian ships, but under no circumstances was he to interfere with the life-blood of any modern armed forces, Italian oil supplies. Fisher was also forbidden to close the Suez Canal to Italian shipping, even though the ships were carrying troops and supplies to support the invasion of Abyssinia. Prompt and decisive action in closing the Suez Canal to Italian supply ships would have brought the invasion to a standstill, resolving the crisis at a stroke.

The time for action passed. Just three years later, in March 1938, tension rose again as Hitler annexed Austria. This time, command in the Mediterranean rested with Admiral Sir Dudley Pound, while aboard *Glorious* as CO was a certain Captain Lumley St George Lyster, a man destined to be one of the most influential in the history of the Fleet Air Arm when it later passed back into naval hands. Pound was soon to be the Royal Navy's first wartime First Sea Lord until his death in 1943. In addition to being the carrier's captain, Lyster also acted as the admiral's air adviser.

Lyster was not a naval aviator, but he was perhaps the next best thing, a career naval officer who had at one time held ambitions to fly. Aided by his Commander Flying, Guy Willoughby, Lyster ensured that the squadrons aboard *Glorious* became highly proficient in night flying, recognising that the lumbering aircraft of the day would be vulnerable in daytime. When asked by the Admiralty which of his squadrons was the ship's night flying squadron, he responded proudly, 'All of them!'

In 1938, as the threat of war with Germany and Italy loomed, Pound asked Lyster to consider a plan for the ship's aircraft to carry out an attack on the Italian fleet at Taranto. There had been consideration of such an attack earlier, but this was the first occasion when serious planning was put in hand. No mention of this was made to the Admiralty in London, and no written communication was ever forwarded to them.

Pound understood that the balance of naval power in the Mediterranean was in Italy's favour, unless his fleet was substantially augmented by units from the Home Fleet and the Far East Fleet. He firmly believed that in the confines of the Mediterranean, with Malta less than twenty minutes flying time for bombers based in Sicily, *Glorious* would not survive long, but at least she could have one strike at the enemy before either being sunk or, hopefully, withdrawn to safety.

Lyster knew that an attack on Taranto had been considered in 1935. He had found the secret papers locked away in his safe and had read them. On receiving Pound's order to plan an attack on Taranto, he had sent for his Commander Flying and the senior observer, Commander Lachlan Mackintosh of Mackintosh. The three of them then set about revising and updating the 1935 plans, while the crews of the ship's three Swordfish squadrons, at that time 812, 823 and 825, soon found themselves in intense training, with night take-offs and landings on the carrier's deck. They also mounted a series of dummy attacks on the Mediterranean Fleet in the Grand Harbour at Malta, where to add realism, the ships and the harbour operated under darkened ship and blacked-out conditions. Before long, Lyster was able to report to Pound that an attack was a possibility.

Many appear to doubt that Pound would have implemented the plan, lacking faith in the Swordfish and having little real understanding of the potential for naval aviation, but in any event the crisis passed. Pound himself felt that the attack would best be conducted by aircraft based ashore in Malta, overlooking the strong possibility that Italian bombers would attempt to destroy British air power first. Later that year when Hitler took the Sudetenland from Czechoslovakia, the United Kingdom and France simply protested and allowed themselves to be bought off by the Munich Agreement. The plan was safely locked away once again aboard *Glorious*, and may even have gone with her to the bottom in 1940. This was to have been the one effective blow before she was overwhelmed by enemy air power. A night attack was favoured. The Commander Flying and his staff also estimated the likely casualties for a raid on Taranto – ten per cent maximum. Although Pound disputed this assessment of casualties, he would have had little choice but to attempt the plan had war broken out in 1938. It is easy to treat Pound's pessimism lightly, but the experience of the early bombing raids over Germany during the war that followed showed that he had good grounds for expecting high casualties. Nevertheless, there can be no doubt in the light of subsequent events that Lyster, his Commander Flying and the rest of his staff all showed a remarkable degree of foresight.

In 1939, Pound was recalled to become First Sea Lord and Admiral of the Fleet to relieve the ailing Admiral Sir Roger Backhouse, also becoming Chairman of the British Chiefs of Staff Committee. He too was to die later while still in post, from an undetected brain tumour. In his new role, Pound was once again to state that shore-based aircraft would be better suited for the attack on Taranto. The RAF's Bristol Beauforts would have been faster and more potent than the Swordfish, but the air bases on Malta rapidly became untenable after Italy entered the war on 10 June 1940, just before the fall of France. At its peak, the bombing campaign was so successful that many fighters were destroyed on the ground as soon as they arrived. The RAF and the British Army had both argued that Malta could not be defended in a war with Italy, and before Italy entered the war had evacuated most British civilians and service dependents. The Royal Navy had argued not only that Malta could be defended, but that it would be an important base for operations against the Axis.

CHAPTER THREE

No Uncertain Sound

Barrow, that isolated town on the Furness peninsula, seems an unlikely spot to have a major warship-building yard. Reaching it from anywhere else in England involves a long detour around the fringes of the Lake District. Yet, though remote from what was formerly the rest of Lancashire, the town lay close to rich deposits of iron ore. This proximity to an essential raw material led to the creation, first, of an iron and steelworks, then a shipbuilding yard handling both warships and merchant vessels. It was to this yard that the first of the Illustrious-class carriers was contracted. Although the new ship was to be the first aircraft carrier built at Barrow, the Vickers-Armstrong yard was to account for many more British fleet carriers in the years ahead, including that developed version of the Illustrious-class, HMS *Indomitable*, while also continuing to build submarines and merchant vessels.

HMS *Illustrious* was ordered on 13 January 1937 and, like all ships under construction, given a yard number, in her case 732. Frantic work on the details for the new ship resulted in the production of some 2,500 plans for the ship alone, with further drawings for her machinery. All of this had to be done before the keel could be laid on 27 April. Soon, the advance guard of the first of many naval personnel would arrive to 'stand by' the ship as she took shape, rising from the slipway and passing through the stage when she looked more like a rusting carcass than a ship, until the basic form of an aircraft carrier hull could be seen. Although the builders were new to the high complexity of carrier construction, work forged ahead at a great pace, and the ship was launched within two years of being laid down, on 5 April 1939. There were some delays, even to this tight timetable; remarkably, these included late delivery of the flight deck, prefabricated away from Barrow and despatched in sections, which were then assembled before two large holes could be cut for the aircraft lifts.

All large ships, and especially major warships, are launched well before completion, partly to avoid tying up valuable slipway capacity, but also because of the increased height of the completing ship. *Illustrious* was no exception. Although she looked like an aircraft carrier as she sat on the slipway, and then slowly glided into the waters of Morecambe Bay amidst a clatter of chains unravelling and air filled with rust dust, she lacked many salient features. On being launched, she was a genuine 'flat-top', lacking her superstructure, the 'island', which accommodated the bridge and flying control, and the single large funnel, or smokestack. All of these features were added in a little more than a year, along with her armament and the million and one items that remained to be completed 'down below'. Warships are complicated and cramped beasts, and aircraft carriers became more so as time passed. Apart from the usual machinery and ammunition hoists, aircraft carriers also required extensive pipework so that planes could be refuelled in the hangars, and this also meant yet more pipework so that adequate fire precautions could be installed. In addition, there were many items of equipment that would not be installed until after her initial sea trials, and still more would be added or replaced, reflecting lessons learned and experience gained during work-up.

Eventually, HMS *Illustrious* was commissioned in the spring, almost nine months after war had broken out in Europe. This was not a moment too soon. The Royal Navy had started the war with seven aircraft carriers, but by spring 1940 *Courageous* had already been lost, torpedoed just a fortnight after war had started. Before long, in June, *Glorious* was also to be lost during the withdrawal from Norway. Only two of the seven pre-war carriers, *Furious* and *Argus*, were to survive World War Two, but as the end approached both were in extremely poor condition and little better than hulks.

STANDING BY

As the ship neared completion, her officers began to assemble, following the old naval tradition of 'standing by' a ship under construction. These relative late-comers joined the select few who had been with the ship from the early days. As work proceeded, more of her officers and senior ratings appeared. This was an essential part of fitting out a ship, with the officers in charge of each department taking a keen interest in the completion of work and installing of equipment, even to the extent of specifying what could and what could not be used. Usually, these officers were standing by the ship well before her commanding officer appeared.

Joining *Illustrious* in February 1940, her new captain, Denis Boyd, was an ideal choice for command of an aircraft carrier at a time when, because of RAF control of naval aviation for so long, there were few senior officers who had actually been naval aviators. In 1911, he had applied to become one of the first of these, but only three a year could be trained at this early stage, and he was among nineteen candidates. The irony is that, had he been accepted, he would probably have been lost to the Royal Navy, like Arthur Longmore who had disappeared into the RAF in April 1918. Instead, Boyd spent World War One in submarines, but returned to take an interest in naval aviation between the wars. When Boyd became director of the Royal Navy's Tactical Division in 1934, he formed a committee that initiated the slow process of persuasion that saw naval aviation handed back to the Admiralty. Boyd's role at the Tactical Division extended to taking a share of the responsibility for the specification of the Illustrious-class.

In common with most major navies, and indeed with many of the more traditional merchant shipowners, the Royal Navy recycled the names of ships, so that over many generations, they came to acquire an impressive list of battle honours. The name *Illustrious* had entered the Royal Navy by an indirect route, as the first ship to bear her name had been a captured French prize, *L'Illustre*, which according to custom was immediately pressed into Royal Navy service. Not only was the name absorbed into the Royal Navy as *Illustrious*, with two further ships bearing the name before the aircraft carrier, but she came complete with her own crest, three brazen trumpets. It was Boyd's brother, a classical scholar, who suggested the motto, *Vox Non Incerta*, 'No Uncertain Sound'.

The other important senior officer of an aircraft carrier was the Commander Flying, Commander J. I. 'Streamline' Robertson. Described as a tiny man who looked like a bird, he had gained the nickname because of his prominent nose and sharp features. Appropriately, Robertson was a naval aviator, having volunteered in 1924. He had qualified by landing an Avro Bison on *Argus* in 1925. His career, instead of the customary involvement with the amphibians and seaplanes carried aboard battleships and cruisers, took him successively to the carriers *Furious*, *Eagle*, *Courageous* and *Glorious*. The most significant of these postings was the last one, in a ship commanded by officers who believed in naval aviation, where the importance of aerial torpedo attacks was at last realised, and serious practice afforded to this and, no less importantly, to night operations.

Robertson was fully aware of developments aboard the aircraft carriers of the United States Navy, where arrester wires were being augmented by a new feature, the crash barrier. Anxious to be as up-to-date as possible, he had spent a month aboard the Royal Navy's newest aircraft carrier, *Ark Royal*, during March 1939, before standing by *Illustrious* from June onward. Here he discovered the new crash barrier system, and saw how it speeded up the process of recovering aircraft. The system was not fully utilised, as many naval airmen, including even the Fifth Sea Lord, in charge of naval aviation, believed that the system would result in substantial casualties, perhaps as high as 40 per cent. One of the ship's officers pointed to the barrier and told Robertson that he 'wouldn't be using that!' Although fitted with the little-used barrier, the *Ark* still did not have a batsman. Robertson determined that his new ship would have both barriers and a batsman, and that the pilots would train hard to gain the necessary discipline to make good use of both innovations. While aboard *Courageous* he had served under a commanding officer who had stressed the need for landing-on to be completed as quickly as possible, pointing out the need in wartime for the flight deck to be free to launch aircraft, and the vulnerability of planes to aerial attack as they landed. 'Streamline' was determined that *Illustrious* should be run as an aircraft carrier from the beginning, and not as another battleship or cruiser that simply happened to carry aircraft.

Under Robertson, the use of bats for landing-on, with illuminated wands employed for landing at night, became compulsory for the first time aboard a British carrier. The new deck-landing control officer, or DLCO, but always 'batsman' to the crew, was Lt-Cdr D. McI. Russell, a Scot known affectionately to everyone as 'Haggis'.

One reason for the late arrival of a commanding officer for a new ship was that there was really not much for him to do until the ship was ready for sea, and especially for the all-important shake-down cruise. The lynchpin of the ship while she was fitting out was her commander, in this case Commander Gerald Seymour Tuck. Although not a naval aviator, but a gunnery expert, Tuck had spent time aboard the aircraft carrier *Eagle*, and was familiar with the routine and organisation of carriers. The CO's job was to be able to fight his ship effectively, and for this *Illustrious* needed her squadrons, as her guns were really only suitable for anti-aircraft use.

THE SQUADRONS

Three squadrons had been detailed to join *Illustrious*. Two were torpedo bomber squadrons equipped with Swordfish, No. 815 commanded by Lt-Cdr Robin Kilroy, DSC, and No. 819 commanded by Lt-Cdr J. W. 'Ginger' Hale. The third was the ship's fighter squadron, No. 806, commanded by Lt-Cdr Charles Evans, DSC, and equipped with Fulmars. These were all experienced naval airmen, and Evans in particular was a happy choice. At a time when British naval aircraft were distinctly plodding, Evans had led the flight of three Skuas of 803 Squadron from *Ark Royal* that managed to shoot down a Dornier Do18 flying boat on 26 September, the first Luftwaffe air-craft to be destroyed by British aircraft during the war. Not content with this, while still in command of 803, Evans had led the squadron from Hatston in Orkney to the raid on the *Königsberg*, for the first time sinking an operational warship in an air attack.

The three squadrons had all been formed recently, indicating the rapid expansion of the Fleet Air Arm. No. 806 had been formed on 1 February 1940, at Worthy Down, near Winchester, initially with a mixed hand of Skuas and Rocs. It had moved to Hatston in Orkney on 28 March, and had seen action over Bergen during the Norwegian campaign, before moving south to help cover the evacuation from Dunkirk, for which it was based at the RAF station at Detling. While the squadron's aircraft were replaced with Fulmars before joining *Illustrious*, it continued at first to have a mixture of types as a number of Gloster Sea Gladiator biplanes were added, doubtless to make up the numbers.

Slightly older was No. 815 Squadron, formed on 9 October 1939, again at Worthy Down, from the survivors of 811 and 820 squadrons that had been embarked in *Courageous* when she was torpedoed. This was something of a false start, however, as the squadron was disbanded in November, then reformed on 23 November, under the same CO, and with nine Swordfish as a spare squadron. It spent time on detachment to RAF Coastal Command, during which Kilroy took over as the CO. By contrast, Hale had formed No. 819 at Ford, near Arundel, Sussex, on 15 January 1940, with twelve Swordfish and crews with experience from both *Glorious* and *Ark Royal*. The squadron had also been detached to Coastal Command for a period, being based at Detling to help protect the Dunkirk evacuation from attack by German U-boats.

Many of the squadrons' aircrew had served aboard *Glorious* in the Mediterranean, and had practised night torpedo attacks. They spent the time waiting for the ship to complete further practice, exercising both night torpedo operations and dive bombing. The venerable Swordfish was no Stuka, and certainly appeared far less menacing to the uninitiated who would have been surprised to discover that it could carry three 500lb bombs, compared with the Stuka's more usual 1,000lb bomb. 'Stringbags' could also suffer considerable punishment and continue to fly. Nevertheless, it was perhaps just as well that the Germans and Italians never managed to commission the aircraft carriers that they tried to build, since a carrier-borne Stuka would have been a potent enemy, and would almost certainly have been rugged enough for carrier operation.

Had Hitler's Germany been able to send carriers to sea, the other component of its air group would have been the Messerschmitt Bf109 fighter. While faster than the Spitfire, and its naval cousin the Seafire, the suitability of the Bf109 as a carrier aircraft would have been questionable. The aircraft might not have been as 'nose-heavy' as the Seafire (or for that matter the otherwise superb Vought Corsair), but it had a weak tail, and this might not have lasted long with frequent arrested landings due to the sharp tug of the wire as it was caught, followed immediately by the aircraft banging down on to the flight deck.

COMPLETION

Life aboard *Illustrious* became increasingly edgy as completion drew near. The big fear was that the Luftwaffe would discover the ship and target her before she was ready. Even when the anti-aircraft armament was fitted, including new multiple pom-poms (sometimes known as 'Chicago pianos'), ratings would close up during an air raid ready to fire if the ship came under attack, but deliberately not firing so as not to draw attention to the ship. In any case, many of them had little prior practice on their new weapons, and ammunition was short while she remained at the builder's yard. Barrow's location helped, as did the relatively short range of the Luftwaffe's bombers, but other cities on Britain's west coast did suffer heavy air raids during the war, including Glasgow and Liverpool, as well as Belfast, even further west in Northern Ireland. The risk of a heavy raid on Barrow was real. Speedy completion was important not simply because of the Royal Navy's desperate need for new ships, but also to avoid the ship spending a day longer than necessary in the fitting-out yard where she was virtually a sitting duck. In the open sea, she could at least make life more difficult for bomber pilots by manoeuvring at full speed.

Most of the ship's personnel did not come aboard until Tuesday 16 April. Among them was Albert Jones, a stoker in the middle boiler room. Even oil-fired ships needed stokers, to regulate the flow of fuel into the fires under the large boilers. It was hot work. Off-duty, there were few comforts, the men living in cramped mess decks where hammocks were slung at night, or during the day for those off-watch, and where meals were served and most entertainment took place. This was a contrast to the restricted but more civilised accommodation for the officers, described by one as 'the best hotel in the world', and by another as 'the only asylum run by its inmates'.

Illustrious first went to sea a little more than a week later, on Wednesday 24 April, heading south for Liverpool on her constructor's trials with a destroyer escort. She also undertook the whole range of essential procedures that a new ship needs to complete before she can become fully functional, swinging compasses, calibrating her pitometer log, testing her echo sounder and, in the open Irish Sea, testing her steering gear and the telegraphs to her three engine rooms. On arrival in Liverpool, she was briefly dry-docked, for the fitting of bilge keels and the replacement of her three cast-iron temporary screws with the permanent bronze variety. This was the time for further tests, of radar, arrester wires and the crash barrier. It was at Liverpool that *Illustrious* received the bulk of her ammunition, and shortly afterwards she was able to test-fire her guns for the first time.

The necessities of wartime and the urgent need for the new ship and her aircraft had meant that her sea trials were cut short, with strict orders that both the cruising and full power trials could be cut to just four hours each if it meant saving a day of trials. Officially commissioned on 25 May 1940, trials and tests continued until the new ship arrived on the south coast at Spithead, at the entrance to Portsmouth, on the morning of 26 May 1940.

The demands of the Norwegian campaign and then of the Battle of France and the evacuation at Dunkirk all combined to keep the carrier's air squadrons away. It was not until early June that they were able to come aboard, and for many of them it meant facing the crash barrier for the first time. The decision to use the barrier had been controversial. During a visit to *Ark Royal*, Captain Boyd had also been counselled against using it, and the matter was discussed with 'Streamline' Robertson. At first, Boyd suggested that the barrier should not be used for the first landings, but eventually 'Streamline' managed to persuade him to try it. The barrier was not really necessary for the plodding Swordfish, which could be relied upon to make a steady approach, catch an arrester wire and come to a stop well before the barrier. The Skua and Fulmar fighters were more problematic.

Charles Evans made the first landing without any difficulty, but the second aircraft missed the wires and was saved by the barrier, as were a number of others that followed. Over the next few days of flying, no less than six of 806's Fulmars were destroyed in landing accidents, due in no small part to the inexperience of their young pilots. These were the days before conversion trainers were known, and after ground training, pilots had eventually to grit their teeth and take a new aircraft into the air. The Fulmar might have lacked the higher speeds of a Hurricane or a Spitfire, but for a fighter the Fulmar was a heavy aircraft, and difficult to land on a flight deck.

Typical of 806's Fairey Fulmar pilots was Sub-Lt Ivan Lowe. Lowe was in his first operational squadron, although he had already flown Blackburn Skuas on dive-bombing raids over Norway, flying from HMS *Sparrowhawk*, the Royal Naval Air Station at Hatston in Orkney. En route to join *Illustrious* in his Skua, the engine of Lowe's aircraft failed and he had no option but to ditch. Provided one survived the experience, ditching an aircraft was not always seen as an unmitigated disaster by those in the Fleet Air Arm. The practice was to write off everything in the aircraft, so many quick-witted observers often found that after a ditching they had acquired a fine pair of official issue binoculars. Aboard ship, hard-pressed air squadron officers responsible for equipment found a ditching a convenient way of writing off equipment that had been missing, but for which they were still accountable.

Ditching whilst flying out to a ship, or even returning from a ship to a new shore station, was a different matter since it also meant that the personal possessions of those aboard the aircraft were at risk. On this occasion, Lowe's air gunner in the back of the Skua was a naval airman named Kensett. Once the aircraft was in the water, they launched the dinghy and instead of clambering in, carefully placed all of their possessions safely inside, including a gramophone which, in wartime, would be hard to replace and would provide much-needed entertainment aboard ship. They then entered the water themselves. In the meantime, they both became separated from the dinghy, which was spotted by a rescue craft which reported, 'No survivors, only suitcases'. Fortunately, they were picked up shortly afterwards.

Charles Lamb later recalled his first impressions after landing on the *Illustrious* in his Swordfish, in which he remained as its wings were folded and it was 'struck down' on the lift to the hangar deck:

> I was looking through the folded wings of almost forty aircraft, all stacked together very tightly, according to some preconceived plans, so that they could all be stowed down below. The wings were almost touching. On the bulkheads, brightly coloured markings indicated fuel points, or connections for high pressure air, oil, water, electric power – all vividly painted in clearly defined colours so that there could be no mistake. Overhead, metal firescreen curtains were rolled and stowed, ready to be dropped in an emergency dividing the hangar into three separate compartments. The whole deck-head was a series of overhead stowages, containing spare aircraft engines, airscrews, long-range tanks, and all manner of objects: but the whole of the hangar deckhead was bristling with little sprinklers a few inches apart, so that in the event of fire at the turn of a switch the curtains would fall and the entire hangar would be sprayed with jets of salt water.

He then joined several of his comrades in 815 Squadron and together they went up to the flight-deck:

> We were astonished at the mount of space available. It had not looked particularly large from our cockpits a few moments earlier, but flight-decks never do look very large from the air … we were joined by Captain Denis Boyd, who surprised me because of the informal way he greeted us and welcomed us on board … he was a famous man, with a great reputation.

One advantage of the slow and stately Swordfish was that it could be operated in little or no wind, and indeed could take off even while the ship was in harbour if she was pointing into the wind. The fighters, with their heavier wing loading, could not, although one of them managed, while *Illustrious* was still at Plymouth, to take off with just eight knots of wind over the flight deck, and nearly crashed into the sea. Determined to run a safe ship, 'Streamline' Robertson promptly ordered that there had to be at least thirteen knots over the flight deck, whether wind or slipstream from the ship's movement, before the fighters could attempt a take-off. While cost was an important factor, since the Fulmars cost £8,000, still more important was the danger of losing scarce naval aircrew in an unnecessary accident. Carrier aircraft, too, were often harder to replace than aircraft ashore, since it was not until later in the war that sufficient spare aircraft could be provided as the fleets moved around the world's oceans.

One naval aviator recalled that, by contrast, flying a Swordfish from a stationary deck, while new to him, was straightforward. The aircraft needed very little space to take off, with its built-in 'headwind' of struts and wires. Landing entailed hitting the arrester wires at around 50 knots, but this was perfectly acceptable for the strong fixed undercarriage of the Swordfish.

OFF TO SEA

After putting into Devonport for revictualling, *Illustrious* set sail for Bermuda for her final working-up. This was intended to ensure that the crew and ship could operate efficiently and was an essential stage in the life of any new ship, or any ship on a new commission after a spell in the dockyard. Bermuda was chosen because it was seen as a secure area, close to the safe haven of the United States, and well away from the main North Atlantic shipping lanes which were the haunts of the German U-boats.

Sea trials are supposed to show up any weaknesses in a ship or her systems. As the constructor's trials had been cut short, it was inevitable that these would appear. An unexpected problem was not long in coming. As *Illustrious* steamed through the Bay of Biscay in darkness, a bad storm developed, with heavy green seas breaking over the flight deck forward. Shortly after midnight, a scuttle on the foc's'le messdeck, or, in layman's terms, a porthole on an accommodation space near the bows, smashed and sea water started to pour in. Shipwrights rushed to plug the damage, but other scuttles followed suit, until in the end a half-dozen or so had been shattered. A new light alloy had been used on the scuttles, and was obviously not strong enough.

The weather worsened as the carrier moved out into mid-Atlantic, with the inevitable result that items of equipment broke loose and were damaged, not all of them small or insubstantial – the most spectacular loss being a 32ft cutter washed overboard, while even the sturdy forward searchlight platforms were bent upward by the raging seas. Less apparent, the anti-magnetic degaussing belt, fitted at Liverpool, was torn, leaving the remains as an untidy mess trailing from the sides. Inevitably, in such bad weather, more scuttles were broken. If life was difficult aboard the carrier, it was worse on the destroyers providing the escort, and eventually these had to be ordered home, leaving *Illustrious* to steam on alone to Bermuda. Fortunately, the bad weather made a submarine attack less likely, while it kept the Luftwaffe's maritime reconnaissance aircraft grounded.

Albert Jones recalls:

We hit heavy weather as soon as we entered the Bay of Biscay. The seas ran so high that the foc's'le cable deck was continuously awash as *Illustrious* dipped through the troughs and then rode the swells … at times the waves nearly came over the flight deck. All around … gear was smashed. Scuttles and deadlights, which are meant to seal portholes to darken ship and for heavy weather, were smashed in. The shipwrights had a very busy time …

BERMUDA

Eventually, calmer waters were reached, and *Illustrious* arrived in Bermuda. Even so, there were dangers to avoid, as the largest ship ever to reach the island was conned through the narrow entrance to the harbour.

The voyage had not been a secret to the Germans, for on the evening of her arrival in Bermuda, Lord Haw-Haw, the Irishman providing propaganda broadcasts beamed to the UK, announced that the ship had been torpedoed on 4 July. The BBC broadcast a denial, stating that the ship had not been sunk. Unabashed, Haw-Haw broadcast that he hadn't claimed that she had been sunk, simply 'torpedoed'.

The stay in Bermuda was not without incident. One Sunday, with a stiffish 17-knot breeze over the flight deck, it was decided to launch the fighters, which had been without any flying practice for some time. Away they went, six Skuas and two Fulmars, with Robertson's blessing. Almost inevitably, the wind died away as soon as they were airborne, leaving the aircraft circling, hoping that the wind would pick up again and allow them to land safely back aboard ship. As their fuel ran low, the safest option was to bat the aircraft in. Both Fulmars and two Skuas managed to land-on safely, despite a minimum approach speed of around 60 knots. The other four landed with such force that their tail hooks were pulled out, and with the crash barrier down, one went over the bows into the sea. Even the capable Charles Evans hit the island, another skidded and ended up with its tail over the port side, and a fourth climbed away. Flying without a tail hook, the aircraft's pilot, Roger Nicholls, signalled for advice. At this time, Bermuda lacked even a rudimentary landing strip, and the only option seemed to be the Mid Ocean Golf Club.

Boyd signalled: 'Hole out on the seventeenth green!'

Nicholls followed this advice to the letter. Unfortunately, the seventeenth was a narrow fairway, straight but bordered on either side by pine trees. The Skua touched down, bounced, hitting first one tree with one wing, and then another on the other side with the other wing, out of control. The aircraft was ripped apart, but the engine continued to surge forward, breaking out of the aircraft and roaring down the fairway to make what one observer described as a 'hole in one'. Fortunately, although it was a summer Sunday morning, no one was hurt; indeed, 806 squadron had been lucky, for despite losing four aircraft, none of the pilots had been hurt. Evans, 806's CO, brought the wreckage back to the ship after presenting the golf club with the wrecked engine as a souvenir. Despite the damage to the green, the club secretary accepted the damaged Bristol Perseus II with good grace as if it were a great honour.

Before leaving Bermuda, exercises were also held, the Swordfish being sent off in company with the remaining Skuas so that the crews could evolve a means of defence if they were caught by enemy fighters. A typical such exercise would involve both aircraft climbing to around 10,000ft, after which the Skua pilot disappeared, getting into position to attack the slower Swordfish in the classic fighter manoeuvre from out of the sun. The Swordfish pilots soon decided that the best means of defence was not to run or dive – leaving the unfortunate TAGs to defend their aircraft from behind with the single machine gun – but instead to make a violent stalling turn to port, standing the aircraft on its tail. The fighter pilot was then in the difficult position of having his target standing still right in front of him, it proving almost impossible to keep the prey in his sights. Often, the fighter pilot would lose control temporarily, and while he struggled to regain control and come in for a second attempt, the Swordfish pilot would enter a steep dive, attempting to get as low as possible before the next attack. The logic of this next manoeuvre was that the fighter pilot could not easily attack an aircraft flying very low because the fighter would 'run out of air', unless he broke off his high speed attack at around 500 or 600ft. The fighter pilot would then resort to a strafing attack, and again, the Swordfish pilot, warned by his observer or his TAG, would attempt another stalling manoeuvre, although by now perilously short of recovery space. The fighter pilot was ultimately forced to make a very low-speed approach, considerably reducing the odds against the Swordfish and the TAG's sole machine gun, while the Swordfish remained the more manoeuvrable of the two aircraft.

On one such exercise over the Caribbean, the fighter pilot misjudged his height above the clear water, failing to spot the surface and not looking at his altimeter, and crashed into the sea upside down. One Swordfish pilot remembers many German fighter pilots later making the same fatal mistake.

The spell in Bermuda allowed much of the damage incurred during the storm to be repaired. Traditional, and reliable, brass scuttles were fitted in place of the alloy scuttles. Even more important, the degaussing strip was replaced, protecting the ship against magnetic mines, often laid in the shallow approaches to major ports.

The voyage home saw much better weather, allowing plenty of flying and enabling the crews to get used to landing behind the crash barrier, which despite its benefits did make the deck seem very short as aircraft raced down towards the arrester wires. The flight deck parties also became accustomed to the routine necessary to recover aircraft quickly. As soon as the landing aircraft taxied over the lowered crash barrier, it was promptly raised again as wings were folded and the aircraft either parked or put on to the lift to be struck down into the hangar. By the time *Illustrious* neared home waters, she was ready for action.

As soon as the carrier returned home, Boyd was summoned to the Admiralty.

CHAPTER FOUR

The Fleet Air Arm in 1940

It would be fair to describe the Fleet Air Arm in 1940 as in a state of metamorphosis; the transition from peacetime to wartime was in many ways clear enough, but much of its maintenance and all of its training was still in the hands of the RAF, and many RAF personnel were drafted aboard *Illustrious* to help maintain the carrier's aircraft. In 1938, anticipating the need eventually to provide its own maintainers – the Admiralty eschewed the description of 'ground crew' for obvious reasons – the Royal Navy had been authorised to implement a 300 per cent increase in the number of personnel in the Fleet Air Arm. In 1938 and 1939, the fleets were trawled for volunteers to become maintainers.

Regular strength of the Royal Navy and Royal Marines in June 1939 totalled 129,000 men, of whom just under 10,000 were officers. In addition, in wartime, it could depend on recalling recently retired officers and ratings, as well as two categories of reserves – the Royal Naval Reserve, RNR, and the Royal Naval Volunteer Reserve, RNVR – which between them provided another 73,000 officers and men in 1939. The Royal Naval Reserve consisted mainly of people drawn from the merchant navy, often bringing with them outstanding navigation and ship-handling skills, although, of course, there were other branches, notably marine engineering and signals. The Royal Naval Volunteer Reserve consisted of people from all walks of life, and was to undergo massive expansion as most wartime recruits went into the RNVR. The old saying was that Royal Navy officers were 'gentlemen trying to become sailors, RNR officers were sailors trying to become gentlemen, and the RNVR were neither, trying to become both.'

There was also some friendly rivalry between pilots and observers. The observers were possessed of that most fundamental of naval skills, navigation, added to which many of them had been trained to assess the fall of shot from the guns of a battleship or cruiser. All very useful, and in quieter spells, many observers would be able to take their turn at watch keeping, sharing this role with the ship's officers. The pilots at this stage often lacked navigational skills, and were often to be described by some observers as 'chauffeurs'.

Included in the 1939 total were 12,400 officers and men in the Royal Marines. The Royal Marines had a number of roles aboard ship, including security and the RM Band Service, but on cruisers and battleships they also manned 'X' turret, one of the aft turrets. Another role, certainly aboard *Illustrious*, was as wardroom attendants, or stewards. The Fleet Air Arm included a significant number of RM pilots and some observers, the naval term for an aircraft navigator. The role of the Royal Marines as commandos was one that was to develop as the war progressed, but in 1940 this had still to come.

In peacetime, a naval officer who wanted to fly would undergo most of his training with the RAF, while the Royal Navy provided catapult training so that he could fly seaplanes and amphibians from battleships, battle cruisers and cruisers. Training for pilots and observers that had taken two years in peacetime was compressed into ten wartime months.

Whereas commissioning from the ranks became significant during and after World War Two, it was a rarity in the pre-war Navy. To obtain a sufficient number of experienced officers for the rapid wartime expansion, many senior ratings, normally chief petty officers – the naval equivalent of a staff sergeant or flight sergeant – were commissioned under the 'Upper Yardman Scheme'.

Another big change was that an Air Branch was established, whose members did not have to carry out the normal shipboard tasks of naval officers. The Air Branch was formed initially for the purpose of accommodating the 1,500 RAF personnel transferred to the Fleet Air Arm, but later wartime recruits, who were members of the Royal Naval Volunteer Reserve, were also allocated to the branch. The inference was that these were airmen who went to sea, rather than sailors who could fly. Air Branch officers were identified by the letter 'A' within the curl of their officers' rings; with (A) following their rank when written. Membership of the Air Branch was a mixed blessing, since it simplified training, but did not confer a watch-keeping certificate; thus no Air Branch officer could ever rise to command a ship, and without such experience, the very highest levels of the service were closed. While observers were expected to fulfil such duties in peacetime, it was often impractical to expect this during combat. At first, training new personnel was restricted since the Fleet Air Arm was dependent on the RAF for training at the outset, but even this was to be overcome later in the war, starting in 1941, with the creation of the Towers Scheme, enabling personnel to be trained in the still officially neutral United States by the USN.

There were many volunteers, ignoring the old service maxim that one shouldn't 'volunteer for anything' in the belief that progress would be quicker if they were in at the start of something new. Others were keen to be involved with aviation. But, without sufficient volunteers, there were also those who were pressed into the Fleet Air Arm. This even happened with officers, not, of course, as pilots, but as observers, special favour being shown to those with a good knowledge of navigation and gunnery practice.

THE TWO-DECK NAVY

By the standards of many of its adversaries, the Royal Navy in 1940 was remarkably democratic, with less of a gap between the so-called upper and lower decks, officers and ratings, as non-commissioned personnel are known in the RN. This is not to suggest that people could move easily between the decks. In the peacetime navy, this had been almost impossible, but under the threat of impending war, and the need to increase the numbers of officers with experience of naval conditions, the Upper Yardman Scheme was introduced to take competent Chief Petty Officers and Warrant Officers into the commissioned ranks. Many of these were to prove extremely successful, and the lessons were borne in mind by the post-war navy.

Albert Jones was one of those who joined *Illustrious* while she was fitting out. As already mentioned, Jones was a stoker, a term retained despite the switch from coal to oil throughout the fleet.

'Shipboard living conditions for ratings below the rank of PO (Petty Officer) were rough and ready to put it mildly,' he recalls. Living cheek by jowl left no room for modesty or privacy. This was a man's world, completely without women yet women and sex were the predominant topic of conversation:

> The lower stoker's messdeck which was below the waterline obviously had no portholes. The upper messdeck which I was in was just above

the waterline so at least while in harbour we had portholes we could open for fresh air during the day. At night, however, it was another story when we had to darken ship and all scuttles and deadlights had to be closed. For air circulation we had only our forced air ventilation through small louvres on the head ducts ... This was wartime and in the hot climate of the Med, or the tropics of the Red Sea ... a crowded messdeck was stifling ... we all needed to sleep somehow so we just sweated it out until it was time to go on watch ...

The Navy had strict standards of hygiene and cleanliness. Messes had to be cleaned and scrubbed out every morning and everything put away. Hammocks had to be properly lashed up and stowed and no gear was to be left lying around. After dinner and supper, dishes and utensils had to be cleaned and stashed away. Before night rounds, messdecks were swept and tidied up by 21.00 ... when the duty officer and PO would do the night inspections.

There was little leisure time for junior ratings when at sea, since life consisted of eating, sleeping, going on watch (duty), cleaning the accommodation and doing laundry, or having a bath by throwing buckets of water over oneself. Most messes had their collection of games, board games and, of course, packs of cards. Aboard aircraft carriers, a popular diversion was watching aircraft take off and land, but it was hazardous, since the superstructure, the island, was often the last resting place for an aircraft that had missed the arrester wires. Yet *Illustrious* did show some progress in naval accommodation, having a recreation room immediately under the flight deck, although this was barely furnished. The NAAFI manager, a civilian, could also sell soft drinks.

At 11.00 each day, the Royal Navy still provided a tot of 'grog', a mixture of one-third rum and two-thirds water, but many would leave this issue until they came off watch.

With a complement of 1,400, fresh water was a problem. The ship had four evaporators, two on each side, but the priority was water for the ship's three boilers. Distilled water was salt free, but tasteless. At times, salt water had to be used for washing and shaving, something of a hardship since it was difficult to raise a good lather.

Catering varied between ships. Older ships such as *Argus* had canteen messing, although the description was misleading since no canteen was provided and all preparation of food was prepared by the 'cook of the day', a member of the mess who had to learn some basic culinary skills very quickly. A victualling allowance was provided monthly and drawn daily, usually tinned goods, with potatoes when available or rice at other times. Once the meal was prepared, it was taken to the galley and handed over to be cooked. The 'cook' would then collect the food when it was ready, take it back to the mess and serve it.

These arrangements permitted some freedom, and if the full allowance was not drawn, the saving would be credited to the men's pay. On a carrier using this system, one rating remembered that their great favourite was to use their outstanding allowance to create 'one pound cake', a dish that could be baked as a cake or steamed as a pudding using a mixture that included one pound of every ingredient available. All went well with this cure for a sweet tooth until an inexperienced 'duty cook' added a pound of yeast. Relations with the ship's cooks were never the same afterwards as he recalls, since on opening the oven door, the 'cake' had swollen so much that it literally burst out of the oven.

Aboard *Illustrious*, a different system was at work. This was general messing, in which everything was prepared centrally and collected by the 'cook of the day' from each mess. Food was plain, but many wartime ratings claim that they fared better than the civilian population at home. One problem that did arise was in the provision of meals outside normal hours for aircrew, especially the ratings. Many a rating complained that on returning to the ship, if someone had remembered to put his food by, it was nothing more than a cold, congealed mess. Others seem to have had their food kept hot, but thoroughly dried out, in an oven. Usually these were members of the ship's company rather than the embarked air squadrons, so that fellow members of, for example, the stokers' mess, would ensure that food was kept hot for those of their messmates on watch at mealtimes.

Living in close proximity to one another for long periods, honesty and thought for a shipmate were as important as high standards of cleanliness, so it was usual for those coming off watch to find that their grog ration was sitting untouched on the mess table waiting for them. Apparently after swallowing a tot of two-and-one grog, almost anything could be eaten.

Such living conditions explain why when a ship was in port, those not on harbour watch would always head ashore. Even when moored alongside, this still meant waiting for the 'liberty boat', a procedure that entailed those going ashore assembling to be inspected before being allowed off the ship.

Further up the rating scale, petty officers and chief petty officers enjoyed better accommodation while their meals were served by stewards, as was the case with the warrant officers, who occupied a kind of no-man's-land between the two decks. After the war, the rank of warrant officer was replaced by that of commissioned rank, such as commissioned airman or gunner; so this was the first step for those commissioned from the lower deck, and the warrant officer's mess was abolished.

For officers, life was even less spartan, but it could still be cramped, with up to three or four to a cabin, especially once the air squadrons were embarked. Being further up in the hull of the ship was a mixed blessing in aircraft carriers, as flying operations involved the frequent shriek of the arrester wire pulleys, followed by the reassuring thump as the aircraft's wheels hit the deck. As in the other armed services, social life when aboard revolved around the mess, known in the Royal Navy, and usually in the Merchant Navy as well, as the wardroom. This normally consisted of an ante-room or bar, and a large dining room. In the larger and more traditional ships, midshipmen, always referred to as 'mister', were not generally allowed in the wardroom, but spent their time off-duty in what was known as the gunroom mess. This rule does not seem to have applied aboard the newer carriers, especially for aircrew midshipmen, although in the wardroom they would find that they were denied spirits. (One officer recalled a session at which they took good care to ensure that a midshipman pilot received an unofficial gin.) Officers were waited on at table by stewards, and if senior enough sometimes had their own, but increasingly under wartime conditions they shared with three or four others a steward who looked after their uniforms and accommodation, in general undertaking similar duties to those of the batman in the Army and the RAF.

The rank of midshipman in peacetime entailed a period of practical training aboard an operational warship, with a range of duties such as command of a ship's boat. It bridged the gap between Dartmouth and life as a sub-lieutenant but, in an increasingly technical age, it could never mark the end of all training. Naval airmen trained between the wars had the benefit of a traditional naval training. For officers this meant a spell at Dartmouth before service with the fleet aboard a large ship as a midshipman. Under wartime pressures different training had to be provided, with much shortened training periods. The rank at which the new officer entered the service depended on his age. Those over twenty-one became Temporary Sub-Lieutenants, those under twenty-one, Temporary Acting Sub-Lieutenants, and those under twenty became Temporary Midshipmen. The last received less money, but they did have equal chances of being shot down and being killed or wounded in action.

Officers of the Royal Naval Volunteer Reserve were known as the 'wavy navy' because they were distinguished from the straight rings with loops on the upper ring denoting rank amongst regular officers by wavy rings. Instead of the white collar cloth of a midshipman RN, his RNVR counterpart had red-colour cloth.

One of 815's observers, Lt Norman Scarlett, was typical of those regular naval officers whose career ambitions were sacrificed to the need for observers, but his predicament of being pressed to train as an observer was rare, as most people were in the Fleet Air Arm because they wanted to fly, or at least wanted to be associated with flying and to work on aircraft.

Naval aircrew felt that they were something special. Taking off from an aircraft carrier, even with the ship turned into the wind and a good speed being provided by a sympathetic commanding officer and an efficient engineering officer, was not for the faint-hearted. Landing was even worse, as the ship itself, so large close up, looked remarkably small from the start of a landing approach, and the stern over which all landings were made might be moving up and down 40 or 50 feet as the ship pitched in the waves. One of four arrestor wires had to be caught by the arrester hook near the tail of the aircraft before the aircraft crashed into the crash barrier, as on *Illustrious* and her sisters, or ploughed on along the flight deck, possibly hitting aircraft parked forward or, if the pilot was lucky and the flight deck was empty, carrying on with the possibility of being able to go around and try again. The arrival of the angled flight deck well after the end of the war, enabling aircraft to do exactly that, was a godsend to naval aviators. Not for nothing did the *Fleet Air Arm Songbook*, that irreverent and witty commentary on naval aviation, have something suitably pithy to say about it:

> 'They say in the Air Force the landing's OK.
> If the pilot gets out and walks away,
> But in the Fleet Air Arm the prospects are grim,
> If the landing's piss poor and the pilot can't swim.'

The big weakness of the Fleet Air Arm during the early years of World War Two was the absence of senior naval officers with first-hand experience of aviation, able to appreciate its problems and its potential. Men such as Boyd were rare, as was Lyster before him. Lyster's successor aboard *Glorious* at the time of her sinking has been mentioned by many as an example of the opposite school, which treated aircraft carriers as an inferior type of cruiser, one that just happened to carry more aircraft than the typical cruiser. Boyd and Lyster were not aviators, but men who had acquired an understanding of naval aviation. It was not just a case of the Royal Navy lagging behind the United States Navy in the quality of its aircraft in 1940; unlike the USN, it had missed a vital generation of naval officers who were naval aviators and had become captains of aircraft carriers, or had reached even higher rank, such as the USN Vice-Admiral Jack Towers and Captain Albert Read. In 1919, Towers and Read had attempted to make a transatlantic flight as part of a formation of three, and while Towers' aircraft did not manage to stay the course, one of the aircraft, commanded by Lieutenant-Commander Albert 'Putty' Read, managed to reach Lisbon via the Azores. Read's later career included the command of aircraft carriers, and those future Fleet Air Arm pilots who were sent to train with the USN found him in command of the US Naval Air Station at Pensacola.

CHAPTER FIVE

War and Peace in the Middle Sea

Italy's dictator Benito Mussolini did not declare war on Britain and France until 10 June 1940. By this time it was clear that Germany's audacious attack on the Low Countries and France, so soon after the invasion of Denmark and Norway, had been a great success, with the former defeated and occupied and the fighting in France almost over. The British had first withdrawn the surviving remnants of the RAF's Advanced Air Striking Force and then the men of the British Expeditionary Force, leaving almost all of their equipment behind. Despite the imminent collapse of French resistance in the north, Mussolini's attempted invasion was countered by fierce resistance from French Alpine units, the Army of the Alps; had these *Chasseurs Alpins* failed, there might not have been a Vichy Republic after the French surrender of 25 July. In Hitler's view, had Italy entered the war earlier, at the same time as the German push through the Low Countries and into France, the campaign could have been shorter and less costly, and victory in France would have been complete. As it was, the Italians had earned his contempt for being late in the war and then asking for help from the Luftwaffe, despite having their own powerful air force, the Regia Aeronautica.

War with Italy had become a possibility during the mid-1930s as that country attempted to carve a colonial empire for itself out of Africa. To Mussolini, the Mediterranean was *Mare Nostrum*, 'Our Sea', an arrogant deceit that ignored the rights of the other nations with Mediterranean coastlines. Despite the recession of the late 1920s and early 1930s, Italy had developed powerful armed forces, mainly to secure her colonial ambitions and to control the Mediterranean; but there had also been, at least for part of the time, an arms race with neighbouring France. Compared with the French, the Italians had the advantage of being able to concentrate almost entirely on the Mediterranean, while the French had in effect to maintain both Atlantic and Mediterranean fleets, as well as ensuring the security of her many colonies in Africa, the Caribbean and South America, South-east Asia and the Pacific.

On entry into World War Two, the Italian Navy had six battleships and seven heavy cruisers, as well as fourteen light cruisers – the difference between heavy and light cruisers being laid down in the Washington Naval Treaty, with 'heavy' cruisers having 8in guns, and 'light' having 6in guns. This was a powerful force for a nation with few maritime pretensions. Lighter forces included 122 destroyers and torpedo boats, and – something usually overlooked – there were 119 submarines, almost twice as many as the German *Kriegsmarine* had possessed in 1939.

Many commentators take the view that although it was a modern fleet, the Regia Navale suffered from many shortcomings. Their warship design-ers had placed more emphasis on style and speed than on effective armament and armour protection, but, more important still, they lacked radar. According to Britain's naval commander in the Mediterranean, the Italians 'were no further advanced than we had been at Jutland twenty-five years before'. Although an aircraft carrier was under construction, it was never finished. The one big success lay with the human torpedoes, known officially as the *Siluro a Lenta Corsa*, or 'slow running torpedo', but to their two-man crews as the *Maiale*, or 'pig'. These were ridden by their operators who sat on top, and once inside an enemy harbour and under the target ship, detached the warhead and fastened it to the hull. The intrepid crew could then make their escape on the torpedo. Apart from the obvious dangers and difficulties of penetrating an enemy harbour at night, getting clear was important since the percussive effects of underwater blast meant that the crew were greatly at risk while close to the target.

The main bases for the Italian fleet were at Taranto (in Italy's 'instep'), Genoa in the north-west and La Spezia, slightly further south, as well as Trieste at the northern end of the Adriatic, close to the border with Yugoslavia. Of these, only Taranto was well placed as a forward base as the war developed. It was near Malta, and also provided the shortest mainland shipping route to North Africa, where Italian ground and air forces needed to be kept supplied. Being close to Greece, ships based on Taranto could also effectively cut the entrance to the Adriatic. Indeed, as the leg of Italy virtually bisected the Mediterranean, an active fleet based on Taranto could cut the Mediterranean in half.

Taranto offered everything a naval base could be expected to provide. It was a sheltered anchorage, with both an outer harbour, the Mar Grande, and an inner harbour, the Mar Piccolo. The outer harbour provided moorings for the battleships, while the cruisers and destroyers could use both harbours. A large breakwater shielded the outer harbour from the full force of the elements, for even the Mediterranean can be unkind in winter. In the inner harbour, ships used what was known as 'Mediterranean mooring', i.e. instead of berthing alongside, they were berthed stern to the quayside, packed close together 'like sardines in a tin', as one British airman put it. This had the incidental advantage of making a torpedo attack on any one ship very difficult.

A seaplane station was also provided at Taranto, largely for the aircraft that would be used by the battleships and cruisers once they were at sea, literally the 'eyes of the fleet', and in the absence of radar the only eyes for Italian warships other than their own lookouts. The ship-repair facilities were enhanced for wartime by the use of floating docks. There was also a large oil storage depot.

Italy's geographical position, aided by air bases in Sicily, Sardinia and the Dodecanese, meant that the absence of an aircraft carrier in the Italian fleet was not as serious a drawback as it might seem. Italian aircraft could cover the entire Adriatic as well as a substantial proportion of the Mediterranean from shore bases, especially after Greek islands began to be occupied, and, of course, after the fall of Greece and then of Crete. Not having an aircraft carrier was certainly not as serious as it was to prove to the Germans in wartime, or for that matter, the Dutch forces in the East Indies.

THE REGIA AERONAUTICA

At the outset, the air force, the Regia Aeronautica, had about 5,400 aircraft, of which some 400 were obsolete or obsolescent types based in the African colonies, but the remainder were present in Italy or supporting ground forces in North Africa after the invasion of Egypt in September 1940. In Italy and North Africa, the front-line strength included 975 bombers and 803 fighters and fighter-bombers, more than 400 reconnaissance aircraft with a further 285 maritime-reconnaissance aircraft, but fewer than eighty transports. There were over 2,000 aircraft in the flying schools and technical and specialist units. Typical aircraft included the Fiat BR20M Cicogna bombers, and CR42 and CR50 fighters. Many of the Italian aircraft were well designed, although their air-cooled engines meant that their potential performance was reduced by drag, and later in the war this was overcome by the supply from Germany of Daimler-Benz water-cooled engines for many types. The RA entered the war with poor air defences, lacking the air defence networks enjoyed by the other combatants. Most significant was the lack of even a rudimentary night fighter operation, largely due to the absence of radar.

The best Italian bomber of the war was the Savoia-Marchetti SM79 Sparviero, or Hawk, which was something of an achievement for a company that had made its name as a manufacturer of seaplanes and flying-boats. Savoia's pedigree included an early Schneider Trophy winner, and the SM55X flying-boat that had set many distance records as well as being used for the mass formation flight of Italo Balbo in 1933. The SM79 had already been used in combat, in the one-sided confrontations between Italian forces and those in Abyssinia, in the late 1930s. After successful experiments during 1938, the first torpedo-carrying SM79s were delivered the following year, and at the time of Italy's entry into the war, several anti-shipping units, *Aerosiluranti*, were operational with this aircraft.

Unusually for a bomber at this time, the SM79 was a tri-motor, built of wood, and with a low wing, usually regarded as restricting the size of bomb that could be carried and in contrast to British and American practice. The three Alfa-Romeo RC34 engines each provided 750hp, and the aircraft cruised at 200mph, with a maximum speed of 225mph – so this heavy bomber was considerably faster than a Swordfish. 'Heavy' has to be a relative term for bombers; the SM79 was able to carry a 2,200lb bomb load, and at this early stage of the war, even the twin-engined Wellington could manage twice as much. (More importantly, it was the Axis powers who failed to produce genuine heavy bombers; the Luftwaffe finally got a heavy bomber, the unreliable Heinkel He177, too late and in too small numbers.) As an alternative to bombs, the SM79 could carry two torpedoes, carried externally rather than in the bomb bay. The three-engined layout of the SM79 meant that the bomb-aimer's position was under the fuselage, part way along it, rather than in the more usual nose position. The aircraft had a poor defensive armament, with four machine guns, one positioned behind the cockpit and able to fire forward, two aft of the wings, with one under the fuselage and the other on top, and a fourth towards the rear of the fuselage, but there was no provision for a tail-gunner as such. The two pilots had the benefit of thick armoured plating behind their seats, but no such provision was made for the wireless operator and engineer sitting behind them.

The other aircraft that played a prominent part in the Mediterranean war in 1940 was the Cantieri Cant Z506B, another tri-motor with a wooden fuselage, but in this case a torpedo-bomber and reconnaissance seaplane. This had much the same power-plants as the SM79, but the drag of the floats meant that the maximum speed was less, at around 195mph. Bombs or torpedoes could be carried inside a bomb bay, with a maximum load of around 2,000lb.

The Italian armed forces dominated the Mediterranean. As already mentioned, those of France, even before the war, had to be divided between the Atlantic and the Mediterranean, not including that country's extensive colonial interests. Greece, with a small population and, at this time militarily backward, could only offer tenacity on the battlefield, aided by the rugged terrain of its own border territory. Spain was poor, under-industrialised and still suffering from the effects of the Civil War, only just ended. The only foreign presence was that of the British, with their strategically located bases in the colonies of Gibraltar and Malta, as well as in Egypt and on Cyprus, over which control had been gained in the late nineteenth century. The British armed forces were even more stretched than those of France, with a combination of colonies and protectorates, and there was hardly a continent without a British presence. To some extent, this was offset by the participation in 'Imperial Defence' of the Dominions, but none of these had taken defence seriously between the two world wars and whereas their contribution in manpower terms was to be considerable, the Australians and New Zealanders in particular looked to the UK for support in time of war.

A weakness of the Italian strategic position was that in addition to forces in Libya, it also had forces in Eritrea and Somaliland, which could only be reached through the Suez Canal, a route controlled by the British.

THE REGIA NAVALE

On paper, major units of the Italian fleet sounded impressive enough. The Andrea Doria-class of battleships, which included the *Conte di Cavour* and the *Caio Duilo*, were vessels from World War One, reconstructed between the wars, as indeed were a number of units in the British fleet, including the much heavier battleship *Warspite*. These ships had a tonnage of 22,964 tons, were capable of 27 knots, and had a main armament of ten 12.6in guns, with a secondary armament of twelve 5.2in, ten 3.5in and nineteen 37mm, the last being primarily for anti-aircraft protection.

More modern and more impressive were the Impero-class, under construction just before the outbreak of war and intended to make full use of the maximum dimensions permitted by the Washington Treaty. The four ships included the *Littorio*. These were ships of 35,000 tons, capable of 30.5 knots. Their main armament consisted of nine 15in guns, with a secondary armament of twelve 6in and four 4.7in, twelve 3.5in, twenty 37mm and thirty-two 20mm. For comparison, the British *Prince of Wales* also weighed in at 35,000 tons, but was only capable of 28.5 knots. Her main armament was ten 14in guns, with a secondary armament of sixteen 5.25in, forty-eight 2-pounder pom-poms, a single 40mm and twenty 20mm.

Domination on paper was not the same as domination in reality. The Italian armed forces had not been faced with a serious conflict since the Balkan Wars thirty years earlier. The Italian Navy had not been engaged in a fleet action since the creation of modern Italy in the nineteenth century. Italy's naval history, such as it was, was that of pre-unification Genoa and Venice, the latter state having played a major role in the important Battle of Lepanto in 1571. The 'leg of Italy' created that unusual phenomenon of a country virtually surrounded by the sea, and yet not a maritime power in the true sense. It was as though Italy had a navy because it was expected, rather than out of necessity, as in the case of the British and the French, or even smaller countries such as the Netherlands, since the Dutch have always been a seafaring race. Italy's unification came so late in the country's history that it had no opportunity to create an empire, and so it was that the country that had ruled almost all of the known world at the start of the first millennium had little overseas territory in the closing decades of the second.

Apart from the deficiencies in their ships, there was that of the ships' companies. Training was poor, and so too was the study of naval warfare by the officers. Britain's naval commander in the 'Med', Admiral Sir Andrew Cunningham, recorded: 'They had not visualised a night action between heavy ships and did not keep their heavy guns manned …' The gap between officers and men was far greater even than that of the pre-war Royal Navy, in which progress between the decks had been so difficult in the inter-wars years as to be virtually unknown. This, combined with poor training, meant that good morale and the sense, as Nelson would put it, 'of all being of one company', was hard to achieve. The older officers were aristocratic, the younger officers who had joined the service during the period of Mussolini, *El Duce*, were described as being boorish, while the ratings were peasants, and looked down upon by their officers. Political infiltration of the Regia Navale by the Fascists was resented by the older officers who were of a predominantly royalist state of mind. German interference was later to make this situation much worse, undermining morale still further.

On the other hand, it would be wrong to overlook the fact that the Italian Navy, and the other Italian armed forces, did excel in using small specialised forces, such as the two-man crews of the human torpedoes. Skill, courage and imagination made such teams a potent threat, but a wider *esprit de corps* was usually lacking. Instances of Italian ships being well fought during the war in the Mediterranean were rare, although Cunningham's autobiography does mention one outstanding destroyer action.

While Italy had a major shipbuilding industry, and in many ways was far better equipped for this task than Germany, the other problem faced by the Italian armed forces was the shortage of fuel. Britain possessed the fuel resources of the Middle East and, at times, North America, even after the loss of those in the Dutch East Indies. Italy depended on the Balkans, and on whatever Germany would offer her increasingly despised ally. Fuel was to be one of the objectives in Germany's ill-judged thrust eastward into the Soviet Union, and later in the war, as this failed, so the Italian war machine also suffered and eventually faltered.

Cunningham's autobiography relates how, in 1938, the two Italian battleships, *Giulio Cesare* and the *Conte di Cavour*, under the command of Admiral Riccardi, paid a courtesy visit to Malta. The nature of such visits was that the hosts and guests embarked on a round of entertaining and inspections. In return for British hospitality, Cunningham and his senior officers were invited aboard.

We lunched on board the *Conte di Cavour* with Admiral Riccardi, and came to the conclusion that he must have embarked the whole catering staff and band from one of the best hotels in Rome, so distinguished was his entertainment. Afterwards he took us round his palatial and highly decorated private apartments, and took some pride in pointing out a book, *The Life of Nelson,* which always lay on a table by his bedside. His subsequent actions during the war showed that he had not greatly profited by his nightly reading.

There it was, in a nutshell. Despite the impressive armament, the *Conte di Cavour* was really an admiral's yacht. By the outbreak of war Riccardi had become Chief of the Italian Naval Staff, based in Rome at the Italian Admiralty, or *Supermarina.* No British naval officer would have boasted *The Life of Nelson* by the side of his bunk; indeed, it would have earmarked him as at best a poser, and at worst, an amateur. A true naval officer did not need to display knowledge of Nelson's life, since this was taken as read, and whereas Nelson's example of leadership remained important, strategy had moved on in 135 years.

While the Italian Navy must have understood that war was likely, and that the United Kingdom would be the most likely opponent from the start of the Abyssinian adventure in the mid-1930s, no official indication was given to the armed forces, until April 1940, that Italy would expect to fight alongside the Germans. Mussolini listened to and consulted the army, who dominated the Supreme Command, leaving the sailors and airmen to do as they were told.

The Chief of the Italian Naval Staff, Admiral Domenico Cavagnari, also held the political post of Under Secretary of State for the Navy, and should have wielded great influence. He wrote to Mussolini, effectively complaining that entering a war once it had already started meant that any chance of surprise had gone. In the circumstances, Italy was in a weak position. Cavagnari thought that Britain and France could block the Mediterranean at both ends and starve Italy of the fuel and raw materials needed to survive, let alone prosecute a war, or seek combat, in which case both sides could expect heavy losses. He stressed the difficulties inherent on being dependent on the co-operation and goodwill of the Regia Aeronautica.

This was a pessimistic forecast but in many ways realistic, certainly more so than that of the Italian Army. That the Army had not properly considered the impact of maritime strategy in wartime soon became apparent. On the eve of war, the Italian Army maintained that it had six months' supplies in Libya. Once fighting started, and especially after Marshal Graziani, Italy's commander in North Africa, began his push towards Egypt on 13

September, the demand for supplies of all kinds soared. A convoy system had to be hastily initiated, but here the lack of Italian preparation was soon to be felt, as often just one or two small warships would guard a number of merchantmen.

FACING THE ITALIANS

While the Italians were possessive about the Mediterranean, their fleet did little to enforce ownership. Early forays proved inconclusive, and indeed the Italians seemed remarkably inept at bringing opposing forces to battle. Cunningham did not hesitate to display British naval power, in a display of confidence that was to be short-lived as Italian air power began to manifest itself in the heavy air raids on Malta. At sea, maritime reconnaissance by air was initially to prove a problem. The Italians used single-engined Cant seaplanes operated by the Regia Aeronautica, while the British used lumbering flying-boats that were easy prey to Italian fighters.

As war threatened, the British Mediterranean Fleet left its peacetime base at Malta, one of the Royal Navy's most popular peacetime postings, and moved to its wartime base at Alexandria, where it could guard the Suez Canal and was well away from enemy air attack. While the strategic position in 1939 meant that Alexandria was a safe haven, it was far from ideal. There was no dry dock capable of accommodating a warship bigger than a cruiser, and a large floating dock had to be sent for from Portsmouth, as the closest available, in Malta, had suffered from neglect. An airfield for aircraft carriers to send their planes ashore while in port also had to be built, and this was in hand with a base at Dekheila, which was later to prove to be a great boon, both for operations against Axis shipping and in support of the British Army in the Western Desert.

Despite the problems affecting British naval aviation between the wars, the practice had been acquired of providing the British Mediterranean Fleet with an aircraft carrier. At first, this had been *Glorious*, but after she was recalled during the Norwegian campaign, she was eventually replaced, as mentioned earlier, by the elderly *Eagle*, a converted battleship with no great speed.

The other mainstay of the Mediterranean Fleet was the World War One-vintage battleship *Warspite*, with her eight 15in guns. A veteran of Jutland, where she had been badly damaged and her steering put out of action, she had been extensively modernised between 1933 and 1936 to improve her performance. In 1940, *Warspite* had a full load tonnage of 36,450 tons, and was capable of more than 25 knots. In addition to her 15in main armament, she had a secondary armament of eight 6in guns, eight 4in guns, thirty-two 2-pounder pom-poms and fifteen 12.7mm machine guns. This was the one warship available to Cunningham on Italy's entry into the war that could fight on an equal footing with the Italian battleships and cruisers.

Cunningham also had two other battleships, but neither had been modernised to the same extent as *Warspite*. These two ships, *Malaya* and *Royal Sovereign*, were both too slow by the standards of 1939. In addition to destroyers, the Mediterranean Fleet also included five cruisers.

Egypt at the time was in theory an independent sovereign state, with its own monarchy and armed forces. Nevertheless, it was run virtually as a British protectorate, if not actually a colony. Alexandria was essentially an Egyptian naval base, but the situation was eased and liaison with the British Mediterranean Fleet simplified by the fact that the Egyptian Navy had a British admiral in command.

The role of Malta in wartime had been a matter of considerable controversy. At the time of the Abyssinian crisis in 1935, the Grand Harbour had AA defences of around twelve guns, with some searchlights, and this defence was hastily increased to twenty-four guns with additional searchlights, but most of them were obsolete 3in weapons. The RAF took the attitude that Malta could not be defended against heavy aerial attack from bases in Sicily, and the Army accepted this view. Both services would have abandoned Malta, but the Admiralty insisted that it could be used as a base for offensive operations, no doubt also appreciating its value to an enemy in cutting the sea lanes across the Mediterranean, although they probably failed to realise that in due course the island could also be isolated.

The attitude of the other two services possibly reflected the defeatist attitude to the bomber that prevailed throughout the 1930s, when the view had become accepted that 'the bomber will always get through'. This fear of a bomber offensive was obviously not to be taken lightly, as subsequent events were to prove, but it was overstated. It may well have been a factor in the reluctance of Britain and France to go to war in 1938, and it certainly was a consideration in the two allies not initiating a bomber offensive during the Battle of France in 1940 as the French feared German retaliation. Incredible as it may seem in retrospect, Malta did not have a single fighter squadron in 1939 or 1940. Four Gloster Sea Gladiators in crate were all that were available. The senior RAF officer on the island asked Cunningham if he could use the four aircraft, and Cunningham readily gave his permission. Three aircraft were assembled, the famous trio of *Faith*, *Hope* and *Charity*, leaving the fourth for spares. These obsolete biplanes gave a good account of themselves as the air war developed over the island, but within a month or so, someone at the Admiralty, ignoring what was being done to protect their base and naval assets, demanded to know who had permitted Fleet Air Arm spares to be handed over to the Royal Air Force.

'I wondered where the official responsible had been spending his war,' Cunningham remarked.

After German forces swept through France, urgent action was taken to create what was in effect a fleet for the Western Mediterranean; this was Force H, based on Gibraltar and under the command of Vice-Admiral Sir James Somerville. Force H also ventured into the Atlantic, as circumstances demanded, and included the still new aircraft carrier HMS *Ark Royal*. By comparison, the Mediterranean Fleet was at first poorly provided for, having only the elderly *Eagle*, with just eighteen Swordfish. Determined to do something about it, her Commander Flying, Commander C. L. Keighly-Peach, an old *Glorious* hand, found three Gloster Sea Gladiator fighters, and put these antique biplanes into service, flying one himself and training two Swordfish pilots in the dark arts of fighter work.

Charles 'K.P.' Keighly-Peach's career reflected the changes in naval aviation between the two world wars. He had joined the Royal Navy in the most conventional way possible, as one might expect of the son of a rear admiral, going first to the college at Osborne in 1915 at the age of thirteen, and then continuing to Dartmouth. After serving in a number of warships, he had qualified as a pilot in 1926, when naval aviation was well and truly under RAF control. His first flying appointment was with the RAF's No. 3 Squadron ashore, but in 1927 he joined what was then 402 Flight, flying Fairey Flycatchers from HMS *Eagle*. He then became a member of that select club who could draw flying pay and submarine pay at the same time, as he flew the diminutive Parnall Peto seaplane off the ill-fated submarine *M2*. In 1930, he served in the cruiser *Centaur*, before joining 408 Flight aboard *Glorious*, flying Hawker Nimrods, and was still with the flight when it amalgamated with 409 Flight to become 802 Naval Air Squadron in 1933. A staff job followed before he returned to sea aboard the cruiser *London*.

His fighter experience was to prove invaluable, giving the Mediterranean Fleet at least some cover while they awaited the arrival of *Illustrious* and her Fulmars.

Rather than sit and wait for something to happen, once Italy entered the war, the Mediterranean Fleet raided Italian ports along the coastline of North Africa, but this failed to draw the Italian fleet to sea. Instead, the Italians seemed more concerned with protecting their convoys crossing the Mediterranean between Italy and North Africa. The sole Italian naval offensive action during this early period resulted in the loss of the light cruiser *Calypso* in a torpedo attack by an Italian submarine.

Cunningham had written to Pound requesting a modern aircraft carrier and a modern battleship, as well as heavy cruisers able to counter the 8in guns of the Italian fleet.

The multiple pom-poms fitted to both *Illustrious* and *Warspite* were to prove a highly effective anti-aircraft weapon, ('probably the best AA defence any ship could have', one naval airman recalls), giving crews great confidence as the war progressed. They were to be needed. The Regia Aeronautica proved to have squadrons specially trained in high-level bombing attacks against warships as well as the torpedo-carrying anti-shipping units. Speed was not much in evidence among many units of the Mediterranean Fleet, and manoeuvrability could be difficult to attain in some of the channels and narrows, especially those close to Malta.

FIRST SHOTS IN THE 'MED'

The situation in Malta was likely to be serious. Cunningham, who had spent much time on the island, was well aware of this. While the Admiralty was determined that the islands should be held, and Cunningham took the same view, he realised that there were many practical measures to be taken. Stores would have to be cut to the minimum necessary to protect the islands, with everything else that was useful moved to Alexandria for the Mediterranean Fleet. A number of civilians and dependents of British servicemen posted away from Malta had already taken a liner home. British civilians, if willing, would also have to be evacuated, along with the wives and children of the naval personnel, many of whom had been scattered as ships were redeployed at short notice as the war developed. This was more than a case of taking them out of harm's way once the bombing started, but also a recognition that they were a drain on Malta's finite resources, unable to produce enough food for its own dense population of around 280,000, excluding British service personnel, in 1940. Traditionally, supplies had come in small quantities, manageable for the limited port facilities, in small craft, many of them still worked by sail, from Italy, Sicily and Tunisia. These sources would no longer exist, and convoys would have to be fought through to Malta from either Gibraltar, having first steamed through the Bay of Biscay from the UK, or Alexandria.

The evacuation of British civilians and the dependents of service personnel was undertaken in July 1940, sending them by sea to Alexandria as a first step in what was to be a long journey home. Two convoys were used, one fast, with the civilians, and the other slow, carrying naval stores regarded as being superfluous as the fleet redeployed eastward to Alexandria, out of range of enemy aircraft. Cunningham took the Mediterranean Fleet westward to protect the two convoys, hoping that the temptation offered by the ships and his own show of force would bring the Italian Admiral Inigo Campioni to battle.

The first response of the Italians was to send the high-level bombers of the Regia Aeronautica to attack the fleet. The people of Malta had grown accustomed to this, but for many of the seafarers aboard the ships it was their first experience of bombing. Dropped from 12,000 feet, the bombs screamed down, while the vessels thudded and shook to the sound and recoil of their own AA guns. Ships disappeared from sight as bombs sent fountains of water, stained black by the explosive, high above their decks, while pieces of shrapnel struck the sides.

'It was a comfort to remember that there was always more water than ship,' commented Cunningham. 'But not very much, for a ship stood up huge, bare and exposed, above the absorbing flat acres of the sea.'

Contrary to popular belief, Italian bombing was excellent. Cunningham recalled later: 'It is not too much to say of those early months that the Italian high-level bombing was the best I have ever seen, far better than the German ... I shall always remember it with respect.' Only one ship, the cruiser HMS *Gloucester*, received a direct hit, although near misses damaged the unarmoured hull plates of destroyers, and the 'mining' effect of close underwater explosions caused internal damage. Damage to the *Gloucester* was serious enough. She was hit on the bridge, killing seven officers, including her captain, and eleven ratings. Prompt action saw the fires extinguished and control regained as she was steered from her emergency position aft.

Not all of the movement around Malta was away from the islands. As the Battle of France developed, the Fleet Air Arm was using Hyères de la Palyvestre in southern France for advanced flying training, with the elderly aircraft carrier *Argus* for deck landings. This task was assigned to 767 Squadron, which arrived in the area in November 1939. Training continued even as the Germans pushed west, and after Italy entered the war on 10 June, nine of the squadron's aircraft were flown by the instructors to bomb the port of Genoa on 13 June.

The fall of France put the squadron in a difficult position. As soon as Italy entered the war, *Argus* had been recalled for her own safety, so returning aboard was not an option. Neither was internment for the duration of the war. In the end, 767's CO took the squadron to Bône in North Africa, after which the less experienced student pilots were sent home via Casablanca and Gibraltar. Six of the squadron's twenty-four aircraft joined *Ark Royal*, with Force H, to be absorbed into her squadrons, while the bulk of the aircraft, twelve in all, went to Malta to what was then the RAF station at Hal Far, and formed the basis of a new squadron, 830, with a new CO, Lt Cdr F. D. Howie. The new squadron soon showed that it deserved its combat '800' series, and proved that those in the Admiralty who believed that Malta had a role as a base for offensive operations were right. Bombing raids were carried out against Sicily, starting with an attack on Augusta on 30 June, and Libya, while on 19 July the squadron sank a U-boat.

Cunningham already knew by 8 July that the Italians had two battleships at sea. The information had come from the submarine HMS *Phoenix*, which had spotted the two ships 200 miles east of Malta and steaming on a southerly course. This was confirmed later by a flying-boat based on the island, with the additional information that they were accompanied by six cruisers and seven destroyers, escorting a large convoy. He changed course towards the Italians, hoping to get between them and their base at Taranto.

The next morning, a flying-boat again reported the Italians as being 145 miles to the west of the Mediterranean Fleet at 07.30. Further confirmation came from aircraft flown off from *Eagle*. By noon, the distance had closed to 80 miles, and it was not until then that Campioni, racing to get under the air cover of aircraft based in Sicily, received his first indication of the British presence from a seaplane catapulted from his own ship, the *Giulio Cesare*.

With most of the British ships other than *Warspite* outgunned by the Italians, the British launched two strikes of Swordfish armed with torpedoes from *Eagle* before noon and then around 16.00. Unfortunately, neither strike scored any hits on the Italians, which might at least have slowed down the larger ships, and could even have proved fatal to cruisers. Meanwhile, just before 15.00, two British cruisers spotted some of the Italian cruisers. A few minutes later, four Italian heavy cruisers opened fire with their 8in main armament, outgunning their British counterparts which had only 6in guns. Fortunately, Cunningham had raced ahead of his other two battleships with *Warspite*, and at a shade under 15 miles, he opened fire, forcing the Italians to withdraw under cover of a smokescreen. As Cunningham waited for his two older battleships and *Eagle* to catch up, two Italian heavy cruisers attempted to attack the carrier, but were dissuaded from doing so by further fire from the 15in guns of *Warspite* and the other two battleships. At 16.00, the two fleets' battleships were within sight of one another, and *Warspite* opened fire again, at a range of nearly 15 miles and almost immediately after the second Swordfish strike. The Italians replied with ranging shots straddling the British ships, but shortly afterwards Cunningham had the satisfaction of seeing a direct hit by a salvo of 15in shells on the *Giulio Cesare*, hitting at the base of one of her funnels. The Italians broke off the engagement, turning away under cover of a heavy smokescreen. Unable to catch the faster Italian ships, and aware of the dangers of being caught by enemy submarines, Cunningham turned, and as his ships followed, Italian bombers finally arrived to attack *Warspite* and *Eagle*, but then bombed their own ships by mistake – an event reported by the jubilant observer aboard the Swordfish floatplane launched by *Warspite* before the start of the action.

So ended what has usually been described as the Battle of Calabria, but which is sometimes also referred to as the Battle of Punta Stilo: the only one in the entire war when two full battle fleets actually engaged one another. The United States Navy was later to come close to such an engagement during the final stages of the Battle for Guadalcanal, but one of the two US battleships suffered an electrical failure and could not fire her guns. The Imperial Japanese Navy attempted to force such an engagement at Leyte Gulf, but again failed as carrier-borne aircraft took over. All other engagements either involved a single capital ship on one side or the other, as with the hunt for the *Bismarck* or the Battle of the River Plate, or had the primary role conducted by aircraft while the opposing fleets were out of sight and out of gun range.

THE FRENCH CONNECTION

The fall of France had created an unexpected problem for the Royal Navy. The ships of their erstwhile ally were scattered at a number of ports, in the Atlantic from Portsmouth to Dakar in West Africa, and in the Mediterranean from Mers-el-Kebir to Alexandria in North Africa. While the Royal Navy was reluctant to take action against the French, the attitude of the new Vichy French government was an unknown quantity. It was important that the ships should not fall into German hands. At Portsmouth, the ships were seized by boarding, while action was taken against those at Dakar and Mers-el-Kebir by major surface units, including aircraft carriers. The ships at Alexandria posed yet another problem for Cunningham.

Cunningham had every sympathy with his French counterpart, Vice-Admiral Godfroy, who knew that he was under orders from his Admiralty to sail, but was trying to confirm that the order was authentic. There was at this stage of the war no Free French force with which to align those ships caught outside France. Naturally, most of the personnel involved wished to return home to their families. No one wanted to be accused of scuttling their ships, or handing them over intact to either the British or the Germans.

Realising that Godfroy would be aware of the action taken against the rest of the French warships elsewhere, Cunningham knew that his only alternatives were to intern the ships or risk unnecessary bloodshed on both sides by sinking them. After initially appearing to accept internment, with the repatriation of most of his ships' companies, while the vessels would be relieved of their fuel and the warheads taken off their torpedoes, the Vichy government's orders to sail forced Godfroy to change his mind. He instructed his ships to raise steam – a process that would take up to eight hours. Cunningham was alerted and, going on deck, saw not only that the ships were raising steam, but that their guns had been uncovered and they were ready for action, with the real possibility of a close-range gun battle in Alexandria harbour. The British warships immediately did the same, removing the tompions (muzzle covers, usually made from steel or brass and often decorated with the ship's crest) from their guns.

Each French warship had been given a British opposite number and it was the job of her commanding officer to maintain liaison with his French counterpart. Cunningham immediately ordered his COs to visit the French, while the flagship signalled each French warship in turn advising them of the British government's offer of repatriation if the warships were put out of use. The visitors to the French warships were not unwelcome. The captain of a cruiser welcoming Captain Rory O'Connor of the *Neptune* admitted: 'When I saw the tompions being removed from your guns, I immediately ordered the tompions to be placed in mine.'

In many cases, the decision was taken out of the hands of commanding officers as French ratings held meetings on deck, while the French commanding officers visited Godfroy on his flagship, *Dusquesne*. An hour later, Godfroy asked to see Cunningham. They agreed that all fuel oil was to be discharged from the French ships, their guns were to be disabled, and some 70 per cent of their crews were to be landed and eventually repatriated.

No attempt was made to press the French ships into the Royal Navy. Apart from any question of honour, another consideration was that the French used different gun calibres from the British – 5.1in instead of 6in, and 3.5in instead of 4in or the increasingly common 4.5in – and this would have compounded the problem of inadequate ammunition supplies already being experienced. It was unlikely that sufficient spare personnel would have been available to man them in any case. Leaving small crews behind meant that the ships were maintained ready for the day of liberation.

The French fleet no longer presented a threat by 7 July, allowing the British to leave Alexandria without any concern over possible French action to seize the port or the Suez Canal.

BRINGING THE ITALIANS TO ACTION

Meanwhile, there were occasional actions between other units of both the Italian and British fleets. Typical of these was the action off Cape Spada in Crete on 19 July 1940. In this, two Italian light cruisers, *Bartolomeo Colleoni* and *Giovanni delle Bande Nere*, engaged the Australian light cruiser HMAS *Sydney* accompanied by five destroyers. The Italians had the upper hand at the start of this engagement as their ships outgunned the destroyers and outnumbered the British cruiser. But a direct hit by *Sydney* put the

Colleoni's boilers out of action, and she lost way, before being sunk. While *Bande Nere* managed to hit *Sydney*, the Australian cruiser struck back and damaged the remaining Italian ship, which then took refuge in Benghazi, Libya.

On 15 August, expecting the Italians to move eastward to threaten the Suez Canal, Cunningham took his battleships and the heavy cruiser *Kent*, newly arrived, to bombard coastal positions around Bardia and Fort Capuzzo, near Sollum. RAF fighter support was added to that of *Eagle*'s own fighters operating from a shore base. The fighters accounted for twelve of the Savoia-Marchetti SM79 heavy bombers sent to attack the British ships. A week later, on the night of 22–23 August, destroyers were sent in to bombard the seaplane base at Bomba, west of Tobruk, while three of *Eagle*'s Swordfish, operating from a forward shore base, attacked enemy shipping. The flight of three aircraft was led by Captain Oliver 'Olly' Patch of the Royal Marines. On arrival at Bomba, they found a large Italian depot ship, with a destroyer and a submarine lying on either side, while a second larger submarine lay astern. Patch torpedoed and sank the latter, while the other two Swordfish attacked the submarine and destroyer lying alongside the depot ship, which also sank. Cunningham noted with satisfaction that it was 'a most daring and gallant effort on the part of our young gentlemen from the *Eagle*'.

CHAPTER SIX

Off to the 'Med'

When Captain Denis Boyd arrived at the Admiralty to meet the First Sea Lord, Dudley Pound, he recalls being surprised to be shaken by the hand, something that had never happened in the twenty-four years that the two officers had known each other. He was also well aware of the vast difference in their ranks.

Pound wasted little time. 'I want you,' he explained, 'in view of the desperate situation, to take *Illustrious* through the Straits of Gibraltar and join Andrew. He needs you badly out there.'

Pound had been very pessimistic about the fate of an aircraft carrier once the war reached the Mediterranean, and no doubt this was reflected in his warm welcome for Boyd. He must have felt that he was sending Boyd to his doom. Cunningham later claimed to have been far more optimistic. Both Pound and Cunningham realised that the Mediterranean Fleet was remarkably short of 'air' early in the war. Cunningham particularly felt the need for better aerial reconnaissance. He had also sought the help of the Air Officer Commanding Middle East, Air Chief Marshal Sir Arthur Longmore, in exercises between his bombers and his ships, but due to a shortage of squadrons, Longmore had refused this request. It has to be a reflection of the poor state of British defences that this happened, since no one would have been better placed to understand the threat that air power posed to shipping than Longmore, who, as we have seen, had in 1914 been the first man to drop a torpedo from an aircraft, flying a Short Folder biplane at Calshot, near the mouth of Southampton Water.

Boyd realised the implications of this seemingly simple order. It could only be a matter of time before Mussolini, who was building up his forces in North Africa, attacked Egypt with the objective of seizing the Suez Canal. Boyd also knew that his ship would be bottled up in the Mediterranean, facing a far larger force in the shape of the Italian Navy and the ever present threat of Italy's powerful air force. He realised that *Illustrious* with her Swordfish bombers and Fulmar fighters, and her air defence radar that could provide early warning of approaching enemy aircraft, would be a great asset to the Mediterranean Fleet. The elderly *Eagle*, originally intended to have been replaced by *Illustrious* or one of her sisters, was not up to the task.

Illustrious had arrived home in the middle of the Battle of Britain. For safety's sake she was sent north to Scapa Flow, away from the constant Luftwaffe attacks. Her squadrons were dispersed. No. 815 was sent to the Royal Naval Air Station at Machrihanish, HMS *Landrail*, just west of Campbeltown on Scotland's Kintyre Peninsula – known as 'Machribloodyhanish' to wartime naval airmen because of its bleak and unwelcoming position, and the poor facilities at many of the hastily constructed naval air stations. No. 819 was at RNAS Abbotsinch, HMS *Sanderling*, close to the fleshpots of Glasgow. The fighter squadron, No. 806, was at RNAS Donibristle, HMS *Merlin*, on the other side of Scotland in Fife. The stay at Donibristle enabled Charles Evans to work up the squadron with its new aircraft, as it had now standardised on the Fairey Fulmar. At this stage, Donibristle was relatively safe from attacking German aircraft – a comfort, since the Fulmars, while a big improvement over the Skua, would have had little chance against a Bf109.

LUMLEY LYSTER JOINS *ILLUSTRIOUS*

When she sailed from Scapa on 22 August, *Illustrious* was not going to the Med on her own. Apart from taking the opportunity to provide a heavy escort for a convoy headed for the Cape and the Mediterranean via Gibraltar, she was accompanied by the recently refitted and modernised battleship *Valiant*, a sister of *Warspite*, and the two anti-aircraft cruisers *Calcutta* and *Coventry*, as well as an escort of destroyers for the four ships. As the Mediterranean Fleet would now have two aircraft carriers, it was also decided to appoint a Rear-Admiral Aircraft Carriers. This was none other than Lumley Lyster himself, who had played such a part in developing the night flying and torpedo-dropping skills of the air squadrons aboard *Glorious* only a short time before. Meanwhile, Robin Kilroy, 815's CO, had been promoted to commander and had left the ship. He was replaced by Lt-Cdr

Kenneth Williamson, a survivor from *Courageous*.

An addition to the ship's company that interested many of those aboard occurred at this time, when Lt-Cdr Opie of the United States Navy joined them as a liaison officer. Even Albert Jones recalls encountering Opie, and thinking it strange that a USN officer should be aboard a British ship when the USA was supposed to be neutral. In fact, there are, and always have been, shades of neutrality, and increasingly the United States was doing everything it could do to help Britain, short of actually going to war.

While *Illustrious* was still in home waters, the naval air squadrons joined her on 11 and 12 August. The aircrew had been recalled at short notice, and many of the ship's officers had to abandon plans for leave. Denis Boyd missed his wedding anniversary and left without seeing his wife. Two of 815's observers, Norman 'Blood' Scarlett and Richard Janvrin, were more fortunate, in that it was a fine day and they had gone fishing with their wives. They were interrupted by a little boy, leaning over a stone wall and asking politely: 'Are you from the Navy, sir? Because I think that you're wanted on the phone.' It was to be a last-minute rush to get aboard, what the Navy called a 'pierhead jump'.

Life for the aircrew was exciting, but sometimes unnecessarily so. Carrier aircrew and the handlers on the flight deck and in the hangar need to be kept in more or less constant practice – so much can go wrong and the 'airfield' is rarely without some motion of its own depending on the state of the sea. *Illustrious* was to be no exception. There was the case of a Swordfish pilot who lost his depth charges without realising it on a training sortie, or the time when a Swordfish returned with its bombs, missed the arrester wires, attempted to climb while its tailhook was still down, and caught the barrier, collapsing on to the flight deck, rupturing fuel tanks and skidding across the deck in a shower of blue sparks while the bombs detached from the racks and rolled everywhere. It was a miracle that no one was hurt. On other occasions, bombs were accidentally released while aircraft were on the flight deck, but failed to explode because the arming vanes did not have enough height to work. Still more serious, a Swordfish pilot dropped his torpedo on to the hangar deck: had it rolled over it would have set off the firing whisker. These were serious accidents, all containing the potential for disaster. Nor were the aircrew the only culprits, as a maintainer accidentally fired the eight machine guns of a Fulmar while still in the hangar – an accident that occurred rarely, but when it did on one occasion aboard

Formidable later in the war thirty aircraft were destroyed in the subsequent fire.

Events such as these kept everyone on their toes, although perhaps none more so than the crowd of spectators who would stand on the island in what became known in the Royal Navy as 'goofers' gallery', watching aircraft take off and, even more exciting, land on, in the hope of seeing a mishap. Perhaps the American term for this location, 'vultures' row', was the more apt!

Most members of the Fleet Air Arm, regardless of whether they were aircrew, handlers or maintainers, much preferred life aboard ship to that on shore at the new air stations. Accommodation was cramped, especially given the enhanced wartime complements of warships, and noisy, but it was cleaner and, usually, drier than that ashore.

Despite the mishaps, the reinforcements reached Gibraltar safely on 29 August, where they found *Ark Royal*, part of the Gibraltar-based Force H, still not using her safety barrier or a batsman. 'Streamline' Robertson had ensured that the ship's aircrew were by now flying to a high standard. At this time, a major part of Force H's activities was the escort of convoys eastward as far as Malta, there being convoys both for Malta itself and for Alexandria. It would not be long before convoys for Alexandria would have to take the long and circuitous route via the Cape of Good Hope and the Suez Canal as Italian and German airpower came to dominate the Mediterranean. The irony was that the forces protecting the Suez Canal as a short cut to the East were eventually forced to use it to sustain themselves rather than keeping it open for its original purpose.

BRIEFING

Captain Boyd's style was to keep his officers in the picture. Today, he would be described as being a good communicator, someone who 'walks the talk', always seen and always approachable. During the carrier's short stay at Gibraltar, before sailing, he gave all of the carrier's officers a briefing on the strategic situation in the Mediterranean. This would be the last chance for some time to get everyone together. Once the ship passed into the 'Med', her officers would be engaged in their daily tasks – taking watches, on the bridge or in the engine room, looking after the ship's air defences, waiting for Italian attack and, of course, many of them in the air, maintaining anti-submarine and combat air patrols, or providing reconnaissance, so that the convoy could not be 'jumped' by Italian surface vessels.

Boyd told them that the Italians had been mounting an all-out aerial assault on the Mediterranean Fleet since entering the war on 10 June, using Cantieri, Savoia-Marchetti and Breda aircraft. With bases offshore in Sicily, Sardinia and the Dodecanese Islands, which Italy had occupied in 1912, as well as in mainland Italy and North Africa, they had the ability to dominate the air over most of the Mediterranean. He explained that it was only a matter of time before Italy invaded Greece. The Greeks, while still neutral at this time, had been assured the year before, when Italy invaded Albania, that if Italy invaded, Britain would help her, and had been given a signed guarantee.

He also covered the situation in North Africa, before saying: 'For the next few months there will be no shortage of targets for the Swordfish squadrons. We shall be attacking the enemy from the Dodecanese to Libya. On this passage we are to do a surprise raid on their airfield in the island of Rhodes, called Calato … *Eagle*'s Swordfish will be attacking Martiza at the same time – their other base in the Dodecanese Islands.' The base at Calato had been used for offensive operations against British shipping for a couple of months since Italy had entered the war.

Illustrious was also to ferry new aircraft and other equipment to No. 830 Squadron, the Swordfish unit at RAF Hal Far in Malta. Inevitably, given 830's proximity to Italian bases in Sicily, the squadron had suffered very heavy losses, but had been the only effective striking force within reach of Italian shipping, plying the north–south route between Italy and North Africa while the British attempted to keep open their east–west route. Not for nothing was the sea off Malta the cross-roads of the Mediterranean. Yet, despite its front-line role, 830 did not have blind-flying panels for night operations, and it did not have long-range tanks. These deficiencies were to be made good by the equipment being carried aboard *Illustrious*. It was widely believed that one reason for the heavy losses suffered by 830 during its first few frantic months was the lack of additional fuel tanks, needed to allow for flying in higher temperatures when piston-engined aircraft not only consumed more fuel, but the fuel itself expanded in volume and also evaporated. The lack of blind-flying panels also made operations more hazardous.

Interestingly, Boyd maintained that the Italian bombing was very inaccurate because of the high altitudes maintained during the bombing run – in complete contrast to the views of Cunningham. Whether this was the opinion of a naval officer with a far greater understanding of aviation and its potential than his admiral, or whether he was concerned to maintain morale amongst his ship's company before entering the maelstrom of the 'Med', is a moot point.

The significance of *Illustrious* joining the Mediterranean Fleet was also pointed out. Her radar was better than that on any other ship in the Fleet, and despite the performance weaknesses of the Fulmar, more efficient fighter-direction was possible, and Boyd really felt that 806 could make a big difference. 'It is my guess that 806 Squadron from this ship is going to give the Italians the surprise of their lives in the next thirty-six hours,' he assured them.

Nevertheless, he also pointed out that Commander Keighly-Peach, *Eagle*'s Commander Flying, had taught his pilots fighter techniques, and that the ship's scant force of only three Sea Gladiators had accounted for eleven Italian aircraft. All this was achieved despite their lack of radar.

Later that same day, a shortened version of the briefing was broadcast by Boyd over the carrier's tannoy system, with the addition of 'Mussolini has become boastful; he has got into the habit of referring to the Mediterranean as "Mare Nostrum", which means "our sea". We are going to change all that … we are going to change it to "Cunningham's Pond". I tell you that with no uncertain voice …'

NO UNCERTAIN VOICE

The operation to reinforce the Mediterranean Fleet was known as Operation Hats, and would involve both the Mediterranean Fleet and Force H. The risks of failure were too awful to contemplate.

Leaving Gibraltar on 30 August with Force H, *Illustrious*, *Valiant*, *Calcutta* and *Coventry* were soon spotted by the Italians. This was not surprising, as the Italians had almost certainly been tipped off by Axis sympathisers in Spain who could clearly see movements in and out of Gibraltar, aided by those in Morocco or the Spanish enclaves in North Africa. Before leaving 'Gib', the pilots and observers were warned that any strange aircraft would be hostile. As the ships crossed the Mediterranean, it was judged wise to send the Fulmars on combat air patrols, and on 2 September they quickly caught three Italian bombers and scattered a number of others. Believing that offence is the best means of defence, the Swordfish squadrons were armed with 250lb bombs and sent to attack Cagliari in Sardinia.

In any major warship, only a relatively small proportion of the crew can see what is going on; this is especially true during combat, nowhere more so than with an aircraft carrier, whose aircraft may be engaged in conflict some distance away. Aboard *Illustrious,* the eyes and ears for the whole ship were to be the broadcasts over the tannoy system at such times by the ship's padre, the Revd Henry Lloyd, who gave a running account of the conflict, so that as soon as a fighter shot down an enemy bomber, everyone came to know about it. And thanks to intercepted Italian radio transmissions, those aboard the British ships soon realised that the Italians thought they were facing the much more potent Spitfire, or 'spittyfurers'.

The threat from the air was not the only hazard. Force H left *Illustrious* and the other new arrivals at the start of the Pantellaria Straits, south-west of Sicily, steaming at speed through the night towards Malta, with paravanes deployed to cut mine mooring cables, just in case. The following morning, mine-mooring wires were found on the starboard paravane. Striking one of these could have seriously damaged the carrier, and would have crippled a cruiser.

Now much closer to Italian territory, the CAP provided by the Fulmars proved essential. Having passed through the Pantellaria Straits safely, a heavy attack by Italian high-level bombers was waiting – but one of these fell prey to one of 806's Fulmars. Malta was not the destination on this occasion, and once clear of Sicily, a fresh escort was waiting south of Malta – the battleships and cruisers of the Mediterranean Fleet, with what was to be Lyster's other carrier, *Eagle* – for the second half of the voyage to Alexandria. Nevertheless, the opportunity was taken to put two convoys, one each from east and west, into increasingly beleaguered Malta.

While the Swordfish maintained anti-submarine patrols ahead of the convoy, their crews also ensured that the equipment intended for 830 Squadron at Hal Far was delivered. This required a total of thirty flights, the aircraft taking off in pairs or, occasionally, three at a time, with the new blind-flying instrument panels in the rear cockpit and the long-range fuel tanks slung under the fuselage. They also ferried 830's six new Swordfish.

Again, the Fleet Air Arm made a fighting progress across the Mediterranean. Swordfish were sent into action once more as they progressed eastward. Cunningham split his fleet into two divisions to pass north and south of Crete. Dawn on 4 September saw every available aircraft from both carriers sent on the planned attack against the airfields on the Greek island of Rhodes, notably the Italian airfields at Calato and Scarpanto, whose bomber aircraft had been making nightly raids on Alexandria. Because of the variable winds, *Eagle* was a quarter of an hour late in flying off her aircraft, so that when they arrived, the Italians had had time to put fighters in the air, and were able to shoot down four of the carrier's Swordfish, with the loss of their entire crews. Yet, as before, the slow and lumbering aircraft made their mark, leaving hangars and barracks destroyed, and aircraft on fire. As one pilot put it, being bombed by elderly-looking biplanes must have left the Italians feeling bewildered! To add to their problems, the Australian cruiser HMAS *Sydney* shelled Scarpanto.

Strangely, public announcements of the Fleet Air Arm's bombing activities in the Mediterranean early in the fighting usually gave the credit to the RAF. Officially, this was for security reasons, since an aircraft carrier such as *Illustrious*, though mobile and able to turn up close to a target, almost at will, could steam no more than 30 nautical miles in an hour, or 360 nautical miles in twelve hours, while *Eagle* was at best unable to do more than 480 nautical miles in twenty-four hours. Yet the Italians already knew that the Mediterranean Fleet had at least one carrier, and would definitely have known about the arrival of *Illustrious* by this time.

The Regia Aeronautica, however, certainly did not intend to give the new arrival an easy time. Wave after wave of Italian aircraft struggled to reach the convoy, as 806 squadron operated three watches with aircraft patrolling at 20,000 feet under the control of the carrier's fighter-direction team. A senior naval pilot, on passage to Alexandria to command the naval air station at Dekheila, volunteered his services to a grateful Charles Evans, concerned at the pressure under which his team were being placed. No doubt, being an ex-fighter pilot, the offer was also prompted by boredom and frustration at missing the increasingly hectic action over the Fleet.

The pilot's sortie was uneventful until just before the end, when he was vectored on to a Cantieri reconnaissance aircraft that had been shadowing the Fleet. He promptly disposed of the Cantieri, but then an RAF Lockheed Hudson appeared on the scene, completely unaware that it had blundered into an air-to-air combat zone, flying directly towards the patrolling Fulmar. Approaching him head on, the naval pilot could not see the aircraft's markings, and with no time to check, instinctively fired a quick burst into the intruder. As he pulled away to get into position for a second attack, the Fulmar pilot, to his horror, saw the roundels and recognised the aircraft. Too late, for his first burst had done enough damage. Badly damaged, the Hudson limped away in the direction of North Africa, where its four-man crew became prisoners of the Vichy French.

Of course, the Hudson should not have been anywhere near the Fleet. Throughout the war, ships on the watch for air attack always posed problems for friendly aircraft, and it was not unknown for carrier aircraft to come under AA fire as they approached their own ship to land. The Hudson's crew might also have been better off had the plane been ditched, but the instinct of its pilot would have been to head for land, possibly hoping to keep the aircraft airborne long enough to reach friendly territory. Inevitably, the so-called 'fog of war' played a part, and this was an example of what would today be described as either 'friendly fire' or, officially, 'blue on blue'.

Fighter defences should never be judged simply by the number of 'kills' – their score of enemy aircraft shot down. The primary duty of fighter defences is to break up and disrupt the enemy attack. Likewise, whereas shooting down an enemy fighter in a dogfight might appear to be the more glorious and satisfying outcome, a bomber is a much better target.

At last the Mediterranean Fleet had its reinforcements, two of which brought air defence radar to the Fleet for the first time, so that instead of scanning the sky in the hope of spotting attacking aircraft early enough, they could be detected 40 or even 50 miles away. This meant that the long periods of having anti-aircraft gun crews 'closed up' for action were much reduced. 'A very welcome let up,' as Cunningham noted.

CUNNINGHAM THE COMMANDER

Lyster and Boyd now had a new commander, Admiral Sir Andrew Browne Cunningham, known affectionately in the Royal Navy as 'ABC'. Cunningham is a difficult man to assess. A Scot, he was undoubtedly one of the most successful front-line commanders of the war. Equally, he was able to move from the role of active front-line commander to managing strategy, bureaucracy and politics when he later took over as First Sea Lord. No less a diarist of the war years than General Sir Alan Brooke, later Field Marshal

Lord Alanbrooke, had high praise for Cunningham's leadership; and this from a man who, far from suffering fools gladly, refused to suffer them at all. Cunningham certainly inspired affection in his officers, and Brooke was grateful for the man's bluff good humour, something that must have been a relief in the hot-house deliberations of the War Cabinet and the Chiefs of Staff Committee. For Brooke, Cunningham was also a welcome change from his predecessor, the ailing Dudley Pound.

Without doubt, Cunningham was a hard man to work for. He gave little praise, believing that anything less than perfection and high achievement was a failure to perform one's duty. He maintained the smallest staff possible. He has also been described as having a 'sledge-hammer personality', compelling officers to stand up to him. One of Cunningham's staff officers recalls that all eight officers were driven very hard indeed, with little sympathy from their chief. 'I've never heard of a staff officer dying of overwork,' Cunningham is alleged to have said on one occasion. 'And if he does I can easily get another one.' In fact, the officer concerned eventually had to be returned home on sick leave due to the stress of working for his demanding superior.

Another example of Cunningham's intolerance had occurred earlier in his career, when Charles 'KP' Keighly-Peach, by this time *Eagle*'s Commander Flying, joined the staff of the then Rear-Admiral Destroyers in the Mediterranean in 1935. Rear-Admiral Cunningham looked at 'KP' with distaste and enquired, 'Do you intend to keep that thing on your sleeve while on my staff?' 'Somewhat abashed, I said yes I did; that it was the recognised uniform for the FAA,' recalled Keighly-Peach some years later.

Cunningham's ambivalence towards naval aviation may simply have been a reflection of the attitudes of his generation and of the old 'big gun' navy, coming to a grudging recognition of the part to be played by the fliers. Nevertheless, it was to have a bearing before long on the attitudes of Boyd and others. Certainly, Cunningham displayed many of the characteristics of the old-style naval officer, always wearing 'number ones', the term for the most formal uniform, with long white trousers and high-buttoned jacket during the Mediterranean summer, rather than the open-necked, short-sleeved shirts and white shorts with white knee socks worn by most naval officers. Often, when operating ashore in support of the army or with the RAF, khaki uniforms replaced white.

The career of a professional officer in the Royal Navy between the two world wars had in some respects changed little from the time of Nelson. In peacetime, there were often more officers, especially senior officers, than posts. To give captains and commanders time at sea and command experience, spells at sea were often short. In between posts, officers were sent home on half-pay. This had happened to Cunningham as a rear-admiral in 1933. Such an elevated rank had one advantage, for he was soon recalled and sent on a technical course, as the impact of changing technology dawned on the Admiralty. Had he been a vice-admiral, the next step up in a high-flying naval officer's career, he would have been regarded as too senior for the course.

While on the technical course Cunningham and his 'class mates' visited what was then the Royal Air Force Station at Gosport, later to become HMS *Siskin* after World War Two. Here they found a group of young RAF and RN officers waiting to take them up for a flight – what would today be described as an 'air experience flight'. Cunningham thought that he would be safer in the hands of a naval pilot, who would at least 'have a better idea of the value of a rear-admiral than a young man in the RAF'.

'We had an interesting flight except for a sudden drop of 800 feet which the young man thought I would like to experience,' Cunningham recalled later. 'He was quite in error.' On landing, Cunningham was told that his pilot had been in trouble whilst serving on the China Station for flying between the masts of a cruiser. Such ability would in fact be much prized in the years ahead.

Cunningham went on a tactical course and later was appointed Rear-Admiral (D), Mediterranean Fleet. Commanding the destroyers of the Mediterranean Fleet was the appointment he would have chosen for himself at this stage of his career. Rather than fly to his new posting, at the time it was the practice for service personnel to take passage in a liner, in this case a P&O ship. His departure delayed by tonsillitis, he missed the ship, but caught up with her by crossing France by train.

It is worthy of note that when Cunningham later returned to the Mediterranean Fleet as Second-in-Command and Vice-Admiral commanding the Battle Cruiser Squadron, he was to make little mention in his autobiography of naval aviation, even though his command included responsibility for the Mediterranean Fleet's aircraft carrier, HMS *Glorious*. This time, he flew his flag in the battlecruiser *Hood*, at the time known in the Royal Navy as the 'Mighty Hood', for despite her rating, she was then the world's largest warship.

On the other hand – and with Cunningham, there always was 'another hand' – his views on aircraft carrier operations as part of the fleet showed a remarkable degree of perspicacity. At the time, carrier commanding officers favoured falling out of line with the rest of the fleet when flying aircraft off or landing them on. This had evidently become a habit as many flag officers resented having to change the course of the entire fleet in order to operate aircraft. Cunningham felt that carriers were vulnerable to aerial attack when away from the heavy AA support of the major fleet units, and that when flying aircraft off and landing them on, the entire fleet should share the manoeuvre with the carrier. This inter-relationship between the major fleet units and aircraft carriers, with the former providing heavy AA support for the latter, and the latter providing CAP and anti-submarine protection as well as reconnaissance, was to become standard practice later in the war, especially in the Pacific, where on one occasion the absence of the battleships and cruisers, who were busy bombarding enemy positions ashore, resulted in a heavy Kamikaze strike rate against the Allied carrier fleet.

The picture becomes still more confused, since 'ABC' is also credited with having visited *Illustrious* and told 806's Fulmar pilots that, 'You young men have altered the course of the war in the Mediterranean.'

The contrast with his Rear-Admiral Aircraft Carriers could not have been more complete. Cunningham was austere, slim and stiffly upright. Lyster was plump, but approachable. The story is told of an accident aboard *Illustrious* one night. The last Swordfish to land had been badly damaged and the observer had been injured, after it caught the arrester wire and hit the deck; the undercarriage collapsed and the plane overturned. Quickly, everyone gathered around and pulled the pilot, observer and the telegraphist air gunner from the wreckage. Lyster, too, came over to see what was going on.

'Anyone hurt?' Lyster asked gruffly.

Not recognising Lyster's portly figure in the dark, Lieutenant Ian Swayne, one of 815's pilots, doubtless feeling twitchy in case he ever suffered the same fate, was in no mood for idle chatter. 'For Christ's sake!' he retorted. 'We've only just hauled them off to the sick bay. How the bloody hell do you expect us to know whether they are hurt or not? If you must ask damn fool questions go and ask the PMO.'

Those who had recognised Rear-Admiral Lyster waited with bated breath, expecting a furious outburst. They were in for a surprise. 'All right – all right!' Lyster grumbled, although those around noted that he sounded slightly amused. 'Keep your hair on!'

As Lyster wandered off into the darkness, Swain's mistake was pointed out to him. 'What!' he exclaimed. 'For Christ's sake! I thought it was some dumb Seaman PO! What shall I do? D'you think that I ought to go and apologise?'

'I shouldn't if I were you,' replied Charles Lamb, who had witnessed the entire episode. 'If you do, he'll know who it was. At the moment he hasn't a clue!'

FULMARS FACE THE ITALIANS

The warm welcome afforded *Illustrious* in the Mediterranean was due as much to the arrival of her Fulmars as anything else. Not surprisingly, every-one was tired of being bombed by the Italians without having an effective fighter with which to strike back. Despite the undoubted shortcomings of the Fulmars compared to modern shore-based fighters, they were a big improvement on the Gloster Sea Gladiator biplanes currently available to *Eagle*. In fact, with the new arrivals, the Mediterranean Fleet was to become for a period that rarity in British naval history, a balanced fleet.

The pilots of 806 soon showed that they could make good use of the Fulmar, for on the very day that *Illustrious* joined the Mediterranean Fleet, 2 September, a flight of three aircraft, including Ivan Lowe, shot down a Cantieri Z501 flying-boat in full sight of the Fleet. Even so, the air battles were not one-sided. The Fulmar was not the fastest or most manoeuvrable fighter, and on 29 September, while attacking another Cantieri Z501, Lowe's aircraft was hit by heavy defensive fire from the flying-boat's machine guns and he had to ditch yet again; both pilot and observer were uninjured and were soon picked up by the Australian destroyer HMAS *Stuart*.

At this time, escort carriers had not arrived on the scene. When convoys needed air cover, the large fleet carriers had to provide it, and with only two ships, this was no easy task. There were convoys to be escorted to Malta and, in due course, to Greece, once that country eventually entered the war on the Allied side. War in the Balkans was to prove an unfortunate distraction for both sides. For the British, it took troops away from North Africa, where they had held the upper hand despite being outnumbered by their Italian opponents, and then had been forced to retreat in the face of German attacks. As for the Germans, they had to come to the aid of their Italian allies bogged down in Yugoslavia and Greece, and found themselves fighting partisans after what must have been a pyrrhic victory given the numbers of the forces tied down and the consequent delay in mounting Operation Barbarossa – the invasion of the Soviet Union.

When returning from convoy protection, *Illustrious* sent her aircraft to lay mines in the approaches to enemy harbours, to attack Italian forces in North Africa, or to bomb ports and airfields in North Africa and the Dodecanese. Fighter CAP continued, although 'Streamline' Robertson was alarmed by 806's rapid consumption of ammunition, which always threatened to be scarce. Evans made his point a day after being warned. He went into the attack with his customary cry of 'tally-ho' and then treated those listening to the developing air battle with the cryptic remark, 'One burst, one Wop'.

The radar aboard *Illustrious* was clearly better than none, but reliability and accuracy fell far below the standards of later sets. Much also depended on the experience of the radar operators, and here, too, standards varied. On at least one occasion, the alert was given, and everyone prepared for Italian bombers to attack; then the all-clear was given, with hands stood down from action stations and informed that the impending attack had probably been nothing more threatening than a flock of geese. No sooner had this happened than a heavy aerial attack developed, as ever with that Italian speciality, the high-level attack. So far, however, both carriers seemed to have a charmed life, although there were many near misses which, if sufficiently close or frequent, could cause internal damage to a carrier's vital organs, including the all-important aviation fuel system.

The aircraft also spent time ashore. A carrier moored in port is not the ideal base for air operations, as the Bermuda experience all too clearly showed. For the FAA squadrons, the base ashore in Egypt was RNAS Dekheila, also known by the ship's name of HMS *Grebe*; from here, operations were flown in support of the Army, especially after the Italian invasion of Egypt on 13 September 1940. Swordfish from *Illustrious* attacked Benghazi, the main forward base for landing troops and supplies, dropping mines and sinking a destroyer and two merchant ships. Aircraft from *Eagle* had already attacked Tobruk.

RUNS ASHORE

After being cooped up aboard ship with little room, going ashore was popular with the ship's company. At this early stage in the war, it was still possible to have a 'run ashore' in Malta, which meant Strait Street and its many bars for the ratings, and the Marsa Club and the Hotel Phoenicia for the officers. Malta was the most favoured of the Royal Navy's Mediterranean bases, but it was to become increasingly rare for the carrier crews to visit the island as the war progressed. Gibraltar was also popular, but there was disappointment among the ratings that the attractive Spanish girls were sent back over the border with Spain every night. At the time, many Spaniards worked in 'Gib', including the dockyard, but for security reasons, they were all required to return home for the night and the frontier was closed. Alexandria was the least popular, being described by many as a dump, which was unfortunate as it became the Mediterranean Fleet's base for most of the war. The one place that most naval ratings would make for in 'Alex' was the Fleet Club, although Albert Jones recalls the 'Stella beer' tasting of onions, which he thought might have been an ingredient forced on the brewer by wartime shortages. Onions or not, it is hard to tell whether this was a reflection on Egyptian brewing practices or simply a regular drinker of warm bitter being faced with a lighter lager-like brew for the first time.

Back at sea, on 30 September, two of the Mediterranean Fleet's battleships were taken to sea by Cunningham in the hunt for five Italian battleships and the elusive fleet engagement. Once again, the Italians escaped, racing for the safety of Taranto, which was beginning to look like a thorn in the side of the British. This was the Italian naval port most conveniently situated to menace convoys across the Mediterranean, the closest both to Malta and North Africa for the resupply operation for Italian forces, and the best placed to threaten, or at least tantalise, the Mediterranean Fleet in its base at Alexandria. Taranto was at once a menace and a convenient safe haven whenever the Italian battle fleet was threatened. Given their superior speed, there was no hope that the Italian battleships could be caught by the old ladies of the Mediterranean Fleet.

Again, during the night of 11–12 October, the cruiser *Ajax* met four Italian destroyers and three motor torpedo boats off the coast of Tunisia, and in the action that followed, a destroyer and two MTBs were sunk.

Two nights later, on 13–14 October, aircraft from both carriers bombed

Leros, in the Dodecanese, with the Swordfish dropping nearly a hundred bombs on the hangars and the fuel storage depot, causing considerable damage. Later, as the Mediterranean Fleet neared home, it arrived as an Italian air raid on Alexandria was in full spate. Many of the low-flying aircraft were believed to be carrying torpedoes, and the ships headed through the approaches, the Great Pass, for the relative safety of shallow water, moving at high speed while their AA crews created a blind barrage on each side, guns flashing under the bright sparkle of exploding shells in the night sky.

The Italians had come to realise that while the carriers could send their Swordfish out at night, the fighters were limited to daytime operations for they had no radar capable of directing them on to an enemy bomber. Early on, therefore, a pattern emerged, when the Italians would wait until the last fighters had landed on *Illustrious*, and then mount an attack at dusk. It could have been worse, for at least the Fleet now had radar, and a substantial AA barrage could be mounted, beginning as the Italians approached five miles from the ships.

Despite their ambitions in Greece, which they invaded on 28 October, the Italians did not use their sea power to oppose the British occupation of Crete, which enjoyed a vital strategic position covering the sea lanes of the Eastern Mediterranean. British forces landed in Crete at the invitation of the Greek Government on 31 October, gaining its airfields and ports, especially the naval base at Suda Bay. Crete was also a useful base for retreating British and Greek forces after the fall of Greece, even though they were later to be driven out of the island by the German invasion that started on 20 May 1941.

The message was clear, and it was soon to be heeded. Taranto had to be neutralised.

Lt Michael 'Tiffy' Torrens-Spence, the senior pilot or second-in-command of 819 Squadron, put it very aptly one day as many of the squadron's aircrew sat in the bar of Alexandria's Cecil Hotel. 'I'm afraid that Cunningham will have to do a "Nelson".' The reference was to 2 April 1801, when Nelson had sent his frigates into the harbour at Copenhagen to sink the Danish fleet, which had persistently refused to put to sea and face the Royal Navy in open battle. A true repeat of the Battle of Copenhagen would be impossible, given enemy minefields and heavy coastal artillery combined with a narrow and well-protected harbour entrance. It did not matter. This time, there would be no need for frigates.

CHAPTER SEVEN

Planning and Preparation

Cunningham's reputation of disliking naval aviation was well to the fore in Boyd's thoughts when he was summoned to a conference. He later recalled: 'Carriers and their aircraft were regarded as second rate to the rest of the fleet.'

Boyd feared that 'ABC' might want the carriers to leave the Mediterranean. His fears were groundless. Once his captains had assembled, Cunningham opened the meeting by saying: 'Gentlemen, I have called you together for I want your advice on how we can best annoy the enemy.'

An attack on the Italian Fleet and its base at Taranto was the obvious answer.

Cunningham had been delighted with the arrival of *Illustrious* carrying Lyster as Rear-Admiral, Carriers, Mediterranean Fleet, but apparently this was because the new addition to the chain of command relieved his staff of all responsibilities with regard to the Fleet Air Arm. Once they were safely at Alexandria, the two men met, and Lyster lost no time in bringing up the idea of an attack on the Italian fleet at Taranto. Cunningham maintains that he gave Lyster every encouragement, and indeed the operation had already been mentioned in correspondence with Pound, the First Sea Lord, 'though to him the operation always appeared as the last dying kick of the Mediterranean carrier before being sent to the bottom,' Cunningham maintained. Obviously, Pound had not changed his views on the idea since leaving the Mediterranean. 'To Admiral Lyster and myself the project seemed to involve no unusual danger.'

Lyster no doubt had used the brief time since arrival to refresh his own recollection of the plan that had been hatched in a more peaceful era, revised and updated from his days aboard *Glorious*. The RAF was asked to increase reconnaissance flights over the target and provide up-to-date photographs both of ships in the two harbours – the larger outer harbour or

Mar Grande, and the smaller inner harbour, Mar Piccolo – and of the defences. Both carriers were to take part in the action, and their Swordfish crews found themselves in an intensified programme of night-flying, for this was to be far more important than operations over the Western Desert.

A date was needed. Doubtless someone with a sense of history took the decision, for this would be 21 October, Trafalgar Day. The Fleet Air Arm was to knock out the Italian fleet on the anniversary of Nelson's great victory over the French. There was more to it than this, of course. Because of the lack of airborne radar and of anything approaching the targeting techniques available to the Luftwaffe in its *blitzkrieg* against British towns and cities, a moonlit night was essential to success, thus it was coincidence as much as anything else that favoured 21 October.

Having a target date concentrated minds wonderfully, but then the fates turned against the Mediterranean Fleet and its two carriers. So far, they had trained and operated successfully, their ships' companies gaining in experience and confidence, and had coped with the worst that the Italians could throw at them.

DISASTER AND DISAPPOINTMENT

For the Taranto raid, those Swordfish assigned to torpedo-bombing sorties would have to carry 60 gallon long-range tanks, which would be fitted by means of metal straps into the observer's middle cockpit on each torpedo-carrying aircraft; he, in turn, would displace the TAG in the cramped rear cockpit. The bomber Swordfish would also have an extra tank, but fitted under the fuselage. Apart from pushing the observer into the rear cockpit, the other disadvantage of having the long-range fuel tank in the middle cockpit was that there was a real danger of fuel being vented into the rear cockpit, leaving the observer up to his waist in highly inflammable and explosive high-octane petrol.

Accounts vary as to what went wrong while the long-range tanks were being fitted. One version is that a battery short-circuited, and the spark caught a petrol drip, which caused an aircraft to explode into flames on the hangar deck of *Illustrious*. Another relates how a fitter crouching in a cramped Swordfish cockpit securing the long-range tank stood up and slipped, dropping a screwdriver that fell on to exposed battery terminals, which ignited the air heavy with petrol vapour. Yet another blames a spark from a metal hammer in an atmosphere thick with petrol vapour for starting the fire. This seems the most likely explanation since afterwards the instruction was given that only rubber hammers were to be used while aircraft were being refuelled or when work was being carried out on their fuel systems. Despite the highly efficient sprinkler system in the hangar and prompt action by those present, two Swordfish were completely burnt out, while five more were either damaged or affected by the salt water poured so liberally on to them. All of the surviving aircraft had to be stripped, washed in fresh water and oil, and eventually reassembled. At this early stage in the war, there existed a close relationship between an aircraft's crew and its maintenance team; grounded by this unfortunate accident, several of the pilots helped their mechanics and riggers in the task of reviving the stricken aircraft. In any case, until the planes were ready, there was little flying to be done. There was no alternative but to postpone Taranto, and a provisional new date was set for 31 October, by which time there would be no moonlight.

Not wishing to waste the training of his crews, Cunningham sent Lyster with the two carriers for a further raid on the Dodecanese on the night of 13–14 October, bombing the airfield at Leros after a night take-off. On their return, the report came through that the cruiser *Liverpool* had been torpedoed; although still afloat, she was crippled, while a formation of enemy aircraft was picked up on the radar. The attack was brief, and the other ships were able to retrieve the damaged cruiser, towed back to Alexandria by the cruiser *Orion*.

That the situation in the Mediterranean was on a knife edge was illustrated by the arrival in Alexandria at this time of a Turkish delegation headed by Admiral Ulgin, whom Cunningham had met at Istanbul the previous year. The Turks had endured a difficult overland journey, but admitted that they were in Egypt to assess the strength of the British forces. Turkey had been a German ally during World War One, and Turkish intervention would have made British control of the Eastern Mediterranean still more difficult; later it might well have rendered the defence of the Ukraine by Soviet forces almost impossible. Nevertheless, Cunningham entertained the Turks to lunch aboard *Warspite*, and then as a further courtesy, sent them home aboard a destroyer as far as Mersin, on the coast opposite Cyprus. Whether the Turks were impressed by British strength in the region, or unimpressed by the Italian campaign, the country stayed out of the war.

Greece found herself at war with Italy on 28 October, after rejecting an Italian ultimatum to hand over the islands of Crete and Corfu, as well as the city of Salonika and other territory, to Italian occupation. No nation could accept demands such as these without effectively capitulating. Now the Mediterranean Fleet had to protect Greek merchant shipping in the Eastern Mediterranean, escorting convoys from Alexandria to Greece, and helping the Greeks to maintain shipping links with the many islands, especially Crete. The declaration of war was not unexpected, for already on 15 August an Italian submarine had torpedoed and sunk a Greek cruiser lying at anchor at Tinos in the Cyclades.

Amid the increased pressure on Cunningham's fleet, the operation against Taranto now appeared to be an even better move than before. This was the one chance of curing the imbalance of naval power in the Mediterranean.

With just three days to go, the realisation dawned that with no moon on 31 October, the raid would depend entirely on flares being dropped. This was a major obstacle, since the flare droppers had insufficient practice to ensure success. In fact, the primitive night navigation available on the Swordfish and the lack of radar meant that the observers for the flare droppers would have to be extremely skilled navigators indeed for what effectively amounted to a 'pathfinder' mission, with the heavy responsibility of guiding the other attacking aircraft carefully on to a target, possibly obscured by barrage balloons. It was also clear that a failed attempt would be worse than useless, worse than a waste of time and of men and aircraft, for it would alert the Italians without inflicting any damage. There could only be one attempt, with no second chances. The next moonlit night was that of 11–12 November: the attack was planned for then.

On 29 October, at 01.30, Cunningham took his entire fleet to sea, including both carriers, all four battleships and four cruisers, to cover the passage of ships to Suda Bay in Crete on 31 October. The Mediterranean Fleet was spotted and shadowed by Italian aircraft, but no attack developed until 1 November, when heavy air raids struck Suda Bay and Canae. As always, Cunningham hoped to bring the Italian fleet to battle, but yet again was disappointed. Realising that the set-piece naval battle was unlikely, he left the convoy escort duties to cruisers and destroyers, backed up by shore-based aircraft from Crete.

Meanwhile, RAF reconnaissance of Taranto was well in hand, and given a boost by the deployment to Malta of a flight of Martin Baltimore recon-naissance aircraft, which were better suited to the role than the lumbering Short Sunderlands that had risked so much to keep an eye on the Italians.

'The success of the Fleet Air Arm was due in no small degree to the excel-lent reconnaissance carried out by the Royal Air Force Glenn Martin Flight (No. 431) from Malta, under very difficult conditions and often in the face of fighter opposition,' Cunningham was later to write in his despatch on the Taranto operation.

The raid on Taranto was now given a title, Operation Judgement. The carriers were to leave Alexandria, the port packed with Axis spies, under cover of providing an escort for a number of convoys, including one to Crete and Greece, while Force H would distract the enemy by mounting a raid, including aircraft from *Ark Royal*, on Cagliari in Sardinia, known as Operation Crack. The overall operation was given the code Mike Bravo Eight, MB8. There were no less than four convoys. MW3 consisted of five merchant ships sailing from Alexandria to Malta, with another three ships to be escorted as far as Suda Bay in Crete. Since it was an important part of convoy planning to return the 'empties', there would also be ME3, with four merchantmen returning from Malta to Alexandria. AN6 comprised three tankers carrying fuel from Alexandria to Greece, again with a return convoy of empties, from Greece to Egypt. The operation would also involve the passing through the Sicilian Narrows of further reinforcements for the Mediterranean Fleet – the battleship *Barham*, the cruisers *Glasgow* and *Berwick*, and another six destroyers.

The crews continued training, painfully aware of the importance of the operation. Tension mounted, as everyone knew that nothing must go wrong. It was planned to use a total of thirty aircraft from both carriers, consisting of aircraft from 815 and 819 aboard *Illustrious* and 813 and 824 aboard *Eagle*, while the Fulmars of 806 aboard *Illustrious* would provide the all-important fighter cover as the Mediterranean Fleet steamed westward.

On 4 November, MB8 got under way as AN6 sailed towards Greece, but the strain of the many near misses suffered by *Eagle* during the Italian high-level bombing raids finally took its toll. The elderly carrier's aviation fuel system broke down. It was fortunate indeed that this happened in harbour and that the damage was not more extensive. Nevertheless, further delay while *Eagle* was repaired could not be countenanced. With winter weather, even in the Mediterranean, unpredictable, early attack was essential. Another month would mean opportunities lost, and the risk of something else going wrong.

Meanwhile, on 5 November, MW3 sailed to Malta and Crete, overtaking AN6 the following day.

Eagle might not have been available anyway. Her age was beginning to tell and her boilers were giving trouble. As with so many of the Royal Navy's major ships, war conditions had interfered with the normal cycle of refits, which in any event tended to be lengthy, taking two or three years. It is also worth remembering that pre-war she was scheduled to be withdrawn and replaced by *Illustrious* or one of her sisters.

The loss of *Eagle* for the operation meant that only twenty-four aircraft would be available, including six aircraft borrowed from *Eagle*; four from 813 squadron and two from 824 squadron, to augment those of 815 and 819 aboard *Illustrious*.

No. 813 was one of the Fleet Air Arm's pre-war squadrons, having been formed in January 1937. The outbreak of war had found the squadron embarked in *Eagle* and her Swordfish had taken part in the hunt for enemy shipping in the Indian Ocean. The carrier had arrived in the Mediterranean during late spring 1940, when 813 became a composite squadron following the addition of three Gloster Sea Gladiator fighters. Despite their antiquity, the Sea Gladiators accounted for several Italian aircraft.

By the standards of the FAA, 824 was an old squadron, dating from April 1933, when the 700 and 800 series of numbers replaced the old 400 series flights. It was also aboard *Eagle* at Singapore at the outbreak of war, with nine Swordfish, and took part in the hunt for enemy shipping. The move to the Mediterranean saw the squadron providing ASW cover for Malta convoys and gunnery spotting for the Mediterranean Fleet's battleships.

AT SEA

On 6 November, *Illustrious* set sail from Alexandria accompanied by four battleships, Cunningham's flagship *Warspite*, *Valiant*, *Malaya* and *Ramillies*, as well as an escort of cruisers and destroyers.

Surprise was an essential part of the operation. The merest hint that a major attack might be on its way and the Italians could be counted upon to remove their fleet to safer waters further north, perhaps to Naples or, safer still, to Genoa or La Spezia. Experience thus far had shown that this was the more likely option, as they had shown great reluctance to be drawn into a battle. As the ships steamed westward, the Fulmars of 806 helped to provide cover for MW3, which the Fleet spotted on 8 November. After driving off an Italian reconnaissance aircraft at 12.30, and again at 15.20, seven Savoia-Marchetti SM79 bombers approached at around 16.20 and were attacked by three of 806's Fulmars, which managed to shoot down two of the enemy aircraft and drive off the remainder, which jettisoned their bombs in order to make a hasty retreat. Cunningham – as an added security precaution – deliberately pointed his ships towards Malta rather than further north towards Taranto. On 9 November, Cunningham sent cruisers and destroyers ahead of the main body of the Mediterranean Fleet, ostensibly looking for Italian surface vessels, but perhaps hoping to give the Italians one last chance to sally forth and present him with a major fleet engagement. Meanwhile, *Ramillies* took three destroyers to see the convoy into Malta, and to refuel. Using Malta as a refuelling point, given the many demands on the island's scarce resources, may seem odd in retrospect, but convoys were still getting through to Malta in late 1940. The problem was that British warships were remarkably 'short-legged' – a legacy of having so many fuelling stations in a widespread empire – and the Royal Navy and its fleet train, the Royal Fleet Auxiliary, lagged far behind the United States Navy in the techniques of refuelling at sea at this stage of the war. It was to take the demands of the Pacific War to change this situation.

Up-to-date information was vital. Even before the ships sailed from Alexandria, daily reconnaissance photographs were being taken by the RAF, normally using a Martin Baltimore bomber. All of the combatant nations during World War Two could tell tales of inter-service rivalry and bureaucracy which made the efficient and effective conduct of the war more difficult. In the Mediterranean, the problem lay between the Royal Navy and the RAF. In the run-up to Operation Judgement, the Mediterranean Fleet relied on good aerial reconnaissance. Only the RAF in Malta was in a position to do it. Although the photographs were requested by the naval C-in-C, they were regarded as RAF property. They were flown from Malta to the RAF's headquarters in Cairo, where just one naval officer was allowed to look at them, and was refused permission to take them away. The officer concerned, a young RNVR officer, Lt David Pollock (a solicitor in civilian life who had specialised in photographic interpretation on joining the Royal Navy) made a great show of marking the dispositions of ships and defences on to a map of Taranto, and then when his RAF counterpart was not looking, promptly 'borrowed' the photographs and returned to his ship. The RAF never realised the subterfuge, as the photographs were copied in the carrier's photographic section and replaced the next day.

The copies were taken to Lyster and Boyd. Stereoscopic lenses were used for a close scrutiny, as expert photographic interpretation was a fundamental of good intelligence work, especially in wartime when many other sources were closed. What Lyster and his officers wanted was ships, as many as possible. There would be little point in a raid that did not inflict severe damage on the Italian fleet. They were not to be disappointed. The outer harbour contained five battleships, three of the Cavour- and Duilio-classes, and two of the new Littorio-class. There were also three cruisers in the outer harbour, as well as further cruisers and a number of destroyers in the inner harbour. In fact, only one Italian battleship was missing.

The availability of suitable targets for this unique chance of striking at the Italian fleet solved the main problem, but there was also the matter of the enemy defences. The breakwaters of the Mar Grande were lined with anti-aircraft guns. More worrying, given that the aircraft would have to fly low to drop their torpedoes so they would not shatter on impact with the water, were what looked like a collection of maggots, white against the shades of grey of the reconnaissance photograph; these were the tell-tale signs of barrage balloons flying from barges moored along the mole that sheltered the outer harbour from the sea, and guarding the flanks of the battle fleet that did not have the protection of torpedo nets. Other balloons were attached to barges that lined the shore. The barrage balloons were more of a nuisance than a serious threat, provided the pilots remembered where they were or could see them in the light of the flares, since they were positioned some 300 yards apart, and the wingspan of a Swordfish was a mere 45½ft.

The presence of the balloons and the torpedo nets helped Lyster and his staff officers to determine the nature of the attack. It was decided to attack in two waves, and because of the nets only half the aircraft were to be armed with torpedoes, even though these would normally be the weapons of choice for an attack against large warships. The remaining planes would carry bombs and flares, especially in the first wave, or just bombs. Torpedoes were to be used against the battleships, while the bombers were to attack cruisers and destroyers, including those in the inner harbour. The use of flares at this early stage in the war was an innovation, since the RAF had still to adopt target illumination using specially trained crews – the Pathfinders. It was also decided that the balloon cables would pose less of a threat if the Swordfish were to fly in very low, between the barges – yet another reason for needing flares.

Lyster and Boyd hoped for surprise, but both knew that the Italians would maintain constant reconnaissance flights over the Eastern Mediterranean. On 8 November, seven Italian Savoia Marchetti SM79s attacked. Charles Evans and two of his pilots flew off the carrier in Fulmars and shot down two of the bombers, while the others fled. Given the importance of concealing the ship's course it was more than helpful that on 9 November Evans shot down a Cantieri 506B reconnaissance aircraft before it could report on the whereabouts of *Illustrious*.

Tension mounted as they continued steaming westward across the Eastern Mediterranean, but their luck held. On 10 November, the day before the operation, Lt Charles Lamb was called to see 'Streamline' Robertson. Lamb recalls racing to Flying Control, wondering whether he was guilty of some sin of omission or commission. By this time everyone seemed to be living on their nerves. He need not have worried. Robertson was looking relaxed and cheerful and so was Captain Denis Boyd. Robertson explained that Lamb was to fly to Malta to collect the latest reconnaissance photographs, while Boyd told him that on the operation he would be a flare dropper.

'Not a very glamorous job, and I expect that you would rather drop a torpedo?'

'We have a superstition in the "Branch" sir,' replied Lamb with a shake of the head. 'It is supposed to be very unlucky to volunteer … If we are told to do something, no matter what, that's okay; but volunteer – never.'

'I can understand that outlook,' said Boyd. 'Well tomorrow night you have a roving brief … Kiggell and Janvrin will be dropping the main flares, but we want you to follow along behind them and fill any gaps, or lay a line in another direction – to help the strike pilots down below, in the harbour. In other words, use your own judgement …'

Lamb was then sent to see Lyster. When he arrived on the Admiral's bridge, he found Lyster with his two operations officers, Commander Charles Thompson, and his assistant, the same Lt Pollock who had purloined the RAF reconnaissance photographs.

Lyster explained the importance of the task awaiting Lamb. 'The latest photographs are vital and you are not to come back without them. They will be delivered to you at Hal Far as soon as they have been developed, which may not be until tomorrow morning. Bring them back as soon as you can, but by noon at the latest.'

Almost as an afterthought, Lyster also asked Lamb to bring back some potatoes should he find any in Malta. This was a strange request, but understandable. The enhanced wartime complement of a warship placed huge demands on the available rations, and space was limited, even on an aircraft carrier. After a relatively brief period at sea, potatoes were soon replaced at meals by rice, a source of protein that occupied far less space.

Lamb arrived at RAF Hal Far in Malta to find an old friend from his RAF days in command. Informed that the photographs would not be available until 08.30 on the morning of the raid, he prepared to spend the night, and was offered a game of poker. Taking his chance, Lamb enquired about the availability of potatoes – only to be told that he would have to resort to the black market since there was a shortage.

The evening must have been a great success, and when he boarded his aircraft the following morning, Lamb had both a hundredweight of potatoes and his winnings from the poker game, which had covered his RAF mess bill as well as the potatoes.

On landing aboard *Illustrious*, Lamb took the photographs to Lyster immediately. 'Get any spuds?' he was asked. He replied in the affirmative, and could see that Lyster was pleased. How much had they cost?

'A fiver, I'm afraid sir,' Lamb replied, adding: 'But there's no need to worry – they were paid for by my poker winnings last night. If you agree, I will enter it as a credit to me in the wardroom card book.'

'Don't go putting me down for a loss in your bloody card-book!' Lyster retorted. 'Put it down to Flags and I will settle with him.'

Lamb accepted this solution with good grace, realising that his chances of extracting money from the flag lieutenant were slim indeed. In fact the money was never paid, but this might have been due to subsequent events that were to separate Lamb from the ship.

Any idea that all might in fact be going very well was soon to be dispelled. The operation had been plagued with problems from the beginning, and the naval airmen's troubles were far from over.

The carrier's Swordfish maintained constant patrols, looking for enemy shipping and, in particular, submarines. On 10 November, one of 819's Swordfish was some 20 miles ahead of the ship and her escorting cruisers and destroyers when the engine suddenly cut out. The aircraft turned back, gliding towards the carrier, but the distance was too far and the plane crashed into the sea. The pilot had time to pull the toggle to release the rubber dinghy from the centre of the upper wing and grab flame floats to alert passing ships or aircraft, while the observer, 'Grubby' Going, ditched his bulky Bigsworth chart board, unhooked his retaining strap and dived over the side. Once in the water, Going could see two cruisers in the distance, and managed to light one of the flame floats. The ships, *Gloucester* and *York*, spotted the floats and altered course towards the two men. Rescued, and given a good breakfast in the wardroom, Going had to persuade the ship's commanding officer to request Lyster's permission to return him and his pilot to *Illustrious*. Apart from wanting to take part in the attack on Taranto, Going knew that numbers were important, since anyone not rostered for the Taranto operation would be needed for anti-submarine patrols. Permission granted, Going and the pilot were taken back to their carrier in the cruiser's Supermarine Walrus amphibian.

An isolated incident of engine failure was not of undue concern, other than the fact that it reduced the number of aircraft aboard the carrier, inevitably always limited, still further. But alarm bells started ringing the following morning when another aircraft suffered a sudden engine failure and also had to ditch. Investigation aboard *Illustrious* showed the cause to be fuel contamination. One of the ship's aviation fuel tanks had been contaminated with sea water, most probably as a result of the intensive operation of the sprinkler system during the hangar fire. As flying-off time approached, all of the aircraft intended for the operation had to have their fuel systems drained, and then refuelled.

The reconnaissance photographs had provided up-to-date evidence of the Italian presence at Taranto, including the welcome intelligence that the sixth Italian battleship had entered the outer harbour. The Italians had confidently put all of their eggs in one basket and the entire Italian battle fleet was there for the taking. The reasons for this concentration of force were not known to the Mediterranean Fleet at the time, but it was reported by a Greek diplomat in Ankara that the Italians were planning to invade Corfu.

The carrier's photographic section produced a collection of enlargements to go with the large-scale map of Taranto displayed for the final briefing in the wardroom. Not just the harbour itself, but ships, AA positions and balloons were all shown in clear detail. Also visible were the torpedo nets, hanging down to the level of the keel. These would normally have been a great worry, but not on this occasion. The torpedoes were fitted with the new and still highly secret Duplex pistols, a magnetic device that detonated the torpedo as it passed under the keel, set off by the ship's own magnetic field. The term 'Duplex' was used because the torpedo would still detonate if instead of passing under the ship, it simply struck the hull. As one of those present said, with great satisfaction: 'Heads I win – tails you lose.'

There were all the six Italian battleships in the outer harbour, the Mar Grande, with three heavy cruisers, *Zara, Fiume* and *Goriza*. Two more heavy cruisers, *Trieste* and *Bolzano*, were moored in the centre of the inner harbour, the Mar Piccolo, with four light cruisers and seventeen destroyers, using 'Mediterranean mooring', moored stern-to at the quays.

Leaving nothing to chance, at noon a cruiser force was detached from the main force and sent to reconnoitre the Straits of Otranto. They would also seek targets of opportunity, which could distract the Italians as the attacking Swordfish flew towards Taranto.

Six hours later, Cunningham signalled Lyster to take *Illustrious* and her escorts and proceed 'in execution of previous orders'. Just before she left, Cunningham signalled: 'Good luck then to your lads in their enterprise. Their success may well have a most important bearing on the course of the war in the Mediterranean.'

The operation was on. By 20.00 the carrier was 40 miles, 270 degrees, from Kabbo Point, Cephalonia, and just 170 miles from Taranto.

CHAPTER EIGHT

Waiting for the Green Light

'NEXT STOP TARANTO'. This was the unmistakable message scrawled in chalk on the side of a 500lb bomb, hanging under the wing of the waiting Fairey Swordfish. No housewife's stringbag had ever contained anything like this. Other bombs carried similar messages, as did the torpedoes.

The weather was good, almost too good. At 19.45, *Illustrious* increased her speed to 28 knots, as the artificers on watch in the boiler rooms switched on additional burners while their counterparts in the engine rooms turned the valves that ensured extra steam flowed through to the three giant turbines.

As the deadline approached, *Illustrious* neared the flying-off point. Everything was ready, thanks to the maintainers, a mixture of Fleet Air Arm men and RAF personnel, who had worked non-stop for thirty-six hours to get the aircraft ready, a situation that had not been helped by the discovery of the fuel contamination. The ranging of aircraft for the first strike had started at 19.00. Ranging on the flight deck was an important skill. Later, carriers would have small tractors, aircraft tugs, to help in handling aircraft on the flight deck and in the hangar, but at the time it required considerable manpower. The aircraft would come up from the hangar deck, one at a time, using only the forward lift since planes would be parked on the aft lift to allow the leading aircraft sufficient take-off run. Once the aircraft reached deck level, the wings would be unfolded manually and carefully locked in position. (It was not unknown for Swordfish wings suddenly to fold, possibly on take-off or, worse still, while diving on to a target. Whether these accidents were the result of airframe fatigue, or carelessness in locking the wings into position, was not known. Accident investigation techniques were not only rudimentary but also something of a peacetime luxury. Aircraft lost in an area where war was being waged could not safely be recovered for inspection.)

A crowd of sailors would then start to push the aircraft carefully back along the flight deck. Later aircraft would have hydraulically operated wings that remained folded as they were eased back, but the primitive mechanism of the Swordfish had one advantage: pushing the aircraft with the wings unfolded meant that there was plenty of room for those lined up on either side of the fuselage to take hold, heaving against the leading edge of the lower wing. One of the maintainers sat in the front cockpit, ready to apply the brakes, for there was nothing else to prevent the plane going over the edge until it stopped and could be chocked. Aircraft had to be arranged so that they could take off in order, following one another quickly and smoothly. The opportunity for accidents was considerable, not least as the Swordfish, in common with most aircraft at the time, had a tail wheel and the pilot could not see straight ahead until speed picked up enough for the tail to lift. Ashore, pilots managed by zig-zagging while taxiing, but this was not possible in the tight confines of a carrier flight deck, so deck-handling signals had to be given.

A rapid sequence of take-offs enabled aircraft to get into formation quickly once in the air, and reduced the amount of time the carrier was steaming into the wind, vulnerable as she swept along in a straight line. Naturally, while the flight deck was thus occupied, no other aircraft could land, and it was not possible to send fighters into the air if an enemy air attack materialised.

While preparations were going ahead on the flight deck with the first-wave aircraft, aircraft of the second wave were receiving their final preparations on the hangar deck below. The first strike would consist of twelve aircraft, while the second strike was to have nine. Most of the first-strike aircraft and crews belonged to Williamson's own squadron, 815, while those in the second strike were mainly from Hale's squadron, 819. Aircraft and crews 'borrowed' from the unfortunate *Eagle* made up the numbers in each strike. The origin of each aircraft could clearly be seen by their identification number, preceded by the letter 'L' for *Illustrious* or the letter 'E' for *Eagle*.

THE BRIEFING

Williamson's and Hale's aircrews were mustered in the wardroom for a final briefing. Forty-two Swordfish pilots and observers crowded in, some sprawled in chairs, others sitting on the tables or lounging against the bulk-heads. They were joined by those of the ship's officers involved in the operation, and by one unofficial observer, Lt-Cdr Opie, USN. Not only did he act as a liaison officer, despite United States neutrality, but he also had the important task of reporting on the progress of British carrier warfare. Facing them was Commander George Beale, the ship's Operations Officer.

Opie had famously challenged Robertson over the long interval between take-offs in British carriers. 'It's only thirty seconds,' Robertson had protested. 'In our flat-tops they do it in ten,' Opie replied. On discovering that this was no idle Yankee boast, Robertson immediately cut the take-off intervals aboard *Illustrious* to ten seconds. This was not just a matter of effi-ciency. Time spent steaming into the wind could be cut, so that the carrier did not have to disturb the course of the rest of the fleet for longer than was necessary, and spent far less time as a sitting duck. There was another big advantage, as shorter intervals between take-offs also improved the range of the aircraft, with less time and fuel expended by the formation leader flying around waiting for the rest of the aircraft to form up.

Beale climbed on to a chair so that he could be seen over the heads of those sitting near the front. He outlined the plan and also stressed the hazards awaiting the attackers. He explained that the Italians would almost certainly have deployed torpedo nets, but the torpedoes would be set to run deep and explode under the hulls of the warships. He reminded those present that their torpedoes had the new Duplex warhead, so that it would explode whether it hit the target or passed close by. As photographs of the targets were handed around, Beale drew attention to the presence of barrage balloons and stressed the need to avoid their cables, apt to cut off the wings of an aircraft. Fortunately, the balloons were all some distance apart.

The first wave would fly in formation to the target area and then turn for the north of the harbour, when they would split up. The flare droppers would illuminate the battleships so that they could be seen silhouetted against the light by the torpedo-bombers as they flew through the barrage balloons, while the bombers would head for the inner harbour to attack the cruisers and destroyers. Radio silence would be maintained, with the only signal allowed being the terse 'Attack completed' from the wave leader. Silence was required for security reasons, so that the Italians would not be alerted, and also to make it more difficult for them afterwards to find the aircraft or their carrier. Moreover, in the absence of the TAGs whose role normally included telegraphy, it was one less worry for the hard-pressed and cramped observers sitting in the rear cockpit.

Having run through the plan of attack and the targets, Beale added: 'The next thing is the return journey.'

'Don't let's bother about that,' one wag retorted, and the entire assembly broke into nervous laughter.

At 20.00, just as the last of the first strike's twelve Swordfish was about to be trundled off the forward lift, to have its wings unfolded and then ranged in front of its eleven companions, the pilots and observers came out on to the darkened deck in their bulky Sidcot suits and Mae Wests. One by one they clambered into their aircraft and strapped themselves in with the assistance of the maintainers. Earphones were put on, and in the cramped rear cockpits, the observers struggled with their bulky Bigsworth chart boards. Engines were started and revved to warm up, keen eyes examined oil pressure and temperature dials, while the Gosport tube communication between pilot and observer was tested. Just before 20.30, in clear moonlight, Boyd turned his ship to catch what little wind there was and demanded full speed to provide as much lift as possible for the heavily laden Swordfish. A shaded green light from Williamson's aircraft told 'Streamline' Robertson that the formation was ready to go, and he immediately reported this to Boyd, who told him to carry on, in a matter of fact voice, concealing his feelings. The aircraft were ranged as far aft as possible on the flight deck, on both sides, and moved out to begin their take-off run alternately from starboard and port. A green light blinked from the flying control position, a sponson just below the bridge. 'Streamline' was giving the signal for the first aircraft to fly off.

THE FIRST STRIKE

The engine of the first aircraft roared as the leader pushed the throttle forward for full power. This was Lieutenant Commander Kenneth 'Hooch' Williamson of 815, with the then Lieutenant Norman 'Blood' Scarlett as his observer in Swordfish L4A.

Kenneth Williamson had joined the Royal Navy in 1924, but did not qualify as a pilot until some time later, gaining his wings in 1929. He then served ashore until being posted to his first aircraft carrier, HMS *Coura-*

geous, in 1930. On promotion to lieutenant commander in 1938, he took over command of No. 822 squadron. No. 815 was his second squadron, which he had taken over earlier in 1940. If Williamson was an enthusiast for naval aviation, the same could not be said of his observer. Norman J. 'Blood' Scarlett had followed his father into the Navy at Dartmouth in 1924 and then joined the battleship HMS *Queen Elizabeth* in 1928, afterwards serving in cruisers. It was while he was serving in HMS *Penelope* that the Inskip Award was made, giving control of the Fleet Air Arm back to the Admiralty; the Royal Navy found that it suddenly needed more pilots and observers of its own, and there were not enough volunteers among those already serving who saw their careers marked out in such fields as navigation or gunnery. He was later to describe himself as being one of ten 'pressed men' ordered to train as observers. In 1938, he joined 812 Squadron aboard *Glorious* in the Mediterranean. Always a reluctant aviator, he once said: 'I wanted to be in destroyers, not bloody aeroplanes.' At the time of Operation Judgement, he had already made an application to return to general service.

The second aircraft, L4K, was flown by Lieutenant N. McI. Kemp, who was senior pilot of 815 Squadron, that is second-in-command. Neil Kemp was another Dartmouth cadet who had joined in 1927, and qualified as a pilot in 1933. His extensive experience included flying with 812 squadron aboard *Furious* and 820 and 811 squadrons in *Courageous*, before joining 815 in 1940. His observer was Sub-Lieutenant (A) R. A. Bailey, who had switched from being an observer in HMS *York*'s Walrus amphibian to the decidedly more exciting life of 815 squadron.

Squadron seniority had to be amended somewhat to take into account those on loan from *Eagle*'s two Swordfish squadrons, 813 and 824. Swordfish E4F with her pilot and observer were from the cadre transferred from the crippled *Eagle*, but they were from different squadrons. The pilot, Lieutenant M. R. Maund, had joined as a Dartmouth cadet in 1928, and had cruiser and battleship experience before qualifying as a pilot in 1936. He joined 813 in 1938. His observer, Sub-Lieutenant (A) W. A. Bull, had joined 824 in 1939.

Lieutenant (A) L. J. Kiggell had originally joined the Royal Air Force in 1937 while it still included the Fleet Air Arm. Life at sea must have suited him, or perhaps he felt that there was something to be said for being in at the beginning of something new, as Launcelot Kiggell had been one of the

1,500 RAF personnel who had transferred to the Royal Navy. He had joined 815 in 1940. By contrast, his observer in L4P, Lieutenant H. R. B. Janvrin, had pursued a conventional naval training, having started as a Dartmouth cadet in 1929. Richard Janvrin, in some accounts also referred to as Hugh, served in battleships and cruisers before becoming an observer in 1938. Initially, he served in *Ark Royal*, before joining 815 in 1940.

Perhaps one of the most unconventional backgrounds was that of Lieutenant (A) C. B. Lamb in the next aircraft, L5B. Although he was another former RAF officer, Charles Lamb had originally been a Merchant Navy officer. He had taken the unusual change of career during the depressed years of the early 1930s when there were few positions afloat for newly-qualified junior officers and unemployment had threatened. At the time, Lamb decided that the best way forward would be to learn to fly, so he joined the RAF in 1935. He transferred to the Royal Navy in 1938. He had the unsought distinction of having been the last pilot to land on *Courageous* before she was torpedoed and sunk on 17 September 1939. He then had an active war with twenty-nine sorties minelaying, on ASW work and then dive-bombing German troops and attacking E-boats during the Dunkirk evacuation. He had joined 815 in 1940. His observer in L5B was Lieutenant K. C. Grieve, who had joined the Royal Navy in 1927, and had served in a number of ships, including the cruiser *Shropshire* and the battleship *Queen Elizabeth*, before qualifying as an observer in 1938, joining 813 aboard *Eagle*.

Swordfish L4C was also from 815 squadron. Her pilot was Sub-Lieutenant (A) P. D. J. Sparke. Julian Sparke had qualified as a pilot on the eve of war breaking out, and despite being one of the more junior officers, had already gained a Distinguished Service Cross. His observer was Sub-Lieutenant (A) J. W. Neale, who had previously served in *Hermes* and had joined 815 in 1940.

Another 815 aircraft was L4R, with Sub-Lieutenant (A) A. S. D. Macauley as pilot and Sub-Lieutenant (A) A. L. O. Wray, RNVR, as observer. Having also gained his wings on the eve of the outbreak of war, Douglas Macaulay was another naval airman who had been unfortunate enough to have been flying with 822 in *Courageous* when she was sunk. After a brief spell with 763, he joined 815 and embarked in *Illustrious* in 1940. Wray joined 815 in 1940. He was among the early RNVR officers in the Fleet Air Arm, and a rarity at the time before rapid wartime expansion and losses combined to ensure that before long RNVR officers would be in the majority.

L4M's aircrew were Lieutenant (A) H. A. I. Swayne and Sub-Lieutenant (A) Buscall as pilot and observer, both of 815, which they had joined in 1940. Ian Swayne had qualified as a pilot in 1937, Buscall was another RNVR 'new boy'.

Another airman from *Eagle* was also the only Royal Marine officer on the Taranto raid, Captain Oliver 'Olly' Patch of 824 squadron, who had joined it in 1938, having gained his wings the previous year. His role would be to dive-bomb the cruisers in the Mar Piccolo. Olly Patch had already one Italian submarine to his credit, having torpedoed *Iride* in August while she was lying in Bomba Bay, Libya, waiting to embark a team of frogmen tasked with sinking *Eagle* at Alexandria on 28 August. At the time, Patch had been leading a formation of three aircraft, and the other two pilots, Cheeseman and Wellham, also found targets for their torpedoes, attacking a depot ship and a supply ship at anchor with a destroyer, sinking all three. Patch's companion in E5A was Lieutenant D. G. Goodwin, also of 824. David Goodwin had found himself aboard a coal-burning battleship, the elderly *Emperor of India*, when he left Dartmouth as a cadet in 1929, and served in a number of ships, mainly on the China Station, before volunteering to train as an observer in 1936. He passed out top in his course and then attended the School of Naval Co-operation at what was then RAF Lee-on-Solent in 1937. His first carrier had been *Courageous*, flying with 820; he then joined 824 aboard *Eagle* in 1938, in a move that took him back to the China Station before the carrier was called closer to home. On 20 July, Goodwin had been among those giving the Italians a taste of what naval air power really meant when they had sunk the destroyers *Nembo* and *Ostro* in Tobruk Roads.

Joining Patch was another 'composite' crew in L4L, piloted by Sub-Lieutenant (A) W. C. Sarra from 815, who had entered the Royal Navy in 1938 as a Midshipman (A), gaining his wings in 1938. He had joined 815 in 1940 while it was detached to operate under RAF Coastal Command control, supporting the Dunkirk evacuation. He had already experienced night operations against the enemy when, on 16 September, nine aircraft from 815 and another six from 819 had laid mines and dive-bombed enemy shipping at Benghazi, sinking two Italian merchantmen and two destroyers. On October 13, shortly before the original date for the Taranto operation, six aircraft from 815 and nine from 819 had attacked hangars and ships at Portolargo Bay, on the island of Leros. Sarra's observer, Mr Midshipman (A) Jack Bowker, was from 819, which he had joined in 1940 after serving in

Hermes. Their target was to be the seaplane base.

L4H and E5Q were also in Patch's flight, with the allocated target of the smaller ships in the Mar Piccolo, mainly the destroyers, which were expected to be vulnerable to bombing. Sub-Lieutenant (A) A. J. B. Forde in L4H had qualified as a pilot in 1940, and 815 was his first squadron. His observer, Sub-Lieutenant (A) A. Mardel-Ferreira, was a Royal Naval Volunteer Reservist, but he had already served in *Hermes* before joining 815 in 1940. Finally, Lieutenant (A) J. B. Murray flew E5Q from *Eagle*'s 824 squadron, having served with it since April 1939, after earlier flying with 822 aboard *Courageous.* His observer was also from 824, Sub-Lieutenant (A) S. M. Paine, who had joined the squadron in June 1939.

At 20.30 sharp, Williamson's engine roared, and the wheel chocks were pulled away as his aircraft rumbled down the flight deck, slowly gaining speed, then over the bows, sinking at first as air speed built up and then starting a long, slow climb. One after another, the remaining eleven aircraft followed. Eight miles out from *Illustrious,* they formed up on the leader's aircraft, already on course for the target.

There was no lull after the last aircraft had departed. Lifts started bringing up the second-wave aircraft, and as these started to be ranged on the deck, the pilots and observers underwent their briefing in the ready room.

THE SECOND STRIKE

Almost an hour later, it was the turn of Hale's second wave. At 21.20 *Illustrious* turned once again into the wind. Once again, the green light signalled that all was clear.

The second strike was led by 819's CO, Lieutenant-Commander J. W. 'Ginger' Hale in L5A. A Dartmouth cadet who had joined in 1920, he qualified as a pilot in 1930, joining 440 Flight aboard *Courageous* in 1931. He later served in the carrier *Furious* and the battleship *Ramillies,* before becoming CO of 825 aboard *Glorious* in 1938. A keen rugby player, before the war he had played both for the Royal Navy and for England. He joined 819 as CO in February 1940. His observer, Lieutenant G. A .Carline, had joined the Royal Navy in 1927, seeing service in a number of ships, including a battleship and a cruiser, then joining *Courageous* as an observer in 1938, and moving to the new *Ark Royal* later that same year. He joined 819 in 1940.

Hale's aircraft was followed by E4H, flown by Lieutenant (A) G. W. L. A.

Bayley of 824 squadron. Bayley had originally served as a midshipman aboard the battleship *Resolution* in 1932, becoming a pilot in 1938, and had joined 824 in February 1938. His observer, Lieutenant H. J. Slaughter, was also from *Eagle*, but from the ship's 813 squadron. He had served in both *Courageous* and her sister *Glorious*, as well as the cruiser *Penelope* and the new *Ark Royal* before he joined 813 in 1939.

Lieutenant (A) C. S. E. Lea in L5H had served in *Glorious* in 1939 before joining 819. Spencer 'Sprog' Lea was another officer with an unorthodox history, having been apprenticed to an Australian sheep farmer before finally joining the Royal Navy. His observer, Sub-Lieutenant (A) P. D. Jones, had started his flying career with 819 in May 1940. Peter Jones had joined HMS *Hermes* as a midshipman (A) in 1939, and in 1940 had joined 819 aboard *Illustrious*.

Lieutenant (A) J. W. G. Wellham in E5H was another of the pilots loaned from 824 squadron aboard *Eagle*. He had joined the squadron in 1939 and, as mentioned, was another officer who had already made his mark in the war, winning the DSC as one of the flight accompanying 'Olly' Patch on the daylight attack on Bomba Bay in Libya, in which he torpedoed and sank an Italian supply ship. His observer, Lieutenant P. Humphreys, had joined as a Dartmouth cadet in 1927. Pat Humphreys had served in a number of ships, being awarded the Empire Gallantry Medal (a decoration replaced by the George Cross in 1940) in 1937 while serving aboard a destroyer during the Spanish Civil War. After the destroyer had struck a mine, with a petty officer he helped rescue seriously injured men from a compartment flooded with water and oil. He had joined 819 in 1938.

A tall Ulsterman, Lieutenant F. M. A. Torrens-Spence was senior pilot, second-in-command, of 819 Squadron, flying L5K, with Lieutenant A. W. F. Sutton as observer. Widely recognised as one of the Fleet Air Arm's best pilots, Michael 'Tiffy' Torrens-Spence had joined the Royal Navy as a cadet in 1932, and become a pilot in 1936, and again he was one of those who had passed through *Glorious*, flying with 802 Squadron. 'Alfie' Sutton had been a midshipman in 1931 aboard the battleship *Repulse*, and saw service in a number of smaller ships before qualifying as an observer in 1938. His first carrier was *Glorious*, after which he joined 819 in 1940.

L5B was flown by Lieutenant R. W. V. Hamilton of 819 squadron, which he had joined in 1940. Hamilton had originally joined the Royal Navy as a Dartmouth cadet and had served in several ships, including two battleships, before becoming a pilot in 1938. His first flying appointment was with 825 aboard *Glorious* in 1938. Sub-Lieutenant (A) J. R. B. Weekes flew as L5B's observer. Weekes had originally served as a midshipman in *Hermes* before joining 819 in 1940.

L4F was flown by Lieutenant (A) R. G. Skelton, who had flown with 823 aboard *Glorious* from 1938, before joining 819 in 1940. His observer, Sub-Lieutenant (A) E. A. Perkins, another of the few RNVR men, had only joined 815 on 10 August 1940.

Lieutenant E. W. Clifford of 819 flew L5F with his observer Lieutenant G. R. M. Going. Clifford had been a midshipman aboard the battleship *Rodney* in 1932, and started training as a pilot in 1935, joining 812 in *Glorious* in 1937. He had joined 819 in January 1940. 'Grubby' Going had been a midshipman in the cruiser *Exeter* in 1932, before serving in the battleship *Nelson* and the submarine *Starfish*, and then qualifying as an observer in 1938. He joined 819 in 1940.

Lieutenant (A) W. D. Morford of 819 flew L5Q. He had joined 802 aboard *Glorious* in 1938, before joining 819 in 1940. His observer was Sub-Lieutenant (A) R. A. F. Green, who had originally been aboard *Hermes* in June 1939, before joining 819 in 1940.

Everything seemed to be going smoothly, but then, as the last aircraft on the starboard side moved out, its wing-tip caught that of Clifford's aircraft, L5F, tearing the fabric and, worse, breaking several of the ribs inside the wing. Without delay, the aircraft was taken out of service and struck down into the hangar. Frantic, Clifford rounded up the riggers, demanding that they repair the damage. His observer, 'Grubby' Going, dashed into the Air Intelligence Office, cursing and telling David Pollock that they must go to Taranto. Lt-Cdr Opie, the ship's USN liaison officer, was there and suggested that he should see the CO.

Going saw Boyd, repeating his request to go to Taranto.

'But my dear fellow, you've smashed your bleeding aircraft,' retorted Boyd.

'We can repair the damage in ten minutes if you'll let us go, sir. I know we can catch up with the others,' came the reply.

Boyd reluctantly agreed, but sent them to see Lyster first. Both the CO and the Flag Officer knew that every aircraft was vital, with little more than two-thirds of the planned number of aircraft available that night. Lyster agreed. Inevitably, given the damage, it was not ten minutes but thirty minutes before L5F could rumble down the flight deck. Few aircraft could have been repaired so quickly. A Swordfish could fly with almost all of its fabric gone, but it would have been foolhardy in the extreme to have attempted to take off with damaged ribs.

The second-wave aircraft seemed to be fated. Equally unlucky were Morford and Green in L5Q. As a bomber, the aircraft had an external long-range fuel tank rather than having it fitted in the middle cockpit. The tank had broken loose twenty minutes after leaving the ship as they flew in formation, falling into the sea and leaving loose fittings banging on the fuselage. Then the engine cut out, and the aircraft began losing height, but Morford managed to restart it. They now had no choice but to return to the carrier while they still had sufficient fuel, nursing a sickly engine. Observing radio silence, nearing the carrier, they fired a red Very light. Both *Illustrious* and the cruiser *Berwick* opened fire, but Green quickly fired the two-star identification signal of the day, and the shooting stopped. The carrier turned into the wind and L5Q landed on.

Hale was now down to seven aircraft, and had no idea what had happened to L5F. He pressed on, aware that by now the ships and base at Taranto would be expecting him. The element of surprise was over.

Flying on alone, this thought also occurred to Clifford and Going. What was worse, every gun would be trained on their solitary aircraft. As the RAF was to discover over and again, in any air raid there is safety in numbers for the attackers, as it forces the defenders to spread their fire over many targets.

CHAPTER NINE

Hour of Judgement

Meanwhile, the aircraft of the first strike had encountered thick cloud, and climbing through it, the formation broke up, with three of the four dive-bombers and one torpedo-bomber having disappeared once the formation came out above the clouds at 7,500ft, flying in sub-flight V formations of three aircraft each. The flight to the target was hazardous in its own right, as aircraft could, and sometimes did, collide when flying in cloud. It was also very cold in the open cockpits. Maund, shortly after the raid, recalled:

Six thousand feet. God how cold it is here! The sort of cold that fills you until all else is drowned, save perhaps fear and loneliness. Suspended between heaven and earth in a sort of no-man's land – to be sure, no man was ever meant to be here … Is it surprising that my knees are knocking together? We have now passed under a sheet of alto-stratus cloud which blankets the moon, allowing only a few pools of silver where small gaps appear. And, begob, Williamson is going to climb through it! As the rusty edge is reached I feel a tugging at my port wing, and find that Kemp has edged me over into the slipstream of the leading sub-flight. I fight with hard right stick to keep the wing up, but the sub-flight has run into one of its clawing moments, and quite suddenly the wing and nose drop and we are falling out of the sky! I let her have her head and see the shape of another aircraft flash by close overhead. Turning, I see formation lights ahead and climb up after them, following them through one of the rare holes in this cloud mass. There are two aircraft sure enough, yet when I range up alongside, the moonglow shows up the figure 5A – that is Olly. The others must be ahead. After an anxious few minutes some dim lights appear amongst the upper billows of the cloud, and opening the throttle we lumber away from Olly after them. Poor old engine – she will get a tanning this trip.

The sub-flight is reassembled now at 8,000 feet. We have come to the edge of the cloud. The regular flashing of a light away down to starboard claims attention. 'There's a flashing light to starboard, Bull, can you place it?' 'Oh, yes' and that is all – the poor devil must be all but petrified by the cold by now.

A few minutes later Bull was indeed able to tell Maund that they had approximately forty minutes to go.

The two flare-droppers managed to maintain formation, however. The planes that had become detached from the first-wave formation made their own way directly to Taranto. One of them, Ian Swayne, flying with Buscall in L4M, reached Taranto fifteen minutes before anyone else. Not wanting to be the first guest at the party, he flew around waiting for the main strike, a wise decision, but his aircraft was detected by Italian listening devices and the ships in the harbour were kept on alert.

Navigation towards the target was simplified once the port's anti-aircraft defences opened up at around 22.50, shooting at a patrolling Short Sunderland flying-boat of 228 Squadron, sent from Malta by the RAF. As they arrived over Taranto, Williamson sent the two flare-droppers to drop their flares with a signal from 'Blood' Scarlett's dimmed Aldis lamp.

Unknown to the attackers, fate had played a hand and there had been a stroke of good fortune during the day. That morning, the Italian fleet had readied for sea, for gunnery exercises. The crews of the warships had spent much of the morning in the tedious chore of removing the torpedo nets that surrounded the ships. Then, for some unknown reason, the admiral had called off the gunnery exercises. No one had given the order to re-rig the nets.

Even so, the Italians were not caught completely off their guard. A succession of alerts and all-clears had broken up the evening, but this was not unusual in a major target area in wartime. Then they had had the visit of the RAF Sunderland that had obligingly given the approaching Swordfish confirmation that they were on course. The evening's entertainment had started at around 19.55, when a report had come in that the sound of aircraft engines had been heard off the coast. This was assumed to be just another reconnaissance flight. Shortly after 20.00, there were more reports of aircraft engines from listening stations, and the alarms were sounded, with gun crews rushing to their posts while the civilians ashore raced for the air raid shelters. Further noises came later, most of which were caused by 228 Squadron's Short Sunderland patrolling dutifully in the Gulf of Taranto, always watchful for any movement by the Italian fleet. The alarm went off for a second time. At 22.45, more noises were picked up, but no doubt Swayne and Buscall were playing a part in this. There was no immediate action until after a further twenty-five minutes had elapsed, when it was clear that something was happening as the noises became louder.

At 22.50, Williamson saw the massive AA barrage sparked off by the listening posts around Taranto, and a couple of minutes later he sighted Taranto. The formation broke up at 22.56 as aircraft flew off on their particular missions.

'A burst of brilliance on the north-eastern shore, and then another and another as a flare-dropper releases his load, until the harbour shows clear in the light he has made,' Maund recorded. 'Not too bright to dull the arc of raining colour over the harbour where tracer flies, allowing, it seems, no room to escape unscathed.'

Williamson in L4A led his flight of L4R and L4C up the Gulf of Taranto, flying at 8,000ft, and in the moonlight, filtered by eight-tenths thin cloud, they spotted Swayne's aircraft, L4M. The flare-droppers, L4P and L5B, were given the signal to deploy.

Richard Janvrin was in L4P with Kiggle on the flare-dropping mission:

We had a grandstand view so we didn't go down to sea level. We dropped our flares at about 8,000 feet. And in fact we were fired at considerably. We had a fair amount of ack-ack fire and most extraordinary things that looked like flaming onions ... one just sort of went through it and it made no great impression. One didn't think that they would ever hit you ... there was always fear but I think in the same way one always had butterflies in the tummy beforehand, but when things were actually happening you don't seem to notice the butterflies much ...

The torpedo aircraft went down and they attacked in two sub flights. The leader took his sub flight of three and attacked. And he ... attacked a Cavour-class battleship, launched his torpedo, which hit and was shot immediately afterwards ... we had bombs as well, and we dive-bombed some more fuel tanks ... and then we returned to the carrier ...

Janvrin had seen Williamson's aircraft on its torpedo-dropping run, and had then seen it appear to be struck by AA fire as it attempted to make its escape at low level across the harbour.

The two flare-droppers each carried sixteen parachute flares and four bombs. After dropping their flares, their next target was to bomb the fuel storage tanks.

As assistant flare-droppers, Lamb and Grieve remained at 5,000ft while Kiggell dropped the first flares. Giving the rudimentary navigation and targeting of the day, what happened next was impressive. The first flare burst into a yellow orb just as the first attacking aircraft reached the entrance to the harbour.

Williamson had swept through the barrage balloon cables, later maintaining that neither he nor Scarlett had noticed them, heading for the destroyers *Lampo* and *Fulmine*, which welcomed him with a barrage of machine-gun fire, before turning towards the massive outline of a battleship and dropping to only 30ft before releasing their torpedo. In fact, they felt the splash as the torpedo hit the water, so it is likely that they were even lower. There was no time to wait and see, they had to escape the intense AA fire, but a few minutes later the night was shattered by a massive explosion. Their torpedo had found its mark and they had sunk the *Conte di Cavour* in shallow water. Struggling to get away, while turning in the middle of the harbour to escape, the Swordfish crashed, although neither crew member could later be certain whether this was caused by Italian AA fire or an accident. The observer, Scarlett, later recalled:

We put a wing tip in the water. I couldn't tell. I just fell out of the back into the sea. We were only about 20 feet up. It wasn't very far to drop. I never tie myself in on these occasions.

Then old Williamson came up a bit later and we hung about by the aircraft, which had its tail sticking out of the water. Chaps ashore were shooting at it. The water was boiling, so I swam off to a floating dock and climbed on board that. We didn't know we'd done any good with our torpedo. Thought we might have because they all looked a bit long in the face, the Wops.

Williamson in the pilot's cockpit had found escape extremely difficult. He might have lost consciousness for a brief spell as he was aware of his head throbbing, suggesting that he had struck it on the instrument panel as the aircraft finally plunged into the water. It seems almost certain that the aircraft was indeed shot down.

Struggling in the water, his lungs bursting, Williamson was surprised to find his parachute falling off easily as he unfastened it, and then the button of his Sutton harness released that in an instant. He kicked out, and was free of the cockpit, shooting up to the surface. As he gulped in mouthfuls of air, he realised that someone else was in the water with him, and recognised Scarlett.

He later recalled thinking that it had started to rain, then he realised that the tiny splashes of water around them were in fact the splashes of machine-gun rounds.

Williamson and Scarlett spent a good half-hour clinging to the tail of their aircraft. Whether much of the gunfire that splashed around them was aimed at them or was due simply to the Italian gunners having to depress the elevation of their weapons as far as possible to catch the low-flying Swordfish was probably immaterial – sitting in the water clinging to nothing more substantial than the tailplane of a fairly rudimentary aircraft was far from the best position in the middle of an air raid.

Williamson's attack in L4A was just one of the many in progress at much the same time.

Sparke and Macauley had originally planned to attack the *Vittorio Venteto*, but were too far south, so both aimed instead at the *Conte di Cavour*, but missed her; their torpedoes ran on to explode close to the *Andrea Doria*, without causing any damage.

Leading the second sub-flight, during a lull in the AA fire from the cruisers, Kemp aimed at the battleship *Littorio*, and at around 1,000 yards dropped his torpedo. He had the satisfaction of seeing the silver streak of bubbles as it raced towards its target, before climbing steeply as the defences burst into life again. Swayne, who had rejoined his sub-flight leader after becoming detached from the rest of the first wave in thick cloud, now followed his leader. Crossing the harbour as he lost height before making a sharp turn to port as he reached the end of the mole, Swayne dropped his torpedo only 400 yards from the *Littorio*. Despite the aircraft, L4K, leaping upward as its heavy load dropped, he only just managed to clear the battleship's masts. Buffeted by exploding shells, Swayne and his observer Buscall had the satisfaction of seeing a column of smoke shoot up by the smoke-stacks of the *Littorio* herself, hit just seconds after Kemp's strike.

Italian gunners were largely concentrating on shooting at the parachute flares, a fairly pointless exercise, not least because the flares had a delay action, not igniting until they had dropped a thousand feet. A great deal of ammunition was wasted in this way. When it came to shooting at the planes, they faced a terrible dilemma, as the torpedo-carrying aircraft were flying so low that AA fire was beginning to rake the decks and superstructure of the ships in the harbour, risking serious damage and heavy casualties to their own side. Afterwards, many of the pilots were to criticise the Italians for not using searchlights. The view was that had they done so, they could have shot down every aircraft. Lamb, who had a bird's-eye view of the opening stages of the attack, disputed this. The aircraft were so low that had the Italians used searchlights, they would only have served better to illuminate the battleships and cruisers. Another problem was that searchlights could have blinded the AA gunners.

Maund was the last torpedo-dropper of the first strike:

We are now at 1,000 feet over a neat residential quarter of the town where gardens in darkened squares show at the back of houses marshalled by the neat plan of the streets that serve them. Here is the main road that connects the district with the main town. We follow its line and, as I open the throttle to elongate the glide, a Breda AA gun swings round from the shore, turning its stream of red balls in our direction. This is the beginning. Then another two guns farther north get our scent – white balls this time – so we throttle back again and make for a black mass on the shore that looks like a factory, where no balloons are likely to grow ... We must be at a hundred feet now and must soon make our dash across that bloody water ... I open the throttle wide and head for the mouth of the Mar Piccolo, whose position ... can be judged by the lie of the land. Then it is as if all hell comes tumbling in on top of us ... the fire of one of the cruisers and the Mar Piccolo Canal batteries ...

Maund favoured a sister ship to the south of the *Littorio*:

We turn until the right hand battleship is between the bars of the torpedo sight, dropping down as we do so. The water is close beneath our wheels, so close I am wondering which is to happen first – the torpedo going or our hitting the sea – then we level out, and almost without thought the button is pressed and a jerk tells me the 'fish' is gone.

His target turned out to be the *Vittorio Veneto*, a battleship that appeared to be leading a charmed existence that night as the torpedo ran aground in the shallow harbour waters before reaching its target. In attempting to escape while evading the AA fire, Maund nearly struck the fo'c'sle of a destroyer, which had not noticed him at that time.

Many compared the scene over Taranto with the eruption of a volcano, because the AA fire was so intense, and the Italians favoured tracer shells, known to the aircrew as 'flaming onions'. Italian AA gunnery seems to have been very inaccurate, but from the point of view of the attackers, the use of tracer was welcome, simply because they could see it coming and take evasive action. Goodwin was later to describe it as a 'wonderful Brock's benefit', alluding to the name of a well-known fireworks manufacturer.

The bombers were also busy. Patch had arrived over San Pietro Island at 23.06 at 8,500ft, and headed for the cruisers and destroyers moored in the inner harbour, the Mar Piccolo. At first, according to Goodwin, they thought that there was 'nothing much happening', but then the AA defences opened up and they had some difficulty in identifying a target amidst the smoke and flame from the AA barrage. At last Patch saw his chance and pushed E5A into a dive. Levelling out at masthead height, he dropped six bombs, before turning east to escape, throwing his aircraft around so violently that at one stage Goodwin was thrown out of his seat and only his 'monkey's tail' wire stopped him from falling out of the aircraft.

Sarra in L4L dived from 8,000ft to 1,500ft over the Mar Piccolo, looking for a target; unable to distinguish anything in the flame and smoke as he roared over the dockyard, his attention was caught by the hangars and slipways of the seaplane base. He dropped to 500ft and then swept over the seaplane base and dropped his bombs. There was a large explosion and the hangars burst into flames. This alerted the AA batteries to his presence, but he was able to escape to the south, eventually returning to the carrier with one of the few aircraft to escape completely unscathed that night.

Forde in L4H had lost contact with the rest of the group, but arrived as Kiggell began dropping his flares. He saw ships in the Mar Piccolo, sterns against the jetty 'like sardines in a tin', and dropped his bombs at 1,500ft. No hits were observed, so he went round and repeated the attack in case his bombs had not been released. Murray and Paine in E5Q should have been more successful, running across the destroyers at 3,000ft, seeing their bomb strike the destroyer *Libeccio*, but it failed to explode.

Meanwhile, Charles Lamb and his observer Grieve were in L5B, likewise a flare-dropper. They saw aircraft 'flying into the harbour only a few feet above sea level – so low that one or two of them actually touched the water with their wheels as they sped through the harbour entrance. Nine other spidery biplanes dropped out of the night sky, appearing in a crescendo of noise in vertical dives from the slow moving glitter or the yellow parachute flares.'

Kemp, in L4K, was among those flying low over the water. Ahead lay the battleship *Caio Duilio*. Almost blinded by the intense AA fire, heavy with tracer shells, he launched his torpedo less than half-a-mile from the target, and than changed course abruptly to make his escape.

Lamb decided not to drop his flares, as the harbour was brilliantly lit up already. He toyed with the idea of dropping a few over the Mar Piccolo, but held back as he could see another plane starting to bomb the cruisers and destroyers, and he had no intention of illuminating the aircraft for the AA gunners. Lamb was tempted to drop his bombs on the cruisers and destroyers, but remembered that 'Streamline' Robinson had been emphatic about everyone obeying orders, and headed instead for the oil storage tanks, his allotted target. He dive-bombed the oil tanks, asking Grieve to report any explosions, although he realised that this was unlikely as his bombs were semi-armour piercing and would explode deep inside the storage tanks. As he departed, he dumped his remaining flares to give the Italians some more target practice.

The dive-bombers had the task of striking at the lightly armoured cruisers and the destroyers, many of which were in the inner harbour, where space was far tighter and AA fire continued to be intense. Dive-bombing, as exemplified in the course of the German blitzkrieg, can be lethally accurate and effective, particularly when unopposed. But against well-drilled and experienced AA gunners with the nerve to withstand the attack, dive-bombing is an extremely hazardous occupation. The torpedo-bombers had to come in low since, if dropped from too great a height, their torpedoes risked breaking up on impact with the water. Moreover, one advantage of a torpedo over bombs, as an American admiral famously put it, was 'that it is much easier to get water into a ship from the bottom than from the top'. At

Three trumpets, the ship's crest
of HMS *Illustrious*.

Captain Denis Boyd, the first commanding officer of
HMS *Illustrious*. Well respected and liked by his men,
he later rose to the rank of Admiral. (*FAAM PERS 28*)

Always dressed formally, Admiral Sir Alexander Browne Cunningham, almost certainly on the deck of his flagship, HMS *Warspite*, at Alexandria, with the veteran carrier HMS *Eagle* in the background. (*FAAM PERS/315*)

The idea for the raid had originated when HMS *Glorious* was the Mediterranean Fleet's aircraft carrier; here a formation of Swordfish fly past the ship. (*IWM HL46164*)

Pre-raid reconnaissance was handled by the RAF in Malta, using Martin Baltimore bombers such as this, although the airman in the photograph is a naval officer. (*IWM A8223*)

Illustrious parts company with the 3rd Cruiser Squadron, ready for the raid on Taranto; from a painting by the Admiralty war artist, Lieutenant Rowland Langmaid, RN. (*IWM A9763*)

Outclassed by contemporary land-based fighters, in skilful hands the Fairey Fulmar could still make a difference in defending the fleet from air attack or the attentions of reconnaissance aircraft; here a Fulmar 'hooks on' aboard a carrier. (*IWM A8351*)

Illustrious at sea with Swordfish on her flight deck. The aircraft with wings unfolded has just landed. The forward 4.5in AA turrets can be seen clearly. (*FAAM Carrier, I/171*)

The Swordfish was one of a generation of aircraft in which everything had to be done by hand, including unfolding the wings. This machine is ashore, probably at Dekheila in Egypt. (*IWM A8581*)

A Swordfish being 'struck down' into the hangar on the lift aboard one of the older carriers, probably HMS *Furious*. (*FAAM SWFH 14*)

A damaged Swordfish, probably at Dekheila, showing the position of the long-range fuel tank in the observer's cockpit. (*FAAM Taranto 31*)

Lieutenant-Commander Kenneth 'Hooch' Williamson of 815 Squadron led the raid, flying off with the aircraft of the First Strike. (*FAAM PERS 370*)

Lieutenant Richard Janvrin in full dress uniform, in a photograph almost certainly taken just before the outbreak of war. Post-war, he rose to become an admiral. (*FAAM PERS 241*)

A lieutenant at the time of the raid, Norman 'Blood' Scarlett was Williamson's observer. (*FAAM PERS 254*)

Looking like a head boy with a grumpy head-master, 'Streamline' Robertson is pictured (left) with Lumley Lyster, a rare shot of both taken after the event and after both had been promoted, Robertson to captain and Lyster to vice-admiral. (*FAAM PERS 316*)

Captain 'Olly' Patch of the Royal Marines flew one of the bombers of the First Strike. He had already won a DSO for an earlier operation. (*FAAM PERS 253*)

far right: 'Tiffy' Torrens-Spence flew with the Second Strike and his torpedo may have damaged the battleship *Littorio*, for which he was belatedly awarded the DSO. (*FAAM PERS 623*)

A reconnaissance photograph of the outer harbour at Taranto, taken by the RAF the day before the operation. The next day, a sixth battleship entered. (*FAAM Taranto 2*)

NEXT STOP TARANTO: writing messages on bombs is nothing new. These 500lb-bombs are waiting to be slung under the aircraft. (*FAAM Taranto 19*)

The battleship *Littorio* four days after the attack. (*FAAM Taranto 6*)

The *Littorio* down by the bows. (*IWM HU52334*)

The battleship *Caio Duilio* sits on the bottom of the outer harbour after the attack. (*IWM HU2059*)

Another shot of the damaged *Caio Duilio*. (*IWM HU2058*)

The *Conte di Cavour*, the third Italian battleship to be hit, is likewise sitting on the bottom of the outer harbour the morning after. (*FAAM Taranto 39*)

A formation of torpedo-carrying Fairey Swordfish. (*IWM A3533*)

OPPOSITE

above: Revenge: *Illustrious* under heavy attack on 10 January, 1941. (*IWM A4160*)

below: At times the ship seemed to disappear, hidden by the spray thrown up by near misses. (*FAAM Carrier, I/ 145*)

above: The bomb-damaged flight deck, looking aft from the flying control position. Down below, the hangar was ablaze, with many airmen dead. (*FAAM Carrier, I/43*)

Bomb damage by the island of *Illustrious*. The wreckage in the foreground was that of a small mobile crane. (*FAAM Carrier, I/37*)

While staying in Malta for emergency repairs, *Illustrious* once again became a target for the Luftwaffe, with the raids reaching a peak on 16 January. (*FAAM CAMP 415*)

Morford
Hale
Torrens-Spence
Sarra
Sutton
Williamson
Janvrin
Charles Evans
Going
Spencer Lea

Robertson
Grieve
Admiral Boyd
Admiral Lyster
Charles Lamb

The survivors at a post-war 'Taranto Night' dinner aboard *Illustrious* just before she was withdrawn from service in 1954. Admirals Boyd and Lyster are prominent in the centre of the group. (*FAAM Taranto 25*) this low level, the planes presented a difficult target. The dive-bombers had to dive from altitude and release their bombs while still high enough for the bombs to arm themselves before hitting the target. Apart from being clearly visible from the ground, it was not unknown for a Swordfish to have its wings ripped off in a dive.

Now it was the turn of the second strike to arrive, while the first wave was still hard at work. This was to lead to some subsequent confusion as to who took the credit for what.

THE SECOND STRIKE

The cloud that had hampered the formation flying of the first strike had disappeared as Hale's aircraft lined up. He took them to 8,000ft at 22.50 and twenty minutes later they had their first sight of the volcano of flak erupting around the port. The second-wave pilots could see the fires started by the first wave's bombs while they were still 60 miles away.

As news spread that another formation of aircraft was on its way, the gunners spurred themselves on to even greater exertions, although they were firing blindly into an empty sky. Hale arrived with the second wave of seven aircraft, arriving in the opposite direction from the first wave, detaching L5B and L4F, his flare-droppers, at 23.55. Hamilton in L5B dropped sixteen flares at intervals of fifteen seconds, followed by L4F with Skelton, who dropped another eight. They then turned their attentions to the oil storage depot, attacking from different directions and successfully started a fire before they left for the carrier.

Hale in L5A flew over Cape Rondinella at 5,000ft before beginning his dive, jinking the aircraft from side to side as the flak began to swing towards him. Aiming at Italy's newest battleship, the *Littorio*, he levelled out at a mere 30ft. Skimming low over the water, with the huge ship towering above him, he dropped his torpedo at 700 yards, banked steeply to starboard, and only just missed a barrage balloon cable as he made his exit.

Torrens-Spence, with Sutton, flew low through the harbour entrance looking for his target. Sighting the *Littorio*, he lined up on her, and dropped his torpedo, one of three to hit the ship that night. Both Torrens-Spence in L5K and Hale in L5A dropped their torpedoes at around the same time, and no one can be sure exactly who did the damage. In the mêlée of fire and flares, and aircraft doing their best to avoid gunfire while going for their targets, it was a miracle that there were no collisions. Indeed, as Torrens-Spence and Sutton wheeled away, they suddenly saw Bayley and Slaughter, in E4H of the second strike, heading straight towards them and had to dive to avoid hitting them. In making their escape, Torrens-Spence flew so low that at one point the wheels of his aircraft touched the water and only a quick pull back on the control column saved it from cart-wheeling tailplane over mainplane into disaster. Bayley and Slaughter were less fortunate. As E4H prepared to torpedo the heavy cruiser *Gorizia*, it received a direct hit, and Lamb in L5B, saw the plane burst into flames before falling into the harbour.

Lea and Jones in L5H wisely decided that the flak that had greeted the first two torpedo-droppers of their strike was distinctly unwelcoming and turned in a complete circle to starboard while losing height to get beneath the gunfire. This put them just above the water and heading towards the *Caio Duilio*, which loomed up ahead of them. At around 800 yards, they dropped their torpedo, which struck the ship. Turning to escape, flying at just 30ft above the water, they nearly struck the masts of a fishing boat, and then ran the gauntlet of flak as they passed between the two cruisers *Zara* and *Fiume* before clearing the northern tip of San Pietro Island.

Meanwhile, Wellham in E5H had flown over Taranto itself, skirted the balloon barrage and almost sneaked in unnoticed until he entered the harbour. Raked by heavy machine-gun fire, his aircraft had an aileron damaged and he had to struggle to regain control. By the time he was on an even keel again, he was in the centre of a square formed by four battleships, of which the best choice seemed to be the *Vittorio Veneto*. He dropped his torpedo on her port quarter at the close range of just 500 yards. As he turned to starboard his port wing was badly damaged by a 40mm shell that broke several ribs and tore the fabric. Once again the *Vittorio Veneto* saw her luck hold.

Clifford and Going in L5F, meanwhile, arrived as the second strike was beginning its return to the carrier. The AA fire was intense as they approached, but this died down as they got closer. They could see the fires caused by the earlier attacks and that the harbour was already streaked by oil. In the calm, Clifford circled the Mar Grande looking for a suitable target. He eased back the throttle, allowed the Swordfish to drop to 2,500ft and dived towards a line of ships, which promptly greeted him with a hail of fire. At 500ft, he levelled off and headed for two cruisers, dropping his six bombs as he crossed them. There was no explosion and at first he thought that he had missed, but in fact his bomb had gone straight through the cruiser *Trento*, without exploding. Turning north and flying across the Mar Piccolo, Clifford made his escape, crossing the coast five miles to the east of the harbour entrance.

COUNTING THE COST

Inevitably, the long flight back to the ship was something of an anti-climax. The clouds that had helped to break up the first wave on the run into Taranto had dispersed and it was a clear moonlit night. Had the Italians attempted even rudimentary night fighter operations, the aircraft would have been easy targets. Britain's wartime leader, Winston Churchill, was later to note that 11 November was also the day on which Italian bombers, escorted by fighters, had attempted to attack British convoys in the River Medway, adding caustically that the sixty fighters 'might have found better employment defending their fleet at Taranto'.

Aboard L5B, Grieve was struggling first to fix a course back to the rendezvous point off Cephalonia, and then to get the aircraft to pick up the carrier's homing beacon. This was the greater problem, since coming from the elderly *Eagle* he had no previous experience with this useful piece of equipment. An attempt to test it on the outward flight had been unsuccessful, but it was possible that the homing beacon had been switched off at that time so as not to give away the carrier's location.

Lamb soon had other worries as he settled into the flight back. He could not see any other aircraft in the clear night sky. He began to wonder whether his was the only aircraft to survive the raid. He called Grieve on the Gosport tube, the voice pipe linking the two cockpits.

'We may be the only survivors,' he started. 'I doubt whether any of the torpedo or bombing pilots got away with that, and I saw nothing of Kiggell's aircraft after he had dropped that last flare on the far side of the harbour. The Eyeties may have cottoned on to the delay action of the flares and started shooting ahead of them. They would have been very dumb if they hadn't … if he was hit I doubt whether we would have seen it happen, amongst all those other explosions.'

'I'm afraid you are right', Grieve replied. 'But we can't do anything about it now.'

Lamb's next concern was what he should say at debriefing, realising that if they were the sole survivors, they would be expected to give a good account of the damage. Grieve was unable to help. 'You were throwing the aircraft about like a madman, half the time, and every time I tried to look over the side, the slipstream nearly whipped off my goggles! The harbour was blanked out by ack-ack and I had to check with the compass to see which way we were facing.'

Lamb suddenly realised that Grieve must have had a very uncomfortable half-hour, crouched in his small cockpit, with only a thin canvas fuselage between him and the shells whizzing past, and a large petrol tank with its contents slopping away inside in the middle cockpit for company. The observer's lot was not an enviable one, guiding the aircraft to the target, unable to do anything while the action was at its height, and then calmly plotting a course for home afterwards.

Lamb was not the only one with doubts. Aboard *Illustrious*, Lyster and his staff, Boyd and the rest of the ship's company, could have no idea of what was happening. They were waiting anxiously both for news of the attack and to see just how many of the Swordfish might return. Tension rose as the time for the first strike to have been completed came and then passed. There was no signal from Williamson. There could not be. Those aboard the carrier realised that the first strike should have been leaving the target by this time. As they continued waiting for the aircraft of the first strike, eventually the longed-for signal was received from the second strike, 'Attack completed'.

Despite their distinctly hairy departure from Taranto, as they climbed away from the harbour and the heavy AA fire, Lea realised that he had not spoken to his observer for what must have been minutes, but actually seemed like hours. Concerned that Jones might have been wounded, or worse, as they flew through the heavy flak, he tentatively asked him if he was all right. 'Yes thanks,' drawled Jones, proving that it was not for nothing that he had acquired the nickname 'The Imperturbable' among his fellow aircrew in 819. 'Hang on a minute and I'll give you a course back to the ship.'

It was the radar officer, Lt Schierbeck of the Royal Canadian Naval Volunteer Reserve, who first noticed the returning planes on his set. Then, shortly afterwards, two aircraft arrived, their navigation lights switched on, glowing dimly in the dark to reassure those waiting below. Boyd waited until another couple of aircraft had arrived before turning into the wind for the planes to land on, guided by the batsman's glowing wands. One after another the aircraft hooked on, jerked abruptly in the air a few feet above the flight deck and dropped down on to the deck. Then they taxied forward to await their turn to have their wings folded before being struck down into the hangar. Almost before they stopped, excited observers had jumped down and rushed to the ready room for debriefing. Their enthusiasm told the team on deck all that they needed to know. The pilots, staying with their aircraft until they were struck down, were surprised to find that they were riddled with holes, with torn fabric flapping around the fuselage and wings. Later that morning, returning to his plane after snatching some sleep, Sarra counted seventeen shell holes.

When Lamb eventually landed on the carrier, he was still wondering what to say at debriefing. It was not until his aircraft was struck down into the hangar that he realised that he was almost the last to return, despite having been with the first wave. 'Only three to come, sir,' his maintainer Burns reported cheerfully. He had hardly finished when there was the scream of arrester wires running through the blocks followed by the thud of wheels hitting the flight deck above. 'Belay that – only two to come!'

Last to land, Clifford and Going also had the best intelligence on the attack. Flying a single aircraft so long after the second wave, they had been lucky not to be shot down.

The raid had been a complete success. At a time when the RAF was suffering unsustainable losses on its bombing raids over enemy-held territory, the Fleet Air Arm had indeed done well to lose only two aircraft. (The estimate of 10 per cent losses was just about right.) As for their crews, Bayley and Slaughter died, but Williamson and Scarlett survived their ordeal.

Comparisons with RAF bomber missions over enemy-occupied territory early in the war are not strictly fair, since the RAF had to fly lengthy periods when they were constantly harassed by enemy fighters. Better comparisons are with the attacks on German ports and harbours. On 4 September 1939, a mixed force of twenty-nine Bristol Blenheims and Vickers Wellingtons was sent to attack German warships in the Schillig Roads and the Kiel Canal, with the loss of five Blenheims and two Wellingtons. In December, out of twelve Wellingtons sent to attack the *Nürnberg* and *Leipzig* in the Jade Estuary, six had been shot down. Pound's pessimism over likely losses was well founded.

DOWN IN TARANTO

After clinging for half an hour to the tail of their ditched Swordfish, Williamson and Scarlett found the strength to swim 150 yards towards the side of a floating dock. Williamson was sick and dizzy with shock, doubtless concussed, and it was his companion who guided him to a ringbolt. Their position remained perilous as gunfire continued to strike around them, so they attempted to clamber into the dock, soaking and still wearing their Mae Wests. In a moment, they were surrounded by a crowd of shouting Italians, who later proved to be dockyard workers. They were roughly man-handled, their clothes being torn off them in the process, and bundled into a hut alongside the dock. In due course their captors calmed down, and the two prisoners were each given a blanket by the foreman before he disappeared.

It was not for an hour or so that the AA guns fell silent. Then, the door burst open and the foreman reappeared with two armed Italian naval ratings. The pair were again seized and hustled out into the darkness, then prodded into a waiting motorboat, which immediately cast off and made for a destroyer – none other than the *Fulmine*, one of their original targets and most probably responsible for shooting them down. As they clambered aboard, they were greeted by an Italian officer who enquired, 'Sei ferito?', 'Are you wounded?', but this meant nothing since neither of them could understand Italian.

The officer took them down to the wardroom to meet the destroyer's captain and two of his officers, one of whom, a lieutenant, spoke English. He started to interrogate them, but they both steadfastly refused to give more than their names and ranks. The lieutenant then asked for their numbers. It took some time and much argument before the Italians could be convinced that Royal Navy officers did not have numbers. Once this was established, the atmosphere changed completely, and became much more relaxed. The other officer spoke French and offered them a cognac, while the captain went looking for spare clothing. After changing into the clothes, they were given food and beer, before bedding down for the night in the wardroom.

Early the next morning the *Fulmine* moved into the inner harbour where most of the destroyers lay, and the two prisoners were led ashore, blind-folded. They were taken to the headquarters of the local police, the

Carabinieri, where they were ushered into an office to find a naval captain already sitting there, accompanied by an interpreter. They both felt nervous, concerned that Mussolini's men might not be too keen on the Geneva Convention, which restricts the information expected of a captured POW to his name, rank and serial number.

Williamson went first. He was offered a chair, a glass of beer and a cigarette, and accepted all three. 'Now I am going to ask you some questions,' said the affable Italian captain through the interpreter, adding: 'You need not answer them if you don't want to.' Williamson gave his name, rank, home address and next of kin. He refused, however, to say where he had come from. In the discussion that followed, Williamson deduced that the Italians considered Crete to have been the most likely base. The next question was whether or not there had been a third member of the crew, simply because they wanted to know if they had to look for a body, which, they assured Williamson, would be given a military funeral. Williamson informed the Italians that the aircraft carried just a two-man crew.

'Blood' Scarlett was subsequently given the same treatment and asked the same questions. Both men were then held under guard in the police headquarters.

That night, the air-raid sirens sounded, warning of an RAF raid. Conducted to an air-raid shelter, they expected to be roughly handled by the crowd of Italian sailors already there, but instead were treated well, given the only two chairs and offered cigarettes. There was another air-raid warning the following night, but this time their companion in the shelter was an Italian army officer with a steward carrying a silver salver with glasses of Cointreau. No doubt the relaxed atmosphere was due to the fact that the air raid was on Bari, 40 miles away!

After their brief stay in Taranto, they were taken by train to Venice and from there to a prisoner-of-war camp at Sulmona. They were treated reasonably well in the Italian POW camp, but after Italy surrendered in 1943, they passed into the hands of the Germans, and were taken to Germany. Conditions in the German camps were, they discovered, more difficult.

The crew of the other lost aircraft were not so fortunate. Lieutenants Bayley and Slaughter were both killed when E4H blew up under intense AA fire. They were in the second wave, always likely to be the more dangerous as the defences would have been fully alerted, and the AA gunners would have 'got their eye in' against the attacking aircraft. Missing for some time,

Bayley's body was eventually found some years after the war, buried at Taranto, and later moved to the military cemetery at Bari, maintained by the Commonwealth War Graves Commission. Slaughter's body was never found.

Between them, the Swordfish dropped eleven torpedoes and forty-eight 250lb semi-armour-piercing bombs. The Italians had expended 13,489 rounds of high-angle AA fire at the two flare-droppers, as well as 1,750 rounds of 4in and 7,000 rounds of 3in shells at the bombers and torpedo-bombers – all from the harbour defences, while no accurate record was kept of fire from the ships.

Taranto was left in a mess. The outer harbour was covered with burning oil. Ships were on fire and shore installations were also ablaze.

JUBILATION

The crews were jubilant as they returned to *Illustrious*. Yet Cunningham, renowned for taking acts of great bravery as being nothing much more than what was to be expected of naval officers, showed remarkable understatement even for him. As the carrier and her escorts rejoined the rest of the Mediterranean Fleet on 12 November, a hoist of flags was raised aboard *Warspite* saying simply, '*Illustrious* manoeuvre well executed'.

It was three in the morning. Tired and exhausted, the fliers were surprised to be told that they would be going back that night. Their maintainers had been ordered to 'do a major' on the planes during the day, to get them ready for another attack. As one wit put it, 'Even the Light Brigade was only asked to attack once.'

Descending to the wardroom, they found that the stewards had painted a large 'Welcome Home' sign which was hanging from the deckhead – entirely their own idea. As Lamb downed a large whisky and soda pushed into his hand by the Paymaster-Commander, the latter told him he very much doubted whether they would be going back that night. Lyster himself had provided a bottle of whisky to accompany the eggs and bacon breakfast waiting for the returning crews – and the ship's cooks had baked a cake. Worsening weather and the certain knowledge that the Italians would be expecting another attack persuaded Cunningham to turn down the chance to have another go at the target.

Meanwhile, Boyd spoke to the pilots and observers after the briefing. He found that most of them talked about the intense AA fire. 'I didn't take it personally, sir, until they started hitting my aircraft, and then I didn't like it much!' one pilot told him. Amused by this, Boyd thought that it was intended for the 'Line Book', the large scrap book often decorated with a ship's crest that recorded the rivalry between squadrons or between the airmen and the ship's company. Determined to see for himself, he went to see the aircraft, and found its fabric hanging off the fuselage and wings in ribbons.

The cruisers rejoined the fleet at daylight on 12 November having carried out diversionary attacks in the Straits of Otranto. As the carrier steamed eastward returning to Alexandria, Italian aircraft came looking for her – three Cantieri flying-boats which were quickly confronted by 806 Squadron's Fulmars. Lowe shot down two of the planes just three miles from *Illustrious*, but the third went down directly above the fleet like a flaming meteor trailing black smoke, falling out of the sky and into the sea. Had they not been shot down so promptly, there can be little doubt that a substantial bomber force from the Regia Aeronautica would have arrived in a revenge attack.

Two days later, the RAF provided photographs from an aerial reconnaissance taken the morning after the raid. The evidence was clear. In one night, just twenty obsolescent biplanes from a single warship had inflicted more damage on an enemy than Nelson had managed in his famous victory at Trafalgar, and almost twice as much as the British Grand Fleet had inflicted on the German High Seas Fleet at Jutland, without the latter battle's terrible losses. It was the first significant British victory of World War Two.

CHAPTER TEN

A Night to Remember

At Taranto, the Italians had been on a high state of alert for some time before the attack came. They had been woken up by the RAF Short Sunderland from Malta, and kept awake by the stray Swordfish waiting off the coast for the main body of the first strike to arrive. A period of calm ensued.

Some 300 miles to the north, in Rome, the Italian Admiralty maintained an efficient Operations Room at Supermarina, with excellent communications and maintained on a twenty-four-hour basis. On the night of 11–12 November, the duty officer was Commander M. A. Bragadin. Like the others on duty, Bragadin had been aware of the gathering British forces, with Force H to the west and the Mediterranean Fleet to the east. Intelligence reports gave conflicting accounts, although Commander Bragadin was later to say that 'it was learned that the Gibraltar Force had reversed course in keeping with the now classical British operational procedure ... By that evening Supermarina could only conclude, in a general way, that this British force must have been about 300 miles from Taranto and on its way to Alexandria at approximately 15.00 that afternoon.'

Clearly, the consensus at Supermarina was that the British were trying to tempt the Italian battle fleet out into the Mediterranean, hoping yet again to force a major naval engagement. An attack by aircraft from the *Ark Royal* could be discounted, since the planes would have had to fly over Sicily, the element of surprise lost as the defences would have been alerted. Even if this were not a consideration, it would also have put the carrier in a difficult position, within range of aircraft on Sicily and Sardinia to the north. No one seems to have suspected the approach of *Illustrious* – an oversight soon to be exposed. Suddenly, the telephone rang, with the first reports of the attack on Taranto. Bragadin immediately alerted Admiral Cavagni, who hurried down to the Operations Room to see what was happening.

In Taranto harbour the battleship *Cavour* had been first to open fire with her heavy AA armament at 23.14, the tracer shells soaring like fireworks over the destroyer *Fulmine* moored close by. The destroyer's guns also opened up as the crew watched the silhouette of an aircraft diving towards them. The plane, soon recognisable as a torpedo-carrying aircraft, turned to starboard, engine roaring, and then, low on the water, dropped its torpedo towards the *Cavour* with a huge splash. The men could see the wake of the torpedo as it started its run, then the stream of bubbles as it submerged into the harbour waters, running straight towards the larger ship.

Meanwhile, however, the gunners had the aircraft firmly in their sights, and it was soon clear that it had been hit. It staggered past the destroyer as jubilant gunners swung their mountings round to follow it. They saw it lurch in mid-flight, then dive into the harbour, sinking so that just the tail was sticking out of the water.

THE MORNING AFTER

Daybreak at Taranto found Admiral Riccardi and his staff frantically organising salvage and repair parties for the stricken ships. It was to take more than twenty-four hours before a detailed damage report could be given to Supermarina, despite repeated requests throughout 12 November. When it did arrive, the report made depressing reading. Away from the action, in Rome, the news exceeded Supermarina's worst fears. Both harbours were by now covered in fuel oil, giving off a sickly stench and clinging to the many small craft attempting to create order out of the chaos visited upon the port during the night.

The impact on the Italian fleet was considerable. Three battleships were sunk, *Littorio*, *Caio Duilio* and *Conte di Cavour*, although the last was to be refloated and repaired at the end of the war. Three cruisers and two destroyers had also been badly damaged, with two of the cruisers lying in a pool of oil, and two auxiliaries had also been crippled. Both destroyers had been affected by near-misses, the *Libeccio* having a fractured bow, while the *Pessagno* had damage to her hull. The seaplane base and the oil storage tanks had also been damaged by six bombs and were both still burning. The cruiser *Trento* had a lucky escape, as a bomb crashed through the ship and out of the bottom without exploding, although whether this was due to the thinness of her plates, to the bomb not being dropped from high enough for the arming mechanism to work, or simply that it was faulty, is not clear. Her fuel tanks were ruptured, however, and it was her oil that covered the waters of the Mar Piccolo.

As it was, dawn on 12 November found *Littorio*, the pride of the Italian Navy, surrounded by salvage vessels, while a submarine was providing her with electrical power and a tanker was desperately attempting to salvage her fuel, mainly in order to lighten the crippled battleship and counterbalance the flooding. The battleship had received three torpedo hits. During the first attack, two torpedoes had struck, one blowing a hole 49ft by 32ft in the starboard bulge, abreast of No.1 6in gun turret, the other hitting the port quarter by the tiller flat, blowing a hole 23ft by 5ft. A third torpedo had struck the ship during the second wave, again on the starboard side and slightly forward of the earlier blow, making a hole 40ft by 30ft in the bottom plating. In fact, it could have been far worse, since the starboard quarter showed a dent, and investigation showed that this indeed was the mark of a fourth torpedo, one that had failed to explode and was later found stuck in the harbour mud underneath the ship.

Whereas the *Littorio* could claim to have been lucky, the *Conte di Cavour* had been most unfortunate. The first strike had sent a torpedo into her port bow under No. 1 15in turret, blowing a hole 40ft by 27ft, flooding No. 1 and No. 2 fuel tanks and the adjoining compartments. Salvage teams had towed her towards the shore during the night, but she had to be abandoned at 05.45 as she began to settle. By daylight almost the whole of the upper deck was submerged, including the after turret.

The damage was less severe on the *Caio Duilio*, which had received a single torpedo hit low down on her starboard side, abreast of No.1 5.25in gun mounting, blowing a hole 36ft by 23ft between two magazines, Nos 1 and 2. The magazines were flooded, which was fortunate. Had the torpedo hit a few yards either way, the ship could have been blown out of the water. Meanwhile, the flooding had been so severe that, for safety's sake, she had to be beached.

Given the scale of the destruction, Italian casualties were remarkably light. There were twenty-three men killed aboard the *Littorio*, another sixteen in the *Conte di Cavour*, but just one on the *Caio Duilio*. The principal difference in the number of casualties at Taranto compared with Pearl Harbor a little more than a year later can be attributed to one fact: the Italians had been exceptionally fortunate in that none of their ships had blown up. Had a torpedo penetrated a magazine on just one battleship, the death toll would have been very much higher, as would have been the case had a bomb penetrated one of the magazines of the cruisers.

More important than the actual losses, which did much to correct the balance of naval power in the Mediterranean, at least as far as major surface units were concerned, was the impact on Italian naval strategy. Taranto was no longer used as a base for the Italian battle fleet for the remainder of hostilities. The order was given for the undamaged ships to head north, out of harm's way, and RAF reconnaissance photographs showed that the three undamaged battleships and the cruisers had left Taranto on 13 November for Trieste.

LEARNING THE LESSONS

Those present at Taranto were shocked by the extent of the damage, and badly shaken by the events of the night, but Supermarina was suffering from a completely different kind of shock. Just how had a British aircraft carrier, or perhaps even carriers – since the problems afflicting *Eagle* were unknown to the Italians at the time – managed to get within striking distance of the main forward naval base?

Commander Bragadin later explained:

At Supermarina it was taken for granted that if British forces should come within 180 miles operating range of their torpedo planes from Taranto, the Italian forces would sortie to engage the British and prevent them launching an air attack on the harbour. The events of the night of 12 November, added to many other lessons, confirmed in the most obvious way the deficiencies of Italian air reconnaissance. The fact was that large groups of enemy ships had been cruising the whole preceding day in the central Mediterranean and, at sundown, had crossed the Ionian and Adriatic Seas; yet the Italian reconnaissance had not given the slightest warning of their presence.

Part of the problem was that the Italian Navy failed to understand the potential of the aircraft carrier. Many have acclaimed 806's Fulmar fighters for maintaining what amounted to local air superiority over the Mediterranean Fleet; and Cunningham gave them the credit for shooting down shadowers with considerable success. More significant, however, were the shortcomings of Italian intelligence and planning. If reconnaissance aircraft sent in a particular direction failed to return, surely someone should have sought the reason? True, some of the reconnaissance aircraft were shot down, but others were merely driven off; yet the crews were apparently not debriefed to discover what had happened. At this early stage of the war, the long-range escort fighter had still to appear, so the presence of fighters implied that there had to be a base for them within a very short distance.

Obviously, no one seems to have realised that what amounted to an exclusion zone of only 180 miles would not really be good enough. The Swordfish had been flown off *Illustrious* at 170 miles from Taranto. To have been effective, the exclusion zone would have had to have been much greater, perhaps even 360–400 miles.

Another point arises. Cunningham had expended much time and fuel 'trailing his cloak', trying to get the Italians out to sea to draw them into the classical naval 'big gun' engagement, but without success. Would naval forces really have sallied forth from Taranto to engage the British fleet? Possibly the task of keeping the Royal Navy at bay was to be left entirely to the Regia Aeronautica. Perhaps in blaming the failure of aerial reconnaissance we are seeing inter-service rivalry at work.

'The success of the air attack against the Italian fleet in the outer anchorage of Taranto was the first example of the formidable potentialities of torpedo aircraft against large ships in strongly defended bases and confirmed in general the capabilities of aircraft carriers,' explained Admiral Romeo Bernotti after the war. The Italians were later to claim that the air defences of the base were incomplete and the torpedo nets not deep enough at only 26.25ft, but the torpedo nets had not been deployed, and in any case, the Duplex pistols would have dealt with much deeper nets. The Italians were surprised to discover the existence of such pistols from post-raid examination of the single unexploded torpedo. Whereas weapons that do not explode for one reason or another are, understandably, regarded as an opportunity lost, and at worst, if there are too many, the cause of an operation failing, the more serious problem is that unexploded munitions remain to betray their secrets to the enemy.

While the battle had been in progress over Taranto, the cruisers had gone hunting in the Straits of Otranto. Force X comprised Vice-Admiral Pridham-Wippell in his flagship *Orion*, with *Sydney* and *Ajax*, and two destroyers, *Mohawk* and *Nubian*. The destroyers discovered an Italian convoy of four ships escorted by the *Nicola Fabrizi*, a large torpedo boat armed with 4in guns, and a naval auxilary, *Ramb III*, on passage to Brindisi. The destroyers engaged the convoy, and were soon joined by the cruisers. In a brief engagement, all four merchant ships were sunk and the torpedo boat damaged.

CHAPTER ELEVEN

An Ungracious Judgement

Later, in looking back on the war, and the campaigns in and around the Mediterranean in particular, Churchill was to say in connection with the British Army's victory at El Alamein that 'before Alamein we never had a victory. After Alamein, we never had a defeat.' This was just one example of the way in which Taranto was quickly forgotten. Cunningham was later to admit that he had not realised at first just how successful the entire operation had been, and what had been achieved. Perhaps he felt that a second operation was necessary and that it was disappointing that bad weather had ruled this out. The operation was reported and a statement was made to the House of Commons, which apparently 'cheered everyone up'.

The news seemed almost to leak out in an uncoordinated manner. Churchill was told early in the morning of 12 November, and later that day he accompanied the First Sea Lord to an audience with King George VI. The first public announcement came on the BBC Radio news at 18.00 that evening, in the form of a brief statement from the news agency Reuters that the Italians had admitted that a raid had taken place on Taranto, but that little damage had been done.

It was not until the afternoon of 13 November that Churchill rose to address the House of Commons. 'I have some news for the House,' he began with a deadpan expression. Those present were accustomed by this time to hearing nothing but bad news about the progress of the war. Churchill allowed a moment or two to pass, before grinning and saying, 'It is good news!' He then broke the news, emphasising that the Italian Navy had lost half its strength in battleships in one night.

> The result affects decisively the balance of naval power in the Mediterranean, and also carries with it reactions upon the naval situation in every quarter of the globe. I feel sure that the House will regard these

results as highly satisfactory and as reflecting great credit upon the Admiralty and upon Admiral Cunningham, the Commander-in-Chief in the Mediterranean, and above all our pilots of the Fleet Air Arm who, like their brothers in the RAF, continue to render their country services of the highest order.

By this time, the BBC news at 13.00 had included a 330-word communiqué from the Admiralty. This confirmed that three battleships had been crippled. Further information came from the First Lord of the Admiralty, A. V. Alexander, when he broadcast a tribute following that evening's news at 21.00.

Despite these plaudits, recognition of the heroism of those involved was slow in coming. When the first list of decorations for the aircrew who had risked so much were posted on the notice boards of *Illustrious*, angry sailors tore them down. No one was awarded Britain's highest decoration, the Victoria Cross, no one received better than a Distinguished Service Order (DSO), and at first this was only awarded to the squadron commanders and their observers, and Capt 'Olly' Patch and his observer who both received the Distinguished Service Cross (DSC). Later in the war, many of the men of the famous 617 Squadron were to attend an investiture at Buckingham Palace – undoubtedly well deserved – but no such honour awaited the men of 815 and 819 squadrons, and their reinforcements from *Eagle*'s squadrons. Many attribute this to Cunningham, who either failed, as he subsequently claimed, to recognise the achievement fully, or simply expected such operations to be part and parcel of the naval airman's life.

It could also be that the remarkably light losses incurred also diminished the valour displayed in the eyes of senior officers, or to put it more bluntly, in the view of those who had not been there. The famous Dam Busters squadron of the RAF, No. 617, sent nineteen aircraft to the Ruhr dams, of which only eleven returned. These were Avro Lancaster heavy bombers, more than twice as fast as a Swordfish and heavily armed. In any such operation, luck plays a part. The biggest stroke of luck enjoyed by the aircrew who flew from *Illustrious* to attack Taranto was that they did not have to fight their way to the target, or indeed home from it, even though there was a full moon and, later, little cloud. Had the Italians tried harder, had their reconnaissance been good enough to alert them to the carrier's presence, had they put up fighters, the whole operation could have been a disaster, more akin to the raids on Petsamo and Kirkenes that went, as we shall see, so disastrously wrong and for so little impact on the enemy, the following summer.

Cunningham was slow to appreciate what had been achieved, and just how very fortunate the force had been to suffer so few losses, but later, he was to be wholesome in his praise. 'Admirably planned and most gallantly executed in the face of intense anti-aircraft fire, Operation Judgement was a great success,' he later wrote.

> The zeal and enthusiasm with which these deliberate and accurate attacks were carried out in comparatively slow aircraft in the face of intense fire cannot sufficiently be praised. It was a great day for the Fleet Air Arm, and showed what they could do when they had their chance. Taranto, and the night of November 11–12, 1940, should be remembered for ever as having shown once and for all that in the Fleet Air Arm the Navy has its most devastating weapon. In a total flying time of six and a half hours – carrier to carrier – twenty aircraft had inflicted more damage upon the Italian fleet than was inflicted upon the German High Seas Fleet in the daylight action at the Battle of Jutland.

High praise indeed. Clearly, there is no apostle quite like the convert.

The 1941 New Year Honours List saw both Captain Boyd and his counter-part on *Eagle*, Captain Bridge, awarded the CBE, and Lyster the CB. The remaining awards were not announced until May 1941, by which time many of the recipients were dead.

No one among those who had struggled against the odds to get the air-craft ready, or among the escort vessels, received anything.

Lt Cdr Kenneth 'Hooch' Williamson of 815, and his observer, the then Lt Norman 'Blood' Scarlett, in Swordfish L4A, were both awarded the DSO. Sub-Lt Sparke, who already had the DSO, was awarded a bar, while his observer in L4C, Sub-Lt J. W. Neale, was awarded the DSC. Sparke shortly afterwards transferred to 806 Squadron while in Malta, eventually flying Hawker Sea Hurricane fighters, but was killed flying from HMS *Formidable* some six months after the Taranto raid, by which time he had a second bar to his DSO. Sub-Lt Macauley also received the DSC, as did his observer in L4R, Sub-Lt A. L. O. Wray. Macauley died in June 1941, when the wings of his Swordfish were torn off as he dive-bombed Vichy-French shipping.

The flare-droppers Kiggell and Janvrin in L4P both received the DSO. The other 'assistant' flare-droppers Lamb and Grieve, in L5B, did not receive anything at the time, although Lamb was later awarded both the DSO and DSC.

Royal Marine Captain 'Olly' Patch and his observer, Lt D. G. Goodwin, in E5A, had already been awarded the DSC, although 'Olly' was later to receive the DSO for a subsequent achievement. Sub-Lt A. J. B. Forde was simply mentioned in despatches for his part in the attack, although he was later to be awarded the DSC while in command of 810, a Fairey Barracuda squadron; but there was nothing for his observer in L4H, Sub-Lt A. Mardel-Ferreira. Similar treatment was given to the crew of L4L, Sarra and Bowker, with a mention in despatches for the former, nothing for the observer. Both were shot down later, but survived to become prisoners-of-war, with Midshipman Bowker being reunited with Williamson and Scarlett in an Italian POW camp.

Torrens-Spence and his observer in L5K, Sutton, both received the DSC. Sutton was later awarded a bar to his DSC, while Torrens-Spence subsequently received the DSO and the Air Force Cross, AFC, as well as the Greek Distinguished Flying Cross for operations over Crete. In 1941, during what might be described as the preliminaries to the naval action off Cape Matapan, Torrens-Spence pressed home an attack on the cruiser *Pola*, slowing her down so that Cunningham and the Mediterranean Fleet could bring the Italians to battle. His actions earned this comment from the *Pola*'s captain: 'Either that pilot was mad or he is the bravest man in the world.' Kemp and Bailey also both received the DSC. Bailey was later to be killed while flying as observer to Macauley when the wings were torn off their Swordfish.

Despite damaging the destroyer *Libeccio* in a dive-bombing attack, almost certainly in the face of intense AA fire from the ship and from the defences of the crowded inner harbour, Murray and Paine in E5Q received nothing. Buscall and Swayne, whose torpedo dropped from L4M struck the *Littorio*, were given nothing at the time, but later Buscall received the DSC and Swayne was mentioned in despatches. Buscall was killed later in operations from RNAS Dekheila. In E4F, Maund was mentioned in despatches, and was later awarded the DSC, while his observer Bull received nothing.

Maund was another to die later, while flying a Fairey Albacore with 828 Squadron on anti-shipping operations from Malta.

The members of the second strike fared no better. In the lead, Hale in L5A was awarded the DSO, while his observer Carline was awarded the DSC. Carline was later to be killed while a Lt-Cdr aboard the escort carrier (known to the British as an auxiliary carrier) *Audacity* when she was sunk by *U-741* in December, 1941. Skelton and Perkins in L4F received nothing, despite dropping flares and then dive-bombing the oil refinery. More fortunate were Lea and Jones in L5H, who both received the DSC for their successful attack on the *Duilio*. Wellham in E5H with his observer Humphreys received nothing. Humphreys was killed later in the war when collaborating with the RAF on night-fighter operations at West Malling in Kent.

Hamilton and Weekes in L5B also dropped flares and dive-bombed the oil refinery, for which they each received the DSC. They were both killed the following year during a dive-bombing attack on Leros. Clifford and 'Grubby' Going in L5F both received the DSO, although unfortunately their bomb passed straight through the heavy cruiser *Trento*.

Slaughter and Bayley, who were the only casualties during the attack, were both mentioned in despatches. There was nothing for Green or Morford, the unfortunate victims of a mechanical failure as the fastenings for a long-range fuel tank snapped.

Scant recognition at the time, but for those who survived the war, what of their subsequent naval careers?

The most successful by far was Richard, or Hugh, Janvrin, who served until 1971 when he retired as Vice Admiral Sir Richard Janvrin. Goodwin, Olly Patch's observer, eventually reached the rank of commodore before retiring in 1960 after being the UK's Naval Attaché in Washington. Unlike the equivalent ranks in the RAF and the Army, air commodore and brigadier, the rank of commodore was not substantive at the time, so Goodwin became a captain again on his retirement. Williamson served until 1961 when he retired in the rank of captain, having in the meantime returned to *Illustrious* in 1948 as her Commander (Air). Others to attain the rank of captain included Torrens-Spence, who retired in 1961 having earlier commanded the commando carrier *Albion*, while his observer Sutton also reached this rank before retiring in 1964, with a career that included a period as CO of RNAS Hal Far in Malta. Torrens-Spence was to be awarded the DSO for his actions in the Mediterranean the following year, and among his post-war appointments he, too, returned to the *Illustrious* as her Commander (Air) in 1946; later he was chief instructor at the Empire Test Pilots School at Farnborough, and he then served at the Admiralty as Deputy Director of Air Warfare.

Several others reached the rank of commander, equivalent to the rank of lieutenant-colonel in the Army, at which stage a man would command a battalion. These included 'Blood' Scarlett, Kiggell, Charles Lamb and his observer Grieve, Hale, leader of the second strike, and 'Grubby' Going. Others who became lieutenant commanders included 'Olly' Patch, with the Royal Marine equivalent rank of major.

All in all, these were men capable of proving themselves in command as well as in battle. Williamson and Scarlett also had to contend with the gap in their careers left by a spell as prisoners of war. Scarlett's request for a transfer to general service and hopefully his beloved destroyers, had been forwarded from *Illustrious* before the attack on Taranto, and was approved by the Admiralty, but too late, for he was already a prisoner of war. Meanwhile, he had also received a mention in despatches for organising an escape attempt while at Lubeck. Post-war, Scarlett found that he had inherited an estate in Sussex from his brother, Air Vice-Marshal J. R. Scarlett-Streatfeild, who had been killed while on active service, and Scarlett then became Scarlett-Streatfeild himself. He never got his destroyer: after being released from his POW camp in 1945, he became Lieutenant-Commander (Flying) aboard the escort carrier HMS *Fencer* in 1946, before going to the Admiralty in 1947. He did eventually command the frigate *St Austell Bay*, before serving in HMS *Sea Eagle*, the joint service anti-submarine school at Londonderry in Northern Ireland. By contrast, David Goodwin, Olly Patch's observer, did get a destroyer, the Daring-class HMS *Duchess*, as his one and only sea-going command, operating with the Home Fleet and the Mediterranean Fleet for two-and-a-half years from 1954. Scarlett would not have been surprised to learn that Goodwin described the command of *Duchess* as 'the most exciting job I ever did.' It must all depend on one's definition of excitement.

The Germans were the first to appreciate fully what had happened at Taranto, and the first to take positive action. While the Italians moved their major fleet units out of the port to safer havens, the Germans prepared to move their own Luftwaffe units into Italian bases in Sicily. *Illustrious* had changed the balance of power in the Mediterranean and would not be allowed to get away with it.

It was only at a service dinner, some time after the war, that Cunningham admitted he had not realised at the time 'what a tremendous stroke it was'.

CHAPTER TWELVE

Nemesis

Taranto bought a brief respite to the British war effort in the Mediterranean, but it had replaced one menace, the Italian battle fleet, with another, the Luftwaffe. Italian failings both in the Balkans and North Africa were also met by German air and ground forces, so that eventually the war began to swing back against the British. They had control of the seas, but only for as long as it took the Germans to take control of the air. The Germans did not replace the Regia Aeronautica, but they substantially reinforced it.

In fact, while the Italian fleet had sailed northward to the greater security of Naples, the Mediterranean Fleet was also reduced, as the battleships *Malaya* and *Ramillies* were ordered home within a few weeks of the action. Cunningham noted with satisfaction that this move freed up many of his destroyers, which had been hard pressed to provide an effective anti-submarine screen for so many large capital ships.

Back in Alexandria on 14 November with the rest of the Mediterranean Fleet, within a few days Longmore visited *Illustrious* to congratulate the airmen – a gesture by an old RNAS pilot that was much appreciated by the crew.

Aboard *Illustrious*, Neil Kemp became temporary CO of 815 Squadron, until he was replaced on 16 November by Lt-Cdr John de F. Jago, an old *Glorious* hand. At this stage of the war, few naval airmen had extensive night-flying experience, and Jago, who had been away from flying for some time, engaged in extensive practice, with the squadron undertaking night formations flying out of Dekheila until Jago was satisfied that he was up to his squadron's exacting standards.

Italian air attacks on Alexandria were noticeably more frequent and heavier after Taranto, although the Italians often appeared reluctant to press home such attacks while the Mediterranean Fleet was in port, due to the intense curtain of heavy AA fire put up from the ships. Crete was another favourite target for Italian air attack, despite the island's defences being strengthened. There was still much to do to turn Crete into a fortress, for while Suda Bay was protected by anti-submarine nets, it was still vulnerable to aerial assault and to air-dropped torpedoes. On 3 December, in a revenge attack that might be described as a 'mini-Taranto', the cruiser *Glasgow* was hit by two torpedoes dropped from two Italian aircraft in an attack in which the element of surprise was so complete that the planes were not even fired upon by the several British cruisers at anchor. Fortunately, although severely damaged, *Glasgow* was able to proceed to Alexandria for repairs at a stately 16 knots, and then left for permanent repairs in early February.

While this was happening, at the beginning of January, the Luftwaffe moved General Geissler's Tenth Air Corps, *Fliegerkorps X*, from Poland to Sicily. This was a powerful force, concentrated in one strategically important central point and superior to the combined RAF and Fleet Air Arm strength in the Mediterranean, scattered as this was over more than 2,000 miles from Gibraltar to Alexandria. The Tenth Air Corps had 150 Heinkel He111 and Junkers Ju88 medium-bombers and the same number of Junkers Ju87 Stuka dive-bombers, as well as fifty Messerschmitt Bf109 fighters. Its role was not, as many have suggested, primarily to attack Malta. The Luftwaffe had agreed with the Regia Aeronautica that the first priority would be the assault on British shipping, with *Illustrious* – whose fighters could provide air cover and whose bombers had already wreaked such havoc – as the prime target. Malta was next on the list, followed by the base at Alexandria. Finally, the Luftwaffe and Regia Aeronautica would sow mines in the approaches to the Suez Canal. The raids on Alexandria and the mining of the Suez Canal would probably need to await the occupation of Crete, since most Luftwaffe aircraft were short in range and there were limits to the trade-off between fuel and bombs or mines if an effective punch was to be landed on the enemy.

This force was largely responsible for making the British presence in the Mediterranean barely tenable. It showed, too, that Pound had been remarkably prescient in his predictions for the lifespan of an aircraft carrier in the Mediterranean once hostilities had started.

The war in the Mediterranean presented even greater problems of convoy protection than the North Atlantic or even the Arctic convoys to

Russia. The Atlantic convoys could be protected by MAC-ships, merchant-men that carried three Swordfish in the case of a tanker, or four in the case of a grain carrier, in addition to their cargoes. These were later replaced by escort carriers, converted merchant ships, and such vessels were also adequate for the Arctic convoys where fighter as well as anti-submarine protection was desperately required. Convoys in the 'Med' needed more than this; the large fleet carriers were essential, even when escort carriers became available. It was not unknown for Mediterranean convoys to have more escorts than merchant ships, although to be fair, a large number of cargo ships could not all discharge their cargoes at once in Malta, with a population of less than a third of a million and port facilities to match this, and the peacetime custom of sending cargo to the island in small vessels, often using sail as their main means of propulsion.

OPERATION EXCESS

Even after Taranto, Malta's plight remained serious. Italian light forces and submarines kept up the pressure on the island, its population and the garrison, while bombing by the Regia Aeronautica remained constant except on those rare days when the weather intervened. Nevertheless, the breathing space created by the attack on Taranto afforded the opportunity to reinforce and resupply the beleaguered island and the forces based there. Once the success of the raid had been confirmed, most explicitly by the evacuation of the surviving heavy units of the Italian fleet, a convoy was hastily organised. One ship was destined for Malta, carrying 4,000 tons of ammunition, twelve Hawker Hurricane fighters disassembled and in crates, and 3,000 tons of seed potatoes; the others were intended for Alexandria. The convoy sailed from the UK in December, the first leg of its voyage taken jointly with a much larger convoy sailing for the Cape. The convoys were to divide on reaching Gibraltar. On Christmas Day, the German heavy cruiser *Hipper* was sighted, and the convoy scattered. Force H left Gibraltar to provide support. One of the heavy escorts, the elderly battleship *Renown*, was damaged by heavy seas and was delayed in Gibraltar for repairs, while one of the cargo ships intended for Greece was driven ashore by the bad weather.

The convoy, known as Operation Excess, was now running late, and was down to only four ships, albeit fast merchantmen. It was not until 6 January

1941 that the small convoy was finally able to steam eastward from Gibraltar. The delay was to have serious consequences. As with the arrival of *Illustrious* herself the previous year, Force H was to cover the convoy as far as Sicily, and then it would pass to the Mediterranean Fleet, which sailed from Alexandria the following day.

On 8 January, to discourage the Italian Navy, Malta-based Wellington medium-bombers raided Naples, finding both the *Cesare* and the *Vittorio Veneto* there, and managing to damage the former, so that Italians finally took the hint, and both ships moved further north. For their part, the Italians sent ten Savoia Marchetti SM79s to bomb the convoy, with little success and the loss of two of their aircraft to the *Ark Royal*'s Fulmars.

The hand-over date was fixed for dawn on 10 January, although in reality this meant Force H quitting the convoy at dusk on 9 January. To avoid leaving the convoy completely unprotected, the cruisers *Gloucester* and *Southampton*, with two destroyers, were detached from the main force and sent through the Sicilian Narrows in brilliant moonlight. They were challenged by a signal station on the Italian island of Pantellaria, and in changing course, they cut mine cables with their paravanes, being lucky not to explode any of them.

That the whole affair would be no picnic was well known aboard *Illustrious*. The arrival of the Tenth Air Corps, *Fliegerkorps X*, in Sicily during early January had been noticed, both by RAF reconnaissance and by that of *Illustrious* herself. What was less certain at the time was that Geissler's prime target was not Malta – for that could wait – it was the carrier. The Germans wanted revenge for Taranto, and then they could take their time over Malta. The Tenth included many of the Luftwaffe's most experienced anti-shipping aircrew. On the broad reaches of the North Atlantic, such work was left to flying-boats and the long-range Focke-Wulf Fw200 Condors and Junkers Ju290s, for which the Fulmar could prove a match; but over the 'Med', this was for the more manoeuvrable medium-bombers and dive-bombers.

At first, the omens seemed good. An Italian reconnaissance aircraft had been shot down by one of 806's Fulmars as the fleet sailed towards the rendezvous point. On the evening of 9 January, a force of Italian bombers escorted by fighters had failed to find them, and the most the Regia Aeronautica seemed able to do was mount sporadic attacks.

Well before dawn, at 04.30 on 10 January, *Illustrious* was steaming to the north-west of Malta with the battleships *Warspite* and *Valiant*, close to the Pantellaria Straits and ready to pick up the convoy. Previously, this stretch of water had only been passed through at night. That day, the weather was clear, without any clouds. It was dangerous, with limited room for manoeuvre, within easy reach of enemy aircraft and of shore-based artillery. Lyster and Boyd had tried to persuade Cunningham that there was no need to expose the carrier to the threat of air attack, since she could cover the convoy from a distance, while her fighter squadron, 806, had suffered heavy losses. Cunningham insisted nevertheless on sending *Illustrious*, giving as his reason that morale was always high when the ship was in sight. Further proof of the dangers awaiting them, if such was needed, was soon provided that morning when an escorting destroyer, HMS *Gallant*, racing through the seas at high speed to regain her position, struck a mine that blew off her fo'c'sle, which sank immediately, while another destroyer, *Mohawk*, quickly took the stern portion in tow to Malta, although she was never repaired. Eyewitnesses aboard the heavy ships were uncomfortably aware that they had only just traversed this same dangerous stretch of water. Some of the Italian mines seemed to have been passed over by several ships before finally detonating; but whether the mine that crippled *Gallant* had a delayed-action fuse, or an acoustic fuse that was activated by the high speed screws of a destroyer, remained a matter for surmise.

Everyone was on alert, the AA gunners having been closed up at action stations throughout the night. The carrier's Swordfish were already in the air, maintaining anti-submarine patrols and looking out for enemy surface vessels, while a flight of Fulmars maintained a combat air patrol in the skies over the ship, shooting down a shadowing aircraft during the morning. Taking every opportunity to harass the enemy, other Swordfish were on the deck, being readied for an attack against Axis shipping shuttling between Italy and North Africa.

The reconnaissance ahead of the carrier soon paid off, reporting a small enemy convoy of three ships escorted by a destroyer and a smaller vessel. Jago led a flight of Swordfish from 815 Squadron against the convoy, personally dive-bombing the first ship, a cargo vessel, and having the satisfaction of seeing his first bomb disappear into an open deck hatch. His flight then turned its attention to a large troop transport, a liner called up for war service, and this too was promptly despatched, while the third member of the convoy was also sunk. All this happened within minutes, catching the convoy escorts completely off guard, so that AA fire did not start until the aircraft were breaking off the attack and heading back to the carrier.

The planes landed and were struck down into the hangar, while Hale had a flight from 819 Squadron ready for a similar operation. Jago and his aircraft were still down below in the hangar as noon approached, while the carrier was being protected by a flight of six Fulmars patrolling the sky. Other members of the ship's squadrons were in the wardroom having an early lunch before the sorties expected that afternoon. On the flight deck, Fulmars were being ranged to replace those on patrol, after which the current Fulmar patrol would land on.

The carrier started to turn into the wind and to get enough sea room to launch her aircraft and then receive those that had been replaced on the CAP, and which were running short of fuel. Being caught in the air short of fuel is almost always fatal for a fighter. Before any further action could be taken, however, the ship's radar picked up several large formations of aircraft approaching at speed. They could only be hostile.

UNDER ATTACK

Just before 12.30, two Italian torpedo-bombers were sighted flying just above the sea on the carrier's starboard quarter. As the starboard side AA defences opened up, at 400 yards, the bombers let their torpedoes go, while Boyd changed course to starboard to comb the torpedoes: they missed. They also missed the battleship *Valiant*. The anti-aircraft gunners aboard *Illustrious* failed to hit the planes – not surprising since many were new to the ship after more than twenty of her experienced gunners had been posted when she was at Alexandria.

Although two Fulmars on CAP chased the Italian aircraft, shooting them both down, this meant that they had been decoyed to a lower altitude, where they would have difficulty fending off an attack at high level. The carrier turned back into the wind and started to launch the six Fulmars that had been waiting. As the aircraft raced to get into the air, the first Stukas were into their bombing dives. Lowe was last off the flight deck, and as his aircraft struggled to become airborne, a Stuka pulling out of its dive machine-gunned it, wounding Lowe in the shoulder and arm and killing his observer in the back of the cockpit as the plane crashed into the sea.

In the hangar, Janvrin joined Jago to discuss the prospects of another anti-shipping strike that afternoon. Janvrin had just lunched, so Jago went off to eat so as to be ready for a sortie afterwards. No sooner was his meal served than he heard the ship's AA defences start up again and dashed back to the hangar, which served as action stations for any aircrew not in the air during an attack. It was to prove to be the worst place possible for them.

Shortly after 12.30, two groups with a total of 43 Stuka dive-bombers led by Major Enneccerus and Major (later Lt Col) Hozzel swooped down on to the Mediterranean Fleet from 12,000ft. Ten aircraft attacked the two battle-ships, while the rest concentrated on the carrier. The last of the six Fulmars took off amidst the spray of a near miss. The poor rate of climb of the heavy Fulmar with its two-man crew meant that *Illustrious* would have to depend on her guns.

Cunningham later wrote:

We opened up with every AA gun we had as one by one the Stukas peeled off into their dives concentrating almost the whole venom of their attack upon the *Illustrious*. At times she became almost completely hidden in a forest of great bomb splashes.

One was too interested in this new form of dive-bombing attack to be frightened, and there was no doubt that we were watching complete experts. Formed roughly in a large circle over the fleet they peeled off one by one when reaching the attacking position. We could not but admire the skill and precision of it all. The attacks were pressed home at point blank range, and as they pulled out of their dives some were seen to fly along the flight deck of *Illustrious* below the level of the funnel.

I saw her hit early on just before the bridge, and in all, in something like ten minutes, she was hit by six 1,000lb bombs, to leave the line badly on fire, her steering gear crippled, her lifts out of action, and with heavy casualties.

Experts indeed! The Stukas released their bombs as they dropped through 2,300ft down to 1,600ft. They scored six direct hits on the carrier with another three very close misses. The 3in armoured flight deck was designed to withstand the force of a direct hit from a 500lb bomb, but some of the Stukas were armed with 1,000lb bombs, and armour-plating to withstand that force would have been completely impractical.

The first two 1,000lb bombs missed the flight deck. One crashed through the ship, passing unimpeded through several decks to set fire to a paint store, while another hit the P1 pom-pom gun position, killing two men outright, then exploding and killing and wounding many more with blast and shrapnel as it hit the water. Most of the damage was caused by the 500lb bombs. One hit the unarmoured after lift, blowing the lift platform into the hangar, and smashing a Fulmar on the lift along with its young midshipman pilot. Another followed the first and exploded inside the hangar, setting fire to several aircraft. A third 500lb bomb struck the forward lift, causing further serious damage. The sixth and final bomb, of 1,000lbs, breached the flight deck and exploded inside the hangar. The damage knocked out many of the ship's systems.

Meanwhile, the Reverend Henry Lloyd, the padre, was broadcasting his usual running account of the action, calmly and bravely telling those below that 'a bomb is falling and I think that it is going to miss our port quarter – yes – it has', as the bomb exploded. Many claimed that his running commentary between bomb blasts kept insanity at bay. Later, he was to have other work as the ship shook from her wounds, comforting the dying.

Not being on watch in the centre boiler room, Albert Jones went to his action station close to the steering flat beside an armoured bulkhead which separated his position from the wardroom flat. This was not the most comforting position to be in, since he was between two magazines, and also above that for the 4.5in AA guns. Nearby, too, was the ammunition hoist, capable of lifting four shells at a time.

Jones wrote afterwards:

Things then began to happen so fast ... changed to near chaos as the Germans began to score hits on us. With each successive explosion and the gunfire up top, a horrendous cacophony could be heard. Some of the hits were hard to distinguish as individual explosions although they were sufficient to vibrate the ship, causing lights to flicker, and dust from the pipe lagging ... floating down on us ... I could see the keyboard clock above the Marine sentry's head. It was a few minutes before ten to one.

The first bomb to hit the ship had come at 12.38, and another, causing significant damage, only a few seconds later. This first attack lasted ten minutes. The second attack then began, as Jones was to remember:

> Suddenly there was a tremendous explosion and the ship shuddered from stem to stern under the impact as if some unknown force had struck us with a gigantic sledgehammer. The lights went out but seemed to come on again … Everything shook loose, pipes and lagging hung down … clock … stopped. The time was exactly 12.50 … I honestly believed that this was going to be my last day on earth.

The bomb had destroyed the wardroom. Jones and those sharing his position were saved by the armour plating between them and the wardroom, but the entire after part of the carrier was on fire and the rudder jammed, so that *Illustrious* began to steam in circles. It was not until the rudder could be jammed amidships that she could once again make progress, using the engines for steering.

Lowe had managed to get out of his cockpit and inflate his lifejacket as his stricken aircraft sank. He then had the frightening experience of seeing the carrier vanish, although this did draw the German bombing away from him. Eventually, while the ship was still steaming in circles, he saw her reappear with a number of escorts, including the destroyer *Jaguar*, whose crew spotted him and lowered a boat. At first they thought that they were rescuing a downed German pilot, but soon realised their mistake when showered with a string of English expletives as they hauled him out of the water by his wounded arm.

Charles Lamb had been on patrol in his Swordfish ahead of the fleet, flying with his TAG and an unexpected passenger, since his observer, Midshipman Wallington, had climbed into his aircraft by mistake rather than one of his own squadron, 819. At 12.30, he was waiting for his turn to land on *Illustrious*, having dropped his live bombs as a precaution against these dropping off with the violence of the landing, and his TAG had set the depth charge to 'safe' (although this did mean that it would explode when it reached a certain depth). He watched the replacement Swordfish fly off on their anti-submarine patrols, followed by the Fulmars. Then he could see that his time to land had come, as the batsman, 'Haggis' Russell, took up his position on the port side. Suddenly, the DLCO disappeared from sight as the 4.5in guns opened up. Unworried, since he had often landed with the guns firing, Lamb continued his approach, noting that the after lift appeared to be down, but that there was still time for it to be raised. While he was still digesting this information, a Stuka shot ahead of him, so quickly that although he pressed the trigger of his Vickers machine gun, the plane slipped out of his sights, and dropped what was in fact the second bomb into the lift well, blowing the 300-ton lift out into the air, before it subsided back into the hangar floor.

Landing was out of the question, but Lamb had more pressing problems, as the Stuka pilots, seeing the Swordfish as a sitting duck, took turns at trying to shoot him down. Only by repeatedly taking evasive action did he manage to survive. After four attacks, his aircraft had lines of bullet holes and great tears in the wings. Most worrying, one Stuka had managed to shoot away the bright red handle of the locking pin, the primitive, but effective, mechanism that kept the Swordfish's wings from folding, and he was concerned that at any minute his aircraft might collapse around him and plunge into the sea.

Back aboard the carrier, Janvrin recalled:

Action stations went ... for unemployed aircrew were, unwisely as it turned out, in the hangar by their aircraft ... my first indication that anything untoward was happening was when there was a great ... explosion aft, by the after lift well. I was forward ... and half the after lift which was up at the time seemed to buckle ... you could see daylight through it.

And then there was a considerable amount of mayhem and we felt the shudder of near misses and the ship increasing speed as keeling over (as she turned). I remember that there were a number of casualties in the after end of the hangar and I went to my Swordfish and was just unzipping the first aid kit which was on the outside of the aircraft with the vague idea of going to do something with it ... when there was a considerable explosion and a great blast. And the Swordfish and myself were lifted up in the air and moved about twenty yards down the hangar ... this was a 1,000lb armour-piercing bomb that had just come straight into the centre of the flight deck just by me.

The vagaries of the blast of a bomb are extraordinary because people down the far end of the hangar were killed by this bomb and yet I was really one of the closest people to it on my aircraft. And I was just lifted with the aircraft bodily ... I got down from the aircraft and I remember that my left leg collapsed and I couldn't understand why that I couldn't walk on it ... a sailor came along and said, 'Let me help you, sir.' And I put one arm over his shoulders and he lugged me along ... he said, 'Excuse me, sir, you've got something in your side.' And he bent down and plucked something out and he dropped it with an oath ... it was a white hot piece of metal, a fragment from the bomb that had lodged in my side ... but I didn't feel the pain at all.

Janvrin was indeed very lucky, despite being badly wounded. Men threw themselves on to the hangar decks in the hope that shrapnel and all the other bits and pieces blown around the hangar as bombs burst among air-craft would fly over them. They then had to face the fumes from exploding oxygen cylinders and burning acid from damaged batteries, while aircraft started to burn and the fires spread quickly from one to another, setting off machine-gun ammunition. The heat soon became unbearable. The metal hangar fire screens, intended to break the hangar up into three sections to contain any flames, were lowered as a precautionary measure, but became part of the problem, as the bombs blew them to smithereens and sent sharp shards of metal through the hangar.

This proved to be the most unsuitable place possible for the aircrew. Few of the ship's decks escaped serious damage from the first attack, but the hangar below the flight deck had been reduced to a blackened shell with dead bodies plastered against the bulkheads. Luddington, the master-at-arms, realised that the hangar was an inferno and the peril facing those left inside it. A large, strong man, it seems he decided that he could quickly open a door and bring someone out. His body was found in the hangar afterwards, badly burnt. Many took comfort in the thought that he might first have been asphyxiated by the fumes.

The survivors made their way through the airtight hangar doors to the comparative safety of the rest of the ship.

'Grubby' Going had been caught in the open on the starboard catwalk. His uniform cap was blown off by the blast of one of the first bombs. Deciding to do something useful, he went below, but found darkness, so he proceeded to his cabin to collect his torch, and returned to the after flat, where he found the damage control officer dead. Taking over the duties of the latter, Going remained there as the attack intensified, working in dark-ness illuminated by flickering flames and amidst the noise of water cascading down from the decks above. Judging that the fires were under control, he ordered everyone out and was just about to leave himself when a bomb came crashing down. There was a terrible roar as it exploded, then darkness. He recalled clambering up a ladder, then passing out. This bomb had been the second to burst inside the after lift well, finally destroying it and also bursting through to wreck the ship's steering. Only later did Going discover that he had lost a leg.

Other heroes of the raid on Taranto fared far worse. Lt Neil Kemp, who had sunk the *Littorio*, was among those killed by the 1,000lb bomb that exploded in the hangar. He had been talking to Jackie Jago when the first bomb entered the hangar, and Jago suddenly found himself faced with a headless body. Jago had to give the corpse a push before it would lie down. Sub-Lt Mardel-Ferreira, one of the few RNVR officers on the raid, was also killed in the attack. Lt Clifford, the late arrival at Taranto, was badly wounded by bomb splinters while in the hangar; he was moved from the blazing inferno but before anyone could help him with medical treatment, he disappeared and is officially believed to have been blown over the side by a subsequent explosion. Sub-Lt Wray was among those fatally wounded, and died the following day ashore in hospital at Malta. Captain Denis Boyd was with him when he died.

In the wardroom, the 1,000lb armour-piercing bomb that had burst through the hangar deck exploded. It knocked Sub-Lt Perkins unconscious. As he lay there, the wardroom flooded with water from fire-fighting and from the sprinkler system, and he drowned. An RAF liaison officer was without a role during the battle, and doubtless feeling safe, he had settled down in the wardroom to read a newspaper: he was later found headless in a scorched armchair, but still holding *The Times*. Only three officers in the wardroom, including Torrens-Spence who was having lunch, survived the attack. When he eventually did return to the ship, very much later, Lamb recalled the wardroom stanchions twisted into spirals like ornamental candles, though the clock was undamaged.

Morford, disappointed at Taranto, did not escape the German revenge. In the blazing hangar, he was very badly burned, but he survived and returned to service after extensive plastic surgery.

Albert Jones went to the stokers' bathroom, usually the place where they would wash or do their laundry. Next door was a dressing-room, taken over as an emergency first aid station. Lined up in the middle on stretchers lay the seriously wounded and dying, at least half-a-dozen, all waiting quietly without a sound. He was able to help one or two by lighting cigarettes for them and placing them in their mouths.

It was not surprising that Surgeon-Commander Keeble, the senior doctor, received a DSO for his work that day, and over the fortnight that the ship was to spend in Malta, under almost continuous aerial attack in the so-called *Illustrious* Blitz. Many thought he should have been given a VC. Padre Henry Lloyd was another who received a DSO, greeted with shouts of delight by the sailors when it was announced.

DITCHING

Between them, the Fulmars and the AA defences accounted for four of the Stukas. But because of the enemy bomb damage, the only course open to the fighters was to head for Malta. Others, lacking the fuel, tried to hang around, hoping against hope that they could somehow get down on to the ship, but as the lifts were blown out of the flight deck, leaving gaping holes, it soon became clear that this was impossible.

Charles Lamb, relieved at last of having to dodge the Stukas, had an aerial view of the conflict below:

> I saw dozens of men rushing about the flight deck with hoses. Around them the 753 foot length and 93-foot breadth of deck was a mass of steam; the heat from the hangar below immediately turned water into vapour as soon as it touched the hot steel beneath their scorched feet. But all the ship's guns were still blazing away, and I was in danger of being shot down by them, and in any case I was probably in their way. I felt as though I was deserting my home and the people I loved when they were in peril, but there was nothing to be gained by staying, so I turned to the north-east in the vague direction of Malta and concentrated on trying to keep the aircraft stable.

Lamb's aircraft was still flyable, but only just. The starboard lower mainplane had parted from the fuselage and was only kept in position by the struts to the upper mainplane and the control wires. He recalled the aircraft being heavy to handle and requiring heavy opposite aileron. He demanded a course to Malta from his observer, Midshipman Wallington, shouting down the Gosport Tube. The answer came back in a whisper: 'I can't. The Bigsworth Board is floating about in petrol.'

Both Wallington and the TAG were up to their knees in petrol. Had one of the Stukas fired closely enough for the shell still to be hot, or a hot cartridge case splashed out from the TAG's machine gun at this point, both men would have been burnt alive, more than a thousand feet in the air, and without any hope of ditching safely. Lamb checked his fuel indicator, gaping through the hole in the cockpit instrument panel to where the instrument was placed some distance away over the engine. He expected to find that he had around 80 gallons of fuel left, but instead as he looked, the gauge fell from 48 gallons to 47, then to 46. He would have to ditch, immediately.

He looked down. The sea was covered in large fountains of water as high-altitude bombers inflicted their punishment on the ships below, and in between these were the smaller and more plentiful splashes as shrapnel from the ships' AA shells fell back to the sea, obeying the basic laws of gravity.

Taking the Aldis lamp from the hapless midshipman, Lamb flashed at a destroyer below his aircraft and to port. The destroyer answered. He then flashed that he was ditching and wished the destroyer to rescue the occupants of the aircraft. He was relieved when the destroyer flashed back, 'R', meaning that his message was received: even happier to see the ship, HMS *Juno*, turn into the wind and members of her crew racing down the deck to man the falls and lower a boat.

Lamb then had to turn to port, by this time the only manoeuvre possible with his crippled aircraft. At this stage, a moment of black comedy intervened. Another Swordfish formatted on his port quarter and he recognised it as being his observer's proper aircraft, the other *Illustrious* 'Q for Queenie' from 819 Squadron.

'He's just arrived. I think that he's hoping that we'll guide him to Malta as he hasn't got an observer,' explained Wallington, perhaps unnecessarily, in response to Lamb's enquiry about how long Denman Whatley in 819's 'Q' had been there. Whatley shook his fist good humouredly at Lamb, pointing to his own observer in Lamb's middle cockpit. Lamb tried to wave him away, fearing a collision since Whatley could not see the damage to Lamb's starboard mainplane, nor would he realise the dire predicament of the observer and the TAG. Lamb ordered his crew to wave Whatley away, and to point at the sea and give a thumbs-down sign. They could also point him in the direction of Malta, do anything, in fact, that would get rid of the other aircraft.

It was the first time that Lamb had attempted to ditch an aircraft. In training, they were warned that ditching a fixed undercarriage aircraft, or even one with a retractable undercarriage that was down, had to be done tail-first, since if the wheels touched the water there was a great risk of the plane cart-wheeling. Taking a wide turn to port, Lamb noted that the destroyer was already lowering her whaler. He flew as low as possible so that they would not have far to fall if the starboard wing finally did drop off. The weight of the petrol in the two rear cockpits now eased his task slightly, making the aircraft tail heavy. He throttled back, pulling back on the control column to lift the nose still further, then closed the throttle and let the Swordfish glide down towards the sea. The plane seemed to give a little sigh as she stalled, and did a perfect belly flop, sliding briefly through the water before the tail reared upwards and the nose ploughed into the sea. To Lamb, it then felt as if they had hit a brick wall as the aircraft stopped dead, and he saw the two occupants of the rear cockpits catapulted through the air and a couple of splashes about twenty yards out.

Following Lamb's aircraft down, Whatley only just missed putting his wheels in the water, narrowly avoiding catastrophe at the last moment as he climbed away.

Meanwhile, the weight of the engine was dragging the aircraft over, and Lamb was facing downwards. He undid his straps and climbed out, clambering on to the trailing edge of the lower port wing. As his two crew members swam back towards him, he attempted to extract the life-raft from its position in the port wing. The life-rafts in a Swordfish should inflate automatically when immersed in water, using an oxygen cylinder, but in this case the raft had only partially inflated. Nevertheless, as he pulled it out, the raft did inflate fully. Praising his rigger, Brown, for his careful maintenance, Lamb pushed the dinghy into the sea and climbed in.

The whaler, in the meantime, was making slow progress, though Lamb was unsure whether the laborious rowing by those aboard was due to lack of practice or the effects of being bombed for more than an hour. As his two companions joined him in the dinghy, he remembered just in time to cut the cord linking his small craft to the Swordfish, as the aircraft began to sink. Then he suddenly realised that he had forgotten to drop the depth charge before ditching. As the aircraft sank to the pre-set depth, this would detonate, not only blowing them to pieces, but probably the whaler and its crew as well. Fortunately, the whaler arrived in time and they quickly clambered in. Lamb prevented the coxswain from trying to recover the dinghy and took over, standing in the sternsheets and shouting at the oarsmen to row, yelling, 'pull together – in – out…' To avoid possible panic, he did not explain the urgency of the situation, which became evident as soon as they reached the destroyer. Letting the others go first, Lamb had scrambled halfway up the ship's sides when the depth charge exploded. He felt the destroyer heel over with the shock, and the blast pressed him to the side of the ship. The commanding officer was not amused.

ILLUSTRIOUS CRIPPLED

Within ten minutes, *Illustrious* had gone from being a fully operational aircraft carrier, the pride of the fleet and a deadly menace to the enemy, to a blazing cripple, no longer able to operate aircraft and in great danger of not being able to function herself. The hangar deck was an inferno, as aircraft fuelled and ready for take-off blazed. The repercussion of the six bombs that had struck her, and the mining effect of the three near misses, had put the steering out of action, and this problem was aggravated by the flooding of the steering flat by the water from the sprinklers and hoses of the fire-fighters.

Yet, despite all of this, the armoured flight deck and hangar deck had protected her vital organs, the ship's machinery spaces. Despite the temperature in the boiler rooms soaring to over 140°F, they continued to provide power for the fire-fighting mains and the sprinkler pumps, and her speed never fell below 18 knots. The AA guns continued to fire throughout the action, and the ship's hull stayed intact. Fortunately, too, the huge tanks of highly inflammable aviation fuel remained secure, and the magazines of AA ammunition, and bombs and torpedoes for the aircraft, were not set off, otherwise, the resulting explosion would have torn the ship apart. That the engines and boilers continued to function was astonishing; without them, the ship would have been finished. Working below the waterline, stokers kept their boots unlaced so that they could make a quick escape if the worst came to the worst and the order to abandon ship was given. They would have had little chance, stuck down far beneath the aviation fuel tanks and the magazines. Not for nothing is the story told of the stoker who found a war correspondent joining him in the stokehold rather than going on top to get his story: 'Now you'll find out what fear really is.'

At a certain stage, fire had threatened one of the magazines, and Boyd was asked for permission to flood it. There were more Stukas around, and high-level bombing had also begun, so Boyd took a risk and refused permission, just in case they needed the ammunition. He was undoubtedly right. The fire was brought under control, but the attacks continued until darkness fell.

Meanwhile, *Illustrious* reported that she was badly damaged and making for Malta, but it was not until 15.30 that she was able to steer in that direction. Her agony was not over, as between 16.00 and 17.00, the carrier and the battleships were attacked by another twenty-five dive-bombers. Aboard, there were more than 200 casualties. Cunningham wrote:

My heart sank as I watched her, wondering how with all her heavy damage she could stand up to it. I need not have worried. As the attacks developed I saw every gun in the *Illustrious* flash into action, a grand and inspiring sight. Moreover her Fulmar fighters, which had flown on to Malta when their parent ship was damaged, had refuelled and come out again. They managed to shoot down six or seven Stukas into the sea and to damage others.

Ashore in Malta, AA gunners saw aircraft coming towards them. As they drew closer, they thought they were seeing Spitfires or Hurricanes, then the more observant recognised Fulmars. This was the first indication many people on the island had of the plight of *Illustrious*, as those aircraft in the air headed for the nearest available landing spot, joining the RAF's Hurricanes in the defence of Malta. At the Royal Navy headquarters on the island, messages saying that *Illustrious* had been seriously damaged had already been received. The Royal Dockyard was warned to expect the crippled ship for emergency repairs.

At 21.45 that night, *Illustrious* arrived off Malta. Slowly, her decks glowing hot, the carrier limped towards the narrow entrance into Grand Harbour. The men were stood down from action stations.

Officers attempting to reach their cabins found that their deck was flooded with oil and dirty water. The officers' wardroom was flooded. The uninjured survivors gathered in the warrant officers' mess. Another grim job lay ahead. Parties were organised to comb the ship and collect the many dead bodies lying around. Going had seen one in the after flat without head or limbs. Across the ship, there were burnt limbs and other assorted parts of what had once been a shipmate, a father, son or brother. Even this last task was to be delayed, as the gunnery officer, attempting to clear up the hangar deck, found it still on fire. Emergency lighting was rigged to help in the grim hunt. In the fire-blackened cavern that was the hangar deck, charred corpses were plastered against the bulkheads, with the tangled remains of aircraft on the hangar deck. It was not until daybreak on 11 January that all of the casualties had been removed and all of the bodies recovered. Some, such as Clifford, were never found.

Among the more fortunate survivors was Ivan Lowe, who went to hospital and had a large calibre machine-gun shell extracted from his shoulder. In April, while still convalescing, he was awarded the DSC.

There can be no doubt that *Illustrious* was the target for the entire air attack. The battleships were left virtually unscathed, one man being killed and two injured by bomb splinters aboard HMS *Valiant*. With the carrier out of the way, the emphasis changed the next day, and the two cruisers *Gloucester* and *Southampton*, which had protected *Mohawk* as she escorted *Gallant* to Malta, came under heavy aerial attack, which they were ill-placed to ward off since neither had radar to provide adequate early warning. Shortly before 15.00, both ships were attacked by twelve Stuka dive-bombers, plunging towards them out of the sun, this making them virtually invisible until the last minute. A bomb struck *Gloucester*, plunging through her director tower but failing to explode, although it killed nine men and wounded fourteen more. Rear-Admiral Renouf had a narrow escape; once again he was aboard a cruiser struck by a bomb that failed to explode.

Southampton suffered a worse fate. The attack occurred as her gun crews were stood down for a brief respite after being continuously at action stations for a staggering forty-eight hours. Having left Malta some ten hours earlier, her officers must have thought that they were safe, and the men went to tea. Two bombs struck the ship, hitting the wardroom and the petty officer's mess, killing and crippling those best able to lead damage control and fire-fighting. Chaos reigned, and the ship was soon ablaze, with the fires quickly out of control. Shortly after 19.00, she was abandoned and sunk by a torpedo, with her surviving ship's company taken aboard *Gloucester* and a destroyer, HMS *Diamond*.

THE MORNING AFTER

Albert Jones had an uncomfortable first night aboard the carrier as she lay alongside in Malta; he had been trying to sleep on a mess stool. After breakfast and a quick clean-up, the ship's company was mustered on the flight deck by divisions for a roll-call as the grim task began of finding out just who was dead and who was injured. Whenever a name was called out and no one replied, there was a moment's pause, then a CPO would ask if anyone knew anything about them. Sometimes, the answer would come that the person concerned was on watch; more likely, though, he was among those killed or wounded.

Each survivor was later given a telegram form, and told that he could send a brief message to his next of kin, but for security reasons this was kept brief, with little flexibility; there was no room for sentiment or creativity when the options were simply 'Don't worry, I am alright 'or 'I am alright, don't worry.'

As soon as it was daylight, scores of Maltese dockyard workers descended upon the stricken vessel. Their role was simply to make the carrier seaworthy so that she could escape. Repairs to the lifts or to the smashed flight deck would have to wait. Divers went down to inspect the ship below the waterline. Wooden plugs inserted by damage control teams to block shrapnel and bullet holes were removed and metal welded over the holes. Most importantly, attention was given to repairing the damaged steering gear. The ship soon lost her purposeful shape as she disappeared under scaffolding and ladders, almost encased in a shroud of tarpaulins, while the roar of aircraft engines was replaced by the clatter of pumps and generators, the sound of welding and the glow of acetylene torches.

Everyone knew that it was a race against time, that the Luftwaffe would want to finish the job that it had started. A ship in harbour was a sitting duck, virtually out of her element. Speed and skill of manoeuvre would count for nothing within the confines of the creek. Fortunately, this first morning was dull and overcast, with the possibility of rain.

A FORTNIGHT IN MALTA

Illustrious spent two weeks in Malta. At first, bad weather prevented the enemy from flying reconnaissance or bombing sorties, but this changed on

13 January, after which she was subjected to daily air raids by the Luftwaffe and the Regia Aeronautica. When the air-raid sirens sounded ashore the ship's company would uncover the guns and prepare to mount a strong defence, while the dockyard workers made a dash from their working places to the caves in nearby Senglea that served as shelters. Clambering from deep in the bowels of a large warship to safety ashore was no easy task. In the engine room, with only auxiliary power needed, Albert Jones spent twenty-four hours on the ship, and then twenty-four ashore. There was scant entertainment available by now in wartime Malta, but he was so keen to be away from the carrier that he spent his own money on a beer, a frugal meal, and a bed for the night. Certainly, his accommodation aboard afforded little comfort, as shells had been piled up on his mess deck 5ft high to be ready for the next air raid, and convenient for the forward 4.5in guns, the only ones to have survived the attack on 10 January. Jones recalls that the ship stank of cordite, a smell that persisted for weeks.

On 16 January, the air raids reached a new peak. This time the Luftwaffe sent forty-four Stukas, seventeen Ju88s, ten Messerschmitt Me110s, escorted by ten Regia Aeronautica Fiat CR42 fighters, as well as a few Macchi 200s. The attack lasted just a few minutes, but barely a quarter of an hour later, a second wave of attackers arrived. *Illustrious* suffered yet another hit during the first attack, and the surrounding dockyard was left burning and cratered, while the ladders, scaffolding and tarpaulins shrouding the ship were blown away. Overall, during her spell in the Grand Harbour, the ship was hit by 2,500lb bombs, and three others were near-misses, falling into French Creek and flinging her against the Parlatorio Wharf. The bombs were a special for the Stukas which normally carried a much lower warload, and with these it took the aircraft ninety minutes to reach an altitude of 10,000ft. Aboard the ship, her engineering commander, Lt-Cdr 'Pincher' Martin, worked unceasingly to repair the steering, for which he was later awarded the DSC. The engines were in reasonable shape, considering the damage that the ship had suffered, and the engineers were confident that they could get her back to sea.

After the raid of 16 January, it was decided to evacuate the ship, leaving only a skeleton crew aboard, including the stokers on watch. Even the AA gunners were among the thousand or so men put into temporary accommodation at the RAF base of Hal Far. One reason for moving the gunners ashore was that the Army wanted to test a new box barrage system, and found that the ship's AA got in the way.

Although the engines were in good shape, the severe battering suffered during the bombing meant that half of the ship's AA defences were out of action, leaving her dependent on the shore-based AA batteries around Grand Harbour, which had earlier been augmented by those of the old monitor, HMS *Terror*, a veteran of World War One. The Australian light cruiser HMAS *Perth* stayed behind in Malta in an attempt to provide extra AA firepower, but she was punished for her loyalty as she suffered damage below her waterline by a near-miss during the raid of 16 January.

A visitor to *Illustrious* while she was in Malta, Mrs Kathleen Norman, a Navy wife and one of the few British civilians left behind, reported that the ship's guns continued to fire even while she was being repaired, as the Germans and Italians attempted to destroy the ship and the dockyard around her. She recalled:

> Her officers and men came in and out of the tunnel (the dockyard air raid shelter) and the surgery. Their faces looked lined and grimy. They were dressed in old boiler overalls, in grey flannel trousers and sweaters – any odd garment they had managed to save from the wrecks of the cabins. The surgeon of the ship had done wonderful work in the battle at sea. He was pale and his face was very, very sad.
>
> It was the first time I had ever been on board a wounded ship. When I saw *Illustrious*'s great torn decks, the aching chasm that reached into her bowels, the little sick-bay that had known such horror, I felt almost as near to tears as when I talked with her tired seamen ... It seemed impossible that *Illustrious* would put to sea again, but she was in Malta dockyard – the dockyard that just could not be defeated.

While the Germans had lost only four Stukas during the attack at sea, the Hurricanes defending Malta, reinforced with 806's surviving Fulmars, and the island's heavy AA defences, took a heavy toll. Lt-Col Paul-Werner Hozzel, at that time a major in the Luftwaffe, later recalled that each day he expected to lose five or six of his best crews, and one of his two squadrons lost all of its original aircrew during this period. On 16 January, some ten aircraft had been shot down, without any corresponding losses among the Malta-based Hurricanes and Fulmars.

The attack of 16 January was described by many as the first really heavy bombing raid suffered by the islands. This was when Malta faced the concentrated force of both the Regia Aeronautica and the Luftwaffe. The Stuka pilots once again dived through intense anti-aircraft fire, and yet again many were flying below the high fortress walls of Valletta in order to deliver their bombs accurately. It was a close shave for *Illustrious*, for while just one bomb hit her on that day, another hit the engine room of the cargo ship *Essex*, which had reached Malta safely, leaving fifteen dead and twenty-three wounded. Had it struck her cargo, the 4,000 tons of ammunition would have exploded and possibly destroyed Valletta, the dockyard, the celebrated Three Cities, including the town of Senglea on the opposite side of the Grand Harbour, and *Illustrious* as well. The next day, the Germans sent reconnaissance aircraft, and on 18 January began to strike at the airfields, hoping to crush the troublesome fighter defences that rose to meet every raid. The day after that, the carrier again became the target, and a near-miss that exploded on the bottom of the creek had a 'mining' effect, damaging the hull – more work to be made good before she could sail.

Hal Far was certainly not a completely safe haven. As an airfield it was an obvious target, and almost a hundred enemy aircraft raided it on 18 January. They also attacked the surrounding villages, including the nearby coastal resort of Birzebugia, killing and injuring many civilians. Another bad day for air raids was Sunday 19 January, but it also proved unlucky for the Germans, who admitted losing ten aircraft while the Italians lost four, (the British claiming thirty-nine enemy aircraft, another five probables and nine damaged). Seventeen of the Axis losses were attributed to the RAF's Hurricanes and the Fleet Air Arm's Fulmars, while just two British fighters were lost. The Regia Aeronautica sent a Cant Z506 with Red Cross markings to patrol the sea between Malta and Sicily, looking for ditched aircrew.

Most of the ship's company had little idea of the progress being made in getting the carrier seaworthy again, and it was not until they were recalled during the afternoon of 23 January that they realised she was ready to make a break for it. That night, under cover of darkness, with the ship darkened and some repair stages still hanging over her sides, but her temporary repairs completed, she left the Grand Harbour quietly and secretly. The Governor, Sir William Dobbie, was holding a session of the Council of Malta, the island's governing body; as a servant entered and drew the blackout curtains before switching on the lights, someone said: 'She's off – and safe.'

Leaving Grand Harbour, *Illustrious* was anything but safe, but to put as much distance as possible between her and the Luftwaffe, she then steamed at 26 knots through the night, giving *Perth* some difficulty in keeping station and missing a cruiser escort sent to meet her, and onwards to Alexandria, which she reached to a warm welcome on 26 January.

This was the first stage in her journey to the United States where she was given a complete refit at Norfolk, Virginia. Not the least of the changes made to this great ship was the replacement of the hangar fire blinds with curtains, so that these would never again be an additional hazard on *Illustrious*, or any other British carrier.

The fighter squadron, 806, stayed in Malta briefly with twelve Fulmars before moving to Aboukir, but then returned to Hal Far, with a brief spell at Maleme on Crete, before joining HMS *Formidable* in March 1941. From the squadron's arrival in the Mediterranean until joining *Formidable*, it had accounted for twenty German and Italian aircraft.

The survivors of the two Swordfish squadrons based themselves on Hal Far, which those aircraft already in the air had aimed for on 10 January. On 14 January, 819 was disbanded into 815 Squadron. The merged unit remained at Malta until 17 January, when it transited through Heraklion on Crete en route to Dekheila.

Lamb was not among them as his personal own saga was not over. *Juno* had her own orders and could not take him and his crew to Malta, which would have been the preferred option. Her CO had signalled to the carrier that he had rescued the three-man crew of a Swordfish, but he did not give their names since he felt that those aboard *Illustrious* had enough to cope with at the time. When they started the massive task of assessing casualties aboard the carrier and among its aircrew, 'Streamline' Robertson immediately assumed that the downed Swordfish could not have been Lamb's, since he knew that he had taken off with just a TAG for company.

Whatley had reached Hal Far safely, but having seen Lamb and his crew safely aboard *Juno*, he made no mention of the rescue. Lamb and his TAG were both posted as 'missing'. Their families were sent telegrams, and they feared the worst as news bulletins mentioned 'many unknown dead'. The problem was understandable. Many of those killed aboard the ship were unrecognisable. Others had been shot down.

It was not until he arrived at Alexandria, some two weeks after the events of 10 January, that Lamb was able to correct the situation. In the meantime, he had been transferred from *Juno* to *Eagle* and resumed flying. Aboard this elderly carrier, two things struck him. The first was her flight deck was flimsy, so that it seemed to shake if someone jumped up and down on it. The second was that the action stations position for aircrew not in the air was the wardroom anteroom, which he initially felt was a far safer place than the hangar deck, and if not, at least one met one's fate with a glass in the hand! This, of course, was before he knew what had happened to those who had happened to be in the wardroom of *Illustrious*.

Going survived and after treatment returned to active service as an air staff officer aboard the escort carrier, HMS *Activity*, and before the war ended saw service as Carrier Squadron Fighter Director, Eastern Fleet, in both *Illustrious* and *Indomitable*.

The other four ships that had set out from Gibraltar also reached their destination safely.

CHAPTER THIRTEEN

Taranto and Pearl Harbor

As the first attack of its kind, it is tempting to think of Taranto in relation to the attack by the Imperial Japanese Navy on the US Pacific Fleet at Pearl Harbor on 7 December 1941, a little more than a year later. Ignoring the obvious difference, that the United Kingdom and Italy were already at war when Taranto was attacked, while the United States and Japan were not at war on 7 December 1941, how do the comparisons bear up? In short, Taranto was a defensive strike, an attempt to redress the imbalance of naval power in the Mediterranean, while that at Pearl Harbor was an offensive strike. Moreover, Taranto was a night attack, while Pearl Harbor was mounted in broad daylight.

Over the intervening years, many have come to believe that the Japanese took Taranto as a blueprint, and that the idea of a pre-emptive strike against the United States came from Operation Judgement. This is not true. The Imperial Japanese Navy had already war-gamed the attack on Pearl Harbor, unknown to anyone else. What is clear, however, is that the action at Taranto convinced the Japanese that the attack on Pearl Harbor was feasible. As at Taranto, the attackers' fears that the target ships might be protected by torpedo nets were to prove groundless. Again, concerns that the operation would be detected were wrong on both occasions.

Although one of the World War One allies, Japan between the two world wars rapidly set out on to a collision course with the western powers. A principal reason for this was Japanese territorial ambitions, although these were by no means new and had included the occupation of Korea early in the century. Japanese designs in Asia had resulted in the Russo-Japanese War of 1904–5, and this had started without a formal declaration of hostilities.

Nevertheless, in the afterglow of the World War One alliance, Japan, which had been dependent on its wartime allies for aircraft, also enjoyed the support and encouragement of a British Naval Mission between 1919 and 1922. A member of the mission was F. J. Rutland, who as Flt-Lt Rutland (a rank that originated with the Royal Naval Air Service) had flown the plane that had first spotted the German battlecruiser squadron just before the Battle of Jutland. Japan completed her first aircraft carrier, a converted tanker, the *Hosho*, in 1922. Initially, many of the conditions of that year's Washington Naval Treaty were opposed by Japan, which wanted a far larger total tonnage than the 315,000 tons allocated to her, in comparison with 525,000 tons for both the UK and USA. This Japanese standpoint marked the beginning of a cooler relationship between Japan and both powers, and it was a warning of future Japanese ambitions. The Treaty, in fact, was to have no impact at all on her long-term objectives. Japan simply built ships that exceeded the agreed limits.

Between the world wars, Japanese advances and outrages in China from 1931 onward were to provoke strong international reaction against the aggressor. Yet even at this stage Japan envisaged a wider global encounter. Young Japanese naval cadets, including Mitsuo Fuchida, who was later to lead the attack on Pearl Harbor, had already guessed that their future enemy would be the United States. Fuchida himself selected English as his compulsory foreign language during training, and took whatever opportunities arose to observe US ships. It is interesting to note that, in common with many of his contemporaries in the Royal Navy, he had to show determination to become a naval airman in the face of strong opposition from well-intentioned superior officers who had the young man's career interests in mind.

The one strategic factor that both Taranto and Pearl Harbor had in common – apart from using carrier-borne aircraft for the attack – was that both were intended to redress an imbalance of naval power. Even this needs qualification. The Royal Navy was weaker than the Italian Navy in the Mediterranean, but stronger overall, except that its strength was dissipated by being concentrated in three potential theatres of war at once, the Atlantic, the Mediterranean and, as the threat of war with Japan loomed, the Far East. Conversely, the Imperial Japanese Navy was stronger than the United States Navy in the Pacific, but not overall. To some extent, both were campaigns of desperation, but for markedly different reasons. The British not only needed to correct the imbalance in naval power, they also wanted to reduce pressure on Malta and on their land forces in North Africa. The

Japanese realised that unless the US Pacific Fleet could be curbed, their ambitions for territorial expansion would be doomed, and with them their plans to grab the essential oil and raw materials necessary for survival, let alone making war. This, of course, overlooks one of the fundamentals of maritime strategy, which is that warships are highly mobile assets, and can be directed to wherever they may be needed.

Despite American isolationism, war between Japan and the United States eventually became inevitable, after the US imposed an embargo on the sale of scrap metal and war materials to Japan in December 1940, and followed this by freezing Japanese assets in July 1941, after Japan had seized upon the impotence of Vichy France and invaded Indo-China. While much has been made of the 'War Party' in Japan, largely supported by the Army, the Imperial Japanese Navy included many senior commanders who realised the enormity of the task and some who were even opposed to war. One of these realists was the Commander-in-Chief of the Imperial Japanese Navy's First Fleet, Admiral Isoroku Yamamoto, who appreciated that Japan could not match the United States militarily or, no less important in modern warfare, industrially. Yamamoto felt that Japan could win a major victory in the first year of war, but that the United States would have recovered by the second year and could move to the offensive.

The Imperial Japanese Navy therefore needed to deal a 'knock-out' blow to the United States Navy in the Pacific before the Pacific and Atlantic fleets could combine in overwhelming strength. Yamamoto had to find a solution to this problem. He chose to strike a crippling blow at the US Pacific Fleet by attacking its main base at Pearl Harbor, on the Hawaiian island of Oahu. Destroying Pearl Harbor as a base and wiping out major units of the Pacific Fleet at the same time would ensure that the United States needed time to re-establish a significant naval presence. The distances were so vast that naval power had to take precedence over everything else.

PLANNING

One major advantage that the Japanese had over the Royal Navy lay in the resources available. They were able to bring a massive concentration of force to bear on Pearl Harbor such as those attacking Taranto would have regarded as far beyond their wildest dreams. The attack was to utilise not one aircraft carrier with twenty-one obsolescent biplanes, but six aircraft carriers with 423 aircraft between them, of which 353 were to be used in the attack and in providing fighter cover. It was not to be a night operation, but to take place early in the day. All of this might have jeopardised the element of surprise had not the carriers been fortunate to have their movements hidden by a tropical storm, so much so, in fact, that Cdr Mitsuo Fuchida later said that he would have cancelled the operation had it simply been an exercise.

Despite the massive strength of the Imperial Japanese Navy's Air Force, senior officers still did not display the enthusiasm one might have expected for air power. Indeed, later in the war Japanese commanders went to tremendous lengths to try to arrange a major big-gun fleet action at Leyte Gulf, but failed; in the resultant battle, it was naval air power and submarines that saw most of the action. Fuchida's commander, in British terms his flag officer, was Vice Admiral Chuichi Nagumo, an officer with little knowledge of naval air power and even less enthusiasm, leaving Genda and Fuchida with a free hand. By comparison with Nagumo, Cunningham was positively open-minded, and certainly there was no one of the calibre of Lyster to support and encourage the naval aviators. There appear to have been no predictions of aircraft losses, but it is known that Nagumo expected to lose between a third and half of his ships. This is a surprising statistic since the Japanese did not, at that time, have the resources to replace major warships quickly. Japanese intelligence did not believe that the Pacific Fleet's two aircraft carriers would be at Pearl Harbor, and again, this makes the timing of the attack all the more surprising, unless, of course, the senior officers believed that American battleships were a far more serious threat than the carriers.

Fuchida had been volunteered for his task by one of the Japanese planners, his friend Cdr Minoru Genda. Genda was strongly in favour of an aerial torpedo attack, although Fuchida was opposed to this, despite the excellence of Japanese torpedoes, because he felt that the Americans would have protected their ships with torpedo nets, while the water inside Pearl Harbor was also very shallow, at just 40ft deep in places. Genda considered nets to be unlikely, although he had to concede that if the entire Pacific Fleet was in port, many of the ships would be double berthed, and thus many of them would be protected from torpedoes by the ship alongside. The Japanese did not have the advantage of the Duplex pistol in their otherwise excellent torpedoes.

Genda won the argument by pointing out that the bombs dropped by the dive-bombers, no matter how accurately, would be wasted against the armoured decks and gun turrets of the battleships, even though they could inflict substantial damage on cruisers and destroyers. The dive-bombers would also be very useful against the American aircraft carriers, if they were in port.

Japanese aircraft at the time were far superior to any that the Royal Navy could offer. The fighter, the Mitsubishi A6M, the famous 'Zero', was later evaluated by an American officer as being 'a light sports plane with a 1,300hp engine', but it weighed more than a third less than the Supermarine Seafire, and was highly manoeuvrable. In contrast to the Fulmar, the Zero was not weighed down by an observer. The main strike aircraft was the Nakajima B5N, known to the wartime Allies as 'Kate', and was a single-engined monoplane with all-metal stressed skin construction, power-folding wings and retractable undercarriage, capable of a top speed of 230mph against the 100mph or so of the Swordfish. The attack would include forty of these aircraft with torpedoes, and another 103 with bombs. The dive-bomber was the Aichi D3A1, known to the Allies as 'Val', and heavily influenced by German thinking. Like the Stuka, this was a low-wing monoplane with a fixed spatted undercarriage.

Japanese Navy Air Force bombers normally flew their missions in a nine-plane 'arrowhead' formation, but with fifty aircraft available for training exercises, Fuchida decided instead on five-plane formations for the horizontal or level bombers, usually the least accurate method of bombing. This seemed to work since on exercises their accuracy reached 70 per cent, while by contrast, the dive-bombers, supposedly more accurate, could only manage 40 per cent.

By mid-November, the aircrew were ready. Admiral Yamamoto visited the flagship for the attack on Pearl Harbor, the aircraft carrier *Akagi*, on the afternoon of 17 November, to wish the officers good luck. He was concerned that they might underestimate their opponent. 'Japan has faced many worthy opponents in her long history – Mongols, Chinese, Russians – but the United States is the most worthy of all,' he warned. 'You must be prepared for great American resistance. Admiral Kimmel, commander-in-chief of the Pacific Fleet, is known to be farsighted and aggressive. You may have to fight your way to the target.'

SURPRISE ATTACK

Much has been made of the way in which the Japanese attack on Pearl Harbor caught the United States completely by surprise. In fact, it is now known that an American destroyer did sink a Japanese submarine on the morning of 7 December, confirmed by the wreckage having been identified in mid-2002. This makes the element of surprise so much more difficult to accept. As in Malta during 1940, air forces and navies apparently failed to speak to one another. Awareness of the submarine might well have put Hawaii's air defences on a higher state of alert.

After refuelling on 5 December, the Japanese fleet continued on its way to the flying-off position north of Hawaii. They knew that war would break out on 7 December, although no one expected a formal declaration of war. For the Japanese, the dates were officially a day later because of the influence of the International Date Line, so for them 7 December was in fact 8 December.

As at Taranto, the attack was to be made in two waves, although in contrast to Taranto there would also be fighter escorts since the Americans were expected to put up their own fighters in defence. Awake at 05.00, the first-wave aircrew breakfasted as their ships were pitching and rolling in heavy seas. After a final briefing, they went to their aircraft. Fuchida was being flown by Lt Mutsuzaki, leaving him free to direct the operation. As he climbed into the aircraft aboard the *Akagi*, the senior maintenance crewman handed him a white scarf. 'All of the maintenance crew would like to go along to Pearl Harbor,' he explained. 'Since we can't, we want you to take this *hachimaki* as a symbol that we are with you in spirit.' Moved by this gesture of support, Fuchida tied the scarf samurai-fashion around his flight helmet.

By 06.15, the 183 aircraft in the first wave were all airborne and Fuchida gave the signal to follow him to Pearl Harbor. He opened his cockpit canopy to let the *hachimaki* stream out behind him as the sun rose like a red disc – the Japanese naval ensign, and now the national flag – which Fuchida took as a good omen. En route, the weather remained poor, with dark clouds, but they were reassured by a weather forecast from a radio station in Hawaii, allaying Fuchida's fears that they might overfly the target or find attacking difficult because of the clouds.

Reaching the coastline of Oahu at 07.30, Fuchida started to get his formation into position for the attack, calling out the order 'Tenkai'. His confidence soared as their progress continued uninterrupted by any opposition, while on the ground in a radar station that was just about to close down for the day, the duty operator in Oahu dismissed the formation as nothing more than a flock of birds. Fuchida's aircraft remained at altitude while he fired a rocket to signal that the aircraft should now descend to prepare for the attack. He then watched Murata, leading the torpedo-bombers, head down towards the ships at anchor in Pearl Harbor. He saw that one of the fighter formations was staying high and fired a second rocket in case the first had not been noticed, but this was mistaken by the leader of the dive-bombers, Takashi, as an indication that enemy fighters were on their way, and immediately he led his aircraft down towards their targets before they could be shot down. It did not matter: the confusion would make little difference to the outcome, and in fact would make the attack all the more overwhelming.

Fuchida's own aircraft remained at around 10,000ft, while the attack developed. He observed that there were only seven battleships in the harbour rather than the nine expected, and, as anticipated, no aircraft carriers. In fact, all of the battleships were there. Instead of nine, there were eight, with the USS *Pennsylvania* in drydock, while Japanese intelligence had counted the *Utah*, relegated to the role of target ship, as an active battleship.

The signal to start the attack was broadcast by Fuchida at 07.49, still with little sign of fighter defences and no AA fire. This left the Zero fighters free to race across the airfield and the dockyards, in what the Fleet Air Arm would later describe as 'fighter ramrod' attacks, shooting at anything in their sights. The few American fighters that struggled to get into the air were shot down. The dive-bombers swooped down towards Ford Island, hitting harbour installations, so that soon the clear blue skies were stained by smoke from the explosions of their bombs and the fires that they started. On Battleship Row, as at Taranto, the torpedo-bombers came in low so as not to damage their torpedoes as they were launched at the targets. Then Fuchida's horizontal bombers began their high-altitude run over Battleship Row, but by this time the first AA fire was starting and the horizontal bombers had to maintain their course if an accurate delivery was to be made. Fuchida's own aircraft received a single hit and was shaken by a near-miss, but his pilot assured him that everything was well. Fuchida made three passes over his target, the battleship *California*, before deciding that he could drop his bombs accurately. On the second run over the target, he saw an explosion as the battleship *Arizona*, whose air defences had been enhanced the previous year with additional guns and radar, blew up. His plane was buffeted by the blast. 'The flame and smoke erupted skyward,' he was later to recall. 'It was a hateful, mean-looking red flame, the kind that powder produces, and I knew at once that a big magazine had exploded.'

Fuchida now had the dangerous task of remaining behind as the first-wave made their escape back to the carriers while the 170 aircraft of the second wave arrived to continue their deadly work. The first-wave planes rendezvoused so that they could return to the carriers in formation, the bombers providing navigational guidance, the fighters protection. The second wave did not include torpedo-bombers since these were seen as highly vulnerable once the AA defences had been alerted. Fuchida had to direct the attack, which began fifty minutes after the strike by the first-wave. Although the leaders were well briefed and knew what to do, Fuchida had to assess the damage so that he could report to Nagumo. He could see clearly that the *Arizona* was blazing, the *Oklahoma* and *Utah* had both capsized, and both the *California* and *West Virginia* were settling in the water. Further away, he could see the light cruiser *Helena* was crippled.

Fuchida's role at this time cannot be underestimated. Attacking in broad daylight, there was no need for the pathfinder tactics of flare-droppers, but in another unheralded innovation, he was playing what in another year or two RAF Bomber Command would describe as the role of Master Bomber, hanging around to direct the operation. This was extremely dangerous, as the best means of survival in a raid over enemy positions is to be quickly in and quickly out, with no second runs. His three passes over the target were definitely not recommended.

The second wave inevitably had a far rougher reception than the first. While they had made their way to the target area untroubled by the defences, some American fighters had managed to get airborne, and the AA gunners on the ships below had 'got their eye in' and knew what to expect. Most of the twenty-nine aircraft lost by the JNAF at Pearl Harbor were from the second wave.

Below, the Americans were doing what they could to fend off the attack. There was no plan, and individual officers acted as they thought best. The captain of the battleship *Nevada* thought that his ship would be safer at sea.

This was correct in theory, since a fast-moving ship that can manoeuvre in the open sea is a more difficult target than one lying motionless in harbour. The only problem was that he had first to reach open water. Seeing the ship moving towards the harbour mouth, Japanese aircraft swarmed around her, realising that if she could be sunk in the harbour mouth, the entire base would be out of action for some time, with the surviving ships penned in and lost to the Americans. The attack was overwhelming, but the ship's officers managed to beach the *Nevada* in a position where she would not be an obstruction. Meanwhile, the second wave damaged the *Pennsylvania* and two destroyers in drydock.

Casualties among those aboard the ships and ashore were extremely heavy, with a total of 3,581 US naval personnel either killed or wounded. No less than 188 USAAF and USN aircraft ashore had been destroyed.

Fuchida started his return to the *Akagi*. The carriers were busy landing aircraft and striking them down into hangars. In the haste to get all of the aircraft on, any that caused an obstruction were quickly pushed over the side, and some fifteen more planes were lost in this way. At this point, had the Americans known the location of the fleet and been able to mount an attack, all six carriers would have been highly vulnerable.

As Fuchida climbed out of his aircraft, someone pointed to a large shell hole behind the cockpit, through which the control wire was hanging by barely a thread. He had narrowly escaped being shot down. But a worse shock was to come. He had estimated that a third wave, and possibly a fourth wave, which had been planned, would locate plenty of targets. He reported to Nagumo once he had been able to check his findings with the other flight commanders. He went below for lunch, fully expecting to be ordered back afterwards, but while he was eating his bean paste and rice wafers, the decision was taken not to mount another attack on Pearl Harbor. The aircraft had been refuelled and rearmed, many carrying torpedoes so that they could strike at American warships at sea, giving chase. Fuchida protested to Nagumo, but was told curtly by Kusaka, Nagumo's chief of staff, that all objectives had been met.

Nagumo considered that any further assault would suffer severe losses as the American defences would be ready. He was also worried about being attacked by the Pacific Fleet, and in particular, their carrier-borne aircraft. In this, he was undoubtedly right, although with six carriers, he could have put up a good defence provided that combat air patrols were mounted, reconnaissance flights despatched, and at least one flight deck at a time kept free to launch aircraft. Losses might have been heavy if third and fourth waves had been sent, but in their absence, Pearl Harbor remained an operational base, contrary to Fuchida's belief that the main battle fleet would not be able to function for six months. The raid had failed in its major objective of changing the balance of power in the Pacific. Yamamoto himself judged that Nagumo had failed in not ordering a further attack. The Italians had moved their battleships and cruisers out of Taranto to a safer base, further away from any possible action; the Americans, however, had no intention of doing any such thing.

The other fatal mistake made by Japanese commanders is that they failed to follow up Pearl Harbor with measures designed to make it more difficult for the United States Navy to reinforce its Pacific Fleet. An attack on the Panama Canal or, safer still, intensive mining of its Pacific end, would have been helpful, forcing the Americans to send their warships around Cape Horn and the entire land mass of South America. Sabotage of the Panama Canal's extensive lock system would have closed it for months, if not longer. Yet the canal escaped the war unscathed and continued to remain a shortcut between the Pacific and the Atlantic.

CHAPTER FOURTEEN

What Might Have Been – Disaster in the Arctic

After the great success at Taranto, the Fleet Air Arm had finally proved itself to be a valuable element in the Royal Navy. Even the 'big gun' traditionalists had come round to a grudging acceptance that success in naval warfare was impossible without air power, and some were perhaps beginning to realise that their hoped-for major fleet action would never take place.

Of course, the standing of naval air power did not rest on Taranto alone. The successful attack during the Norwegian campaign on the German cruiser *Königsberg* by naval aircraft operating from a shore base on the mainland of Orkney, the group of islands to the north of Scotland, pre-dated Taranto by several months. Then it was quickly realised just how devastating had been the raid at Taranto. The Germans may be excused for not appreciating what might happen and not giving better protection to the *Königsberg*, but the Italians should have seen what could occur and learned from the German experience.

Modern aircraft were still needed, but more of the new fast armoured carriers were entering service and the Fleet Air Arm's supposedly elderly aircraft were proving highly effective. Many also recognised that the aeroplane was the best antidote to the submarine, and although the most efficient planes were the shore-based aircraft of RAF Coastal Command, the long ranges involved meant that carrier aircraft were essential for this duty; and even when submarines were not spotted or attacked, often by aircraft and escort vessels working together, the presence of aircraft did force the submariners to 'keep their heads down', putting them on the defensive. Increasingly, naval officers began to realise just how deficient the Fleet Air Arm was in the performance of its aircraft. The Swordfish did at least show that it could deliver the goods – as at Taranto and later on in the hunt for the German battleship *Bismarck* – but the Fulmar could only offer sturdiness and long range, while what was needed was a high-performance fighter.

Whether it was the growing confidence in the Fleet Air Arm and naval air power, or political pressure, a lesson on just how Taranto might have turned out was waiting within nine months of Operation Judgement.

The German invasion of the Soviet Union transformed World War Two, giving the British a new, not altogether welcome, ally. But it was an unreliable and uncertain alliance: the two nations had nothing in common. Russia was also a demanding ally; having failed to prepare for a German invasion, despite the warnings and despite the signals which had left little scope for misunderstanding Hitler's intentions, it expected the hard-pressed British to demonstrate their commitment to Russia's survival. The British for their part, and not without some cause, were concerned that Russia might try to reach an accommodation with Germany – ceding parts of Soviet territory was considered by Stalin before and immediately after the German invasion.

In these circumstances, the British felt compelled to take action to demonstrate their commitment to the Russians, and to encourage their resistance. Opportunities for doing so were limited – and so the idea of an attack on German shipping in the ports of Petsamo and Kirkenes, north of the Arctic Circle, was born.

PETSAMO AND KIRKENES

Kirkenes, in Norway, was taken by the Germans as they advanced in the spring and early summer of 1940. Petsamo, or Pechenga to the Russians, had changed hands on a number of occasions. Originally belonging to Russia, it became part of Finland as the Finns seized their independence in the wake of the Bolshevik Revolution, but the town was among those lost again as the price of peace in the Russo-Finnish War of 1939–40. After Germany invaded the Soviet Union in Operation Barbarossa in June 1941, Finland was drawn into the orbit of the Axis powers, largely for national preservation on the basis that 'my enemy's enemy is my friend'. This left both ports for German use as the best means of supporting an advance through the north to Moscow. German possession of these ports also made it more difficult for Russia's new allies to ship supplies to her, since the most direct route through the Baltic was naturally impracticable.

Ever since the German invasion, Stalin had been pressing his new allies to take action against the Germans to ease the pressure on his forces. The question of what could be done was a difficult one. The German armies advancing into the Soviet Union were even further beyond the reach of the RAF's heavy bombers than when they had invaded Poland, and there was clearly no opportunity for the British Army to engage the enemy anywhere which would help Russia's plight. Later, Stalin would demand a premature invasion of France to draw German forces westward, but in 1941, the only possible means of making an impact lay with the Royal Navy, and especially with naval air power.

The commander of the Home Fleet, Admiral John Tovey, was urged by Churchill to carry out an attack which would be 'a gesture in support of our Russian allies to create a diversion on the enemy's northern flank'.

Still fresh from its victory at Taranto, the Royal Navy deployed one of its newest aircraft carriers, together with its oldest, for the operation. The new vessel was HMS *Victorious*, a sister of HMS *Illustrious*, the victor of Taranto, while the other ship was the very first aircraft carrier, HMS *Furious*. Aircraft still included the veteran Fairey Swordfish biplanes, but this time they were to be complemented by Fairey Albacore torpedo-bombers, and escorted by Fairey Fulmar fighters. The planes from *Victorious* comprised twenty Fairey Albacore torpedo-bombers from 827 and 828 naval air squadrons, escorted by Fairey Fulmar fighters from 809 Squadron. Their target was Kirkenes. The elderly *Furious* despatched nine Fairey Swordfish of 812 squadron and nine Albacores of 817 squadron, escorted by the Fulmars of 800 Squadron, to Petsamo.

THE OPERATION

It must have been tempting to consider this as a repeat of the mission against Taranto, but with supposedly more modern and more capable aircraft. This proved a vain hope. In the almost twenty-four-hour summer daylight of the far north, the passage of the two ships northward was spotted, and their intentions guessed, by a German reconnaissance aircraft shortly before the aircraft were flown off late in the afternoon of 31 July 1941. Further more, the aircraft from *Victorious* had to fly over a German hospital ship on the way in to the target, and were ordered not to attack, although, of course, this could not prevent those aboard from sending a warning ashore.

Neither port proved to contain the mass of shipping found at Taranto. At Kirkenes, the aircraft, instead of attacking from the sea, had to fly over a mountain at the end of the fjord before diving into the bay, where they found only four ships. After enduring heavy anti-aircraft fire from positions on the cliffs, the raiders were themselves attacked by German fighters, and most of them had to jettison their torpedoes in a desperate bid to escape. They managed to sink just one cargo vessel of 2,000 tons, and set another on fire. The slow and lumbering Fulmars did well to shoot down four Luftwaffe aircraft. Worse still, at Petsamo, the harbour was empty, and the frustrated aircrew could do nothing more than loose their torpedoes at the wharves.

One of the telegraphist air gunners with 828 was Petty Officer Francis Smith, who recalled:

> Eventually we get to the fjord leading into Kirkenes ... we went from one side of Kirkenes Bay, and 827 Squadron went in from the other side. And all of a sudden, there's flaming onions and God knows what else coming down at us – because we're flying up the fjord, and the Germans are firing down, from the cliffs with light ack-ack. Not funny at all.
>
> So we go in so far, and we have to climb over the end of the fjord ... and over the mountain and down into the bay. And there's all this mass shipping – about four little ships. And before anything can happen, there were 110s and Stukas all over the place – they're all airborne ... they're there, waiting for us.
>
> And they start ... By now the ack-ack has stopped firing, they've left it to the Stukas and the 110s, and they're blasting away with cannon-shells and God knows what. Well, almost immediately, my last sub-flight all got shot down ... Everyone jettisoned their torpedoes ... nobody got a chance to fire at any ship.

Having received such a hot welcome – for so little of value in the target area – the attackers attempted to make their escape. This was easier said than done, for the Albacore was no rival to a Me110. Smith was flying in 828's CO's – Lt-Cdr Langmore's – aircraft, and his role was to keep a lookout while his pilot tried to escape from the attacking fighters:

> And the only protection you had in Albacores, or Swordfish, was to go right down on the water and wait ... see the cannon shells hitting the

water, and at the last second, yell out to the pilot, 'hard-a-starboard' or 'hard-a-port'. With which ... he spun left or right and the cannon shells went by you ... In this case, it worked and they didn't hit us. But I did see the cannon shells going by.

While this was going on, Smith could see other aircraft being shot down. It must have concentrated the mind wonderfully. And, as so often happened on carrier air operations, their troubles were not over:

When we got back to the ship, we couldn't land on ... because there was an aircraft on the flight deck – broken its back on landing – we found out afterwards he hadn't broken his back, he was just shot in two, and the telegraphist air gunner was dead in the back – he'd been cut in two, more or less, by cannon shells. So while we're circling, there was five of 827 come back. Now one of them, his lower mainplane was just flapping in the breeze, it was just in tatters and streamers, where he'd been shot up.

In the operation, *Victorious* lost thirteen of her aircraft, while *Furious* lost three. Altogether, forty-four aircrew were lost, seven of them killed, the remainder taken prisoner. Just how bad this was can be gathered from the simple fact that had the losses at Taranto been on a similar scale, seven aircraft would have been lost rather than only two.

Tovey's reaction to this debacle was clear. 'The gallantry of the aircraft crews, who knew before leaving that their chance of surprise had gone, and that they were certain to face heavy odds, is beyond praise ... I trust that the encouragement to the morale of our allies was proportionately great.'

The operation had no bearing on the course of the war. The Taranto raid stopped the Italian Navy from using the port for the duration of hostilities as well as inflicting heavy, tangible losses. In this case, aircraft and their even more valuable and difficult to replace aircrew were lost, without any positive achievement.

CHAPTER FIFTEEN

The Mediterranean After Taranto

The great success at Taranto had been largely undermined by the revenge taken by the Germans on *Illustrious*. Had Cunningham made more than a tactical error by exposing the ship so close to the enemy when her aircraft could have covered the Mediterranean Fleet from a distance? The immediate reaction is to say 'yes', but there are other factors to take into account. As they were to learn to their cost, the ships of any fleet were safer together when faced with air attack than when they were dispersed, since there was greater security with a concentrated force of AA fire. Indeed, as the war developed, it became clear that the most useful task that could be given to a battleship or cruiser was to help provide intense AA cover for the carriers – until, that is, the changing fortunes of war allowed these ships to provide heavy bombardments to cover invading forces.

Taranto had been abandoned as a naval base, with the heavy fleet units moved to greater safety further away. That was a major gain. On the debit side of the account, it had pulled the Luftwaffe into Sicily, threatening Malta and the Malta convoys, and ably supported in the Mediterranean by the arrival of the E-boats and below them, the U-boats. But if Taranto had not been attacked, the Italians could simply have left their battleships there – a brooding presence threatening any and every convoy. They could even have sailed out to bombard the harbours, airfields and cities of Malta. Time and time again, the Fleet Air Arm and the RAF put a maximum effort into attempts to sink the German battleship *Tirpitz*, sitting in a Norwegian fjord. They could not have ignored six battleships, plus their cruiser and destroyer escorts, while they were at Taranto. It was simply a question of how and when, but not of whether it should be done.

In one sense, however, the attentions of the Luftwaffe and the increased German naval presence may be regarded as a plus rather than a minus. German forces drawn into the Mediterranean were forces lost elsewhere, easing the pressure on other fronts, including the UK itself.

Defending Malta was a priority, for had it not been for this base, the Germans and Italians would have enjoyed virtually free access at all times to their forces in North Africa. While convoy lines to Malta were always fragile and costly, and often failed altogether, the same could be said of the Axis north–south convoy route, thanks mainly to Malta-based forces. Without Malta, the Suez Canal would probably have been lost. True, by 1941, Suez was being used to reinforce British forces in Egypt, rather than as a short-cut to the Indian and Pacific Oceans, but it was also the key to the Middle East. The Germans needed oil – and that was one reason for their mounting Operation Barbarossa – but so did the United Kingdom; the Middle East, especially Iran, was a principal source.

A FORMIDABLE ARRIVAL

Despite Pound's gloomy predictions over the fate of an aircraft carrier in the Mediterranean, *Illustrious* left and was replaced two months later by *Formidable*, another ship of the same class. The speed with which this was done showed a marked change of attitude at the Admiralty and growing recognition of the importance of air power in the war at sea. The need for a replacement aircraft carrier, and a modern one at that, was such that *Formidable* was ordered from the South Atlantic to supplement the Mediterranean Fleet within just two days of her predecessor being crippled. The new ship was joined by the Fulmars of 806, whose pilots were doubtless relieved to be done with the near continuous air attacks and primitive conditions they had endured on Malta. *Formidable* had arrived in the Mediterranean by the same route as *Illustrious* had left it, through the 'back door', the Suez Canal, having sailed around Africa rather than taking the direct route via Gibraltar.

The arrival of the replacement carrier was delayed for several days by Axis air attacks on the Suez Canal, dropping mines which over the course of several days accounted for four merchantmen. Clearing the canal of mines proved difficult, and at one stage involved using watchers ashore to spot where mines had entered the water, sending down frogmen to locate the exact position, and then dropping depth charges. In the end, a crippled cargo ship had to be moved to the side of the canal and beached, leaving just enough room for *Formidable* to squeeze past on her way to the Mediterranean, and then for *Illustrious* to make her exit. It was also decided to send *Eagle* away, for apart from the problems with her fuelling system, she was desperately overdue for a refit. A crippled carrier was a liability, worse than no carrier at all.

It is interesting to note that Pound, despite his pessimism over carrier operations in the Mediterranean, had a good sense of the merits of the available ships. Early in 1941, when Cunningham challenged what he thought was the refusal of the Admiralty to allow him to use *Formidable* to transport Hurricanes towards Malta, Pound signalled a tart reply:

> The earliest date of getting Hurricanes to Malta by carrier is 28 March; delivery by this method has at no time been abandoned. Had *Ark Royal* been in *Illustrious*'s place, I am sure that you are in no doubt what her fate would have been, but the risk to the carrier is but one of many factors taken into account ... I trust you will disabuse Longmore that the reinforcement of Malta with Hurricanes will become a routine affair, which I suspect he hopes for. Although glad to use carriers as air transports in grave emergency, I feel that this is wrong when it can be avoided by looking ahead sufficiently.

The crux of the matter was, of course, that the single carrier available could never carry enough aircraft to maintain an adequate defence of the island and engage in offensive operations at the same time. Even without the poor performance of the existing naval fighters, the defences of a single carrier were always likely to be overwhelmed. Putting the carrier at the disposal of the RAF to reinforce Malta was another difficult question, for the ship was at risk on such an exercise. On the other hand, a strong Malta-based fighter force helped to protect convoys and also backed up the carrier's air group.

Again, the strategic position needs to be borne in mind. Fighter aircraft based on Malta had a short life, as many more were destroyed on the ground in the almost ceaseless air raids than were shot down by enemy fighters. To be sure of maintaining adequate fighter defences before a convoy arrived, aircraft had to be in position a few days before the convoy's due date. It was not unknown for fighters to arrive, and be destroyed almost immediately they landed.

Solving these problems was difficult, given the resources available. Nevertheless, the US carrier *Wasp* made two delivery voyages, ferrying aircraft to within flying distance of Malta, prompting Churchill's grateful remark: 'Who says a wasp can only sting once!'

The problem, as the United States Navy demonstrated in the Pacific, could only be solved by operating a number of carriers together at the same time; and long-term survival of Malta-based fighters was eventually ensured by having ground crew ready and waiting, so that as the aircraft landed on delivery, they were refuelled and rearmed and sent back into the air within minutes.

Formidable's own strike forces included the 803 fighter squadron, with Fulmars and Albacores of 826 and Swordfish of 829. Her Commander (Flying) was James 'Skins' Atkinson, who had qualified as a pilot in 1925, and had flown with 406 Flight from *Furious* and 404 Flight from *Argus*. One of his early claims to fame was as an early member of the 'Perch Club', for which carrier pilots qualified by completing a hundred deck landings. He was later the first CO of the famous 800 Naval Air Squadron when that was formed in 1933 from the merger of 402 and 404 Flights.

Previously, on 9 February 1941, Force H had done its best to maintain the pressure on the Axis forces in the Mediterranean. Vice Admiral Somerville, its flag officer, took the battleship *Malaya*, the battlecruiser *Renown* and the aircraft carrier *Ark Royal*, with a cruiser and ten destroyers as escorts, on a raid in the Gulf of Genoa. This was a risky venture, steaming into a relatively confined area close to the enemy's mainland. Confronted by the battleships bombarding Genoa itself, while the *Ark Royal*'s aircraft bombed the port of Leghorn and dropped mines off the naval base of La Spezia, the Italian Navy finally decided to react. The battleships *Vittorio Veneto, Giulio Cesare* and *Andrea Doria*, with three cruisers and ten destroyers, were sent to intercept Force H, which they heavily outgunned and outnumbered, but failed to make contact. This was the closest they came to the decisive naval engagement for which Cunningham had yearned – it would have been irony indeed had this event been handed to his junior, Somerville.

Nevertheless, the naval war was not completely one-sided. Displaying the courage and resourcefulness which seemed to be largely confined to smaller operations rather than those of the fleet, on 25 March, Italian torpedo-boats sank a tanker in the important anchorage at Suda Bay, Crete. The following day, they succeeded in damaging the heavy cruiser *York* so badly that her captain had to run her aground to save the ship. His efforts, although absolutely correct, were to be in vain, for later, as she lay stranded like some giant beached whale, the bombers of the Luftwaffe completed the job and destroyed her. The thin plating of a cruiser offered little protection against bombs.

Impatient that the Royal Navy still survived to fight in the Mediterranean even though the Luftwaffe controlled the skies, the Germans now urged the Italian Navy to cut the supply lines between Alexandria, Crete and Greece. At a stroke, this would ease the pressure on the German campaign in Greece and help secure their convoys sailing from Italy to North Africa. The Germans managed to convince the Italians that the Mediterranean Fleet had just a single battleship, rather than the three actually present. This is an interesting development, for the Royal Navy was convinced that Alexandria was crawling with Axis agents and spies. It also shows once again that Italian aerial reconnaissance was not very effective.

Formidable brought the new Fairey Albacore strike aircraft of her 826 and 829 squadrons to the Mediterranean for the first time. This aircraft, although still a biplane, had enclosed cockpits and was meant to be a replacement for the Swordfish. It was not. The Albacore was to prove to be unreliable, her Taurus engine nowhere as dependable as the Pegasus, giving rise to the ditty in the *Fleet Air Arm Songbook* that:

> 'The Swordfish relies on her Peggy,
> The modified Taurus ain't sound,
> So the Swordfish flies off on her missions
> And the Albacore stays on the ground.
> 'Bring back, bring back,
> Oh bring back my Stringbag to me…'

The Albacore was not the only disappointment. When Fairey eventually did provide the Fleet Air Arm with a monoplane dive-bomber and torpedo-dropper in the misshapen form of the Barracuda, it too was to be outlived by the venerable Swordfish. The Barracuda was described by one rating 'as a maintenance nightmare'.

British reconnaissance was quick to spot the Italians at sea. This was the closest that Cunningham was to get to the decisive naval engagement for which he had longed since Italy's belated entry into the war. As it was, the Italian force was far less threatening than he had hoped, consisting of just one battleship, the *Vittorio Veneto,* but she did have an escort of no less than

eight cruisers, several of them heavy and able to outgun their British opponents, while the Mediterranean Fleet had just four.

While British reconnaissance always seemed to be one step ahead of the
Italians, the same could not be said of the respective intelligence services.
This was because the Allied position was remarkably open to observation
by enemy agents at both ends of the Mediterranean. In Gibraltar, ships
could clearly be seen from Spain, and their progress through the Straits
observed from the mainland or from the two Spanish enclaves in Morocco,
Ceuta and Melilla. Moreover, as mentioned, Alexandria was reputed to be
swarming with Italian and German agents, or at least, those of other
nationalities who could be relied upon to pass information to the Axis.

MATAPAN

Not realising that the Italians really had little true awareness of the strength
of the Mediterranean Fleet, precautions had to be taken. It was decided that
a false trail should be laid. The plan was to encourage everyone in Alexandria to believe that the Mediterranean Fleet was staying in port.

On 27 March, Cunningham himself went ashore during the afternoon
with a suitcase, so that anyone watching would assume that he would be
spending the night there. Many of the senior officers were also sent away,
some of them by air. Guests were invited to dinner aboard the ships, and the
awnings shading the decks were kept spread. As soon as night fell, everyone
hastened back to their ships, dinner invitations were cancelled, and the
awnings were furled. Under cover of darkness, the Mediterranean Fleet
slipped out to sea.

At 06.00 on 28 March, *Formidable* flew off aircraft for reconnaissance,
fighter combat air patrol and anti-submarine patrols. One of the carrier's
senior officers was S. W. C. Pack, later to write a biography, *Cunningham the
Commander*. Pack recalled:

At 07.20 our aircraft reported four cruisers and four destroyers ...
Another reported at 07.39 she had sighted four cruisers and six destroyers ... When it became known that Pridham-Whippell [in command
of the Mediterranean Fleet's cruisers] had been ordered to rendezvous
at 06.30 south of Gaudo Island, the conviction spread that his own
force must have been the subject of the two separate reports from air-

craft ... At 09.39 Cunningham had ordered the *Formidable* to fly off the six Albacores that had been ranged on the flight deck for the last hour. His aim was to attack the Trieste cruisers now being shadowed by Pridham-Whippell ... The attack saved the British cruisers.

In fact, the British light cruisers were being pursued by the Italian heavy cruisers, who were gaining, and had a heavier armament. Worse, Pridham-Whippell was within range of the heavy guns of the *Vittorio Veneto*. The British cruisers made smoke in an attempt to evade their pursuers.

At 11.27, the Albacores of 826 Squadron arrived on the scene, fortunately escorted by Fulmar fighters as two Junkers Ju88 fighter-bombers attempted to attack; the Fulmars shot down one and drove the other away. Braving intense Italian AA fire, the six Albacores dived down to make a torpedo attack on the *Vittorio Veneto*. They failed to hit their target but did succeed in forcing the Italian battleship to break off the action.

A second strike of three Albacores and two Swordfish, mounted by 829 Squadron, was already in the air. The first strike landed on at 12.44, just before two Savoia-Marchetti SM79s attempted an unsuccessful torpedo-bombing attack on their carrier.

Pack takes up the story again:

> *Formidable*'s log for this day shows that flying operations were con-
> ducted on twenty-one separate occasions. Each operation might
> occupy only a few minutes but required an alteration of course into the
> wind which was upsetting when the whole fleet had to conform to these
> movements to ensure that the destroyer screen would remain effective.
> Essential routine operations severely limited the number of aircraft
> that could be made ready for the big strikes. She had a total of only 27
> aircraft on board; 13 Fulmars, 10 Albacores (of which only 5 were fitted
> with long-range tanks), and 4 Swordfish. These had to cover all routine
> requirements, such as fighter protection and anti-submarine patrol in
> addition to the shadowing, mass reconnaissance, and offensive strikes
> needed in battle: a pitiably small force when compared to the large
> forces available in carriers in the Pacific Campaign of 1945.

During the afternoon, Royal Air Force Blenheim bombers operating from bases in Greece attacked the Italian battleship and cruisers on four occasions, but the high-altitude bombing scored no hits, although there were a number of near-misses. Nevertheless, the Italian battleship, *Vittorio Veneto*, which had enjoyed such a charmed existence at Taranto, was to see her luck run out that day.

Meanwhile, the second wave of aircraft from *Formidable*, led by 829's CO Lt-Cdr Dalyell-Stead, had arrived over the *Vittorio Veneto*. The ship's AA defences were surprised by the Fulmars machine-gunning their positions and the bridge, while the three Albacores pressed home their torpedo attack. The leading aircraft dropped its torpedo 1,000 yards ahead of the ship as she turned to starboard to avoid the missile, while the AA fire belatedly concentrated on the aircraft. The torpedo struck the ship almost immediately after the plane crashed. The battleship was hit 15ft below the waterline, allowing a massive flood of water to gush in just above the port outer screw, so that within minutes the engines had stopped.

It took hard work by damage control parties before the *Vittorio Veneto* could start again, using only her two starboard engines, but ninety minutes after the attack she was limping along at 15 knots. A further strike had meanwhile been flown off *Formidable*, led by Lt-Cdr Gerald Saunt, with six of 826's Albacores and two of 829's Swordfish, themselves to be joined by another two Swordfish of 815 Squadron flying from Maleme in Crete, and including Tiffy Torrens-Spence, now the squadron's acting CO, with Peter Winter as his observer. Torrens-Spence had not wanted to be left out, and had flown from his squadron's temporary base at Eluisis, near Athens, where they had been engaged in a highly effective anti-shipping campaign, to the airfield at Maleme, where he had even arranged his own reconnaissance.

Intending to press home their attack in the dark when the Italians would be at a disadvantage, the raiders loitered, waiting for the sun to set. The Italian Admiral Iachino watched. 'They looked like giant vultures,' he said later. 'Flying slowly around their prey until a favourable moment should present itself…'

At dusk, they attacked the Italians, diving down through a dense smoke-screen and then being dazzled by searchlights and the usual colourful Italian tracer barrage; they recorded no hits. After their departure Torrens-Spence spotted a gap in the defences, and headed down towards a heavy cruiser, the *Pola*. He and Winter had the satisfaction of dropping their torpedo and seeing it inflict such severe damage on the *Pola*, that she lost speed and drifted out of position. It took an hour before Iachino became aware of *Pola*'s problems, sending two other heavy cruisers, *Zara* and *Fiume*, with four destroyers to provide assistance.

Iachino had discounted a night action, but knowing his enemy's weakness in night gunnery, this was what Cunningham was preparing for. The two opposing fleets were now off Cape Matapan, usually referred to on modern atlases as Cape Akra Tainaron, a promontory at the extreme southern end of the Peloponnese peninsula. Initially he mistook *Pola*'s radar trace for that of *Vittorio Veneto*, and as his ships prepared to open fire, the Italian rescue force of *Zara* and *Fiume* sped across his path, to be illuminated by a searchlight from a destroyer. In the battle that followed, both *Zara* and *Fiume* and two destroyers were sunk by the 15in guns of the three battleships. *Pola* was despatched in a torpedo attack from two destroyers. In the heat of battle, *Formidable* was nearly fired upon by her own side, as *Warspite*'s secondary armament was trained on her, but the mistake was realised just in time.

Cunningham saw his ships pick up 900 Italian survivors the following morning, before the threat of enemy air attack stopped the rescue; but despite this threat, he relayed the position of the remaining survivors to Rome, saving many more lives. This was the second time he had done this during the course of the war in the Mediterranean. On the previous occasion, it was to rescue the crew of an Italian destroyer and brought forth a sharp rebuke from the Admiralty for alerting the Italians to the position of his force, although, as Cunningham commented, the Italians surely must have realised that the Mediterranean Fleet was at sea, having lost some of their ships!

Despite the naval success at Matapan, within two months both Greece and Crete were lost.

PROTECTING THE CONVOYS

On 18 April, another attempt was made to force oil and aviation fuel through to Malta from Alexandria, and as always, a sizeable and powerful escort was provided. Leaving 'Alex' at 07.00, the escort was headed by Cunningham's flagship, *Warspite*, accompanied by the Mediterranean Fleet's other two battleships, *Barham* and *Valiant*, and the carrier *Formidable*, as well as two cruisers, *Phoebe* and *Cairo*, with a large destroyer screen. All this was to provide cover for a single ship, the *Breconshire*. This demonstrates vividly just how serious the situation had become, and how important Malta's survival was to the war effort. If the operation was successful, the escort would also bring back four merchantmen from Malta. In order to put the ships to the best possible use, the convoy escort duty was to leave the *Breconshire* after dark on the evening of 20 April and bombard Tripoli. This would be preceded by an air bombardment of the port by RAF Wellingtons and Fleet Air Arm Swordfish from Malta. Oddly, the aircraft from *Formidable* were to be limited to flare-dropping and spotting for the guns of the fleet, rather than conducting a 'mini-Taranto' on the port, which would be occupied mainly by merchant ships and their escorts, usually nothing bigger than a destroyer. That this was seen as a substantial and complicated operation may also be judged by the positioning of the submarine *Truant* accurately four miles off the harbour, showing a light to seaward as a navigation mark, in order to ensure accuracy of the bombardment.

Steaming south through the night, the Mediterranean Fleet picked up another cruiser, *Gloucester*, steamed past the surfaced submarine *Truant* during the early morning of 21 April, just before daylight, and in what was literally the darkest hour before dawn, at least for the Italian defenders, from 05.00 to 05.45, in Cunningham's own words, 'pumped 15-inch and 6-inch shell into the harbour and amongst the shipping. The *Gloucester*'s sixteen gun salvoes must have been particularly effective.' Those on the ships could see little of the damage being done, especially as the air raids, which had only just ceased, had created clouds of dust and smoke from the fires started, but *Formidable*'s aircraft reported that five or six ships had been sunk, and it looked as if *Valiant*'s guns had set off an oil fire.

Despite the air raids, the Italians had once again been caught napping. It took twenty minutes before the shore batteries came into action, and most of their shells flew over the attacking warships, which suffered no hits at all. On this occasion, the Mediterranean Fleet was in luck, for the Luftwaffe also failed to put in an appearance, leaving Cunningham to surmise that possibly the radio station at Tripoli had been put out of action. Before the operation, with the agonies of *Illustrious* in January still fresh his mind, he had been expecting anything from the loss of a major ship in an enemy minefield to the destruction of several ships or heavy damage to all of them from a heavy Luftwaffe attack.

On the way back to Alexandria, they were joined by Pridham-Whippell's cruisers and destroyers, which had been attacking coastal targets between Tripoli and Benghazi. Three Junkers Ju88s attempted to attack, but Fulmars from *Formidable* shot down two of them and chased off the third.

Despite the success of the operation, Cunningham appears to have been opposed to using the Mediterranean Fleet for heavy shore bombardments. Whereas the risks already mentioned no doubt influenced his views, he also recalled that the fleet had many other heavy commitments, especially given the grave situation in Greece by this time. He also felt that heavy bombers from Egypt could have achieved as much in a few hours as it had taken his forces to achieve in five days. There was much to be said for this view, although to some extent he was also expressing the opinion that the RAF was shirking its responsibilities and passing the work to the Royal Navy. Cunningham wanted Beaufighters in Malta to provide night-fighter cover, and heavy bombers in Egypt to attack the enemy in North Africa. The first expectation was undoubtedly justified but the second was questionable, not least given the demands on the RAF to attack German industry and communications, and the heavy losses Bomber Command was experiencing at the time. The heavy guns of the battleships could each deliver around a ton of high explosives, and with as many as eight 15in guns firing salvoes, the destruction was likely to have been far more than that of a single bombing raid. It must be remembered that at this time, RAF bombing accuracy was far from good, although the clearer skies of North Africa might have ensured better results than over Germany.

That this was the case was borne out by the resulting flurry of signals between Alexandria and London, when, on 27 April, Churchill himself finally intervened, pointing out that the purpose of the RAF presence in Malta was to protect the naval base. The Prime Minister also pointed out that to deliver the same weight of bombs as Cunningham's ships had fired in shells in forty-two minutes would have taken a Wellington squadron from Malta ten-and-a-half weeks, or a Stirling squadron thirty weeks. This was something of an exaggeration, since the Stirling was a true heavy-bomber and had relegated the Wellington to the role of a medium-bomber, although the former had a mid-wing which had the unfortunate effect of dividing the bomb bay in two. It shows how much heat and how little light could be involved in high-level wartime communication. In the event, this ended the correspondence as Cunningham did not reply, which was no bad thing. In any case, following the fall of Yugoslavia on 18 April, the evacuation of the troops in Greece had started on 24 April. From then until 30 April, the Mediterranean Fleet, in conjunction with merchant ships for which it provided cover, transported a total of more than 50,000 men from Greece, most of whom were taken to Crete, which now assumed prime importance.

By this time, the Axis had effectively cut the Mediterranean into two halves. Malta's plight was desperate; deprived of supplies, the potential capture of the island base would consolidate Axis power and render the Mediterranean, especially the central part, out of bounds to the British. Ships and crews were by this time showing signs of strain; the ships needed refits and repairs, the men needed rest.

Despite this, it was decided to send a large convoy, Operation Tiger, with five large cargo ships through the Mediterranean, carrying tanks for the British Army in Egypt and Hawker Hurricane fighters for the RAF. The escort for the convoy would also include reinforcements for Cunningham, with the battleship *Queen Elizabeth* and the cruisers *Naiad* and *Fiji* sailing with Force H as far as the Sicilian Narrows, where they would hand over the convoy to the Mediterranean Fleet. Cunningham's outward voyage on this occasion was also to provide cover for two convoys from Alexandria to Malta, with one convoy consisting of four large merchant ships carrying supplies, and the other two tankers with fuel for the island. As usual, a side-show was planned; on this occasion Benghazi was to be attacked by a cruiser and three destroyers.

Both Force H and the Mediterranean Fleet were to sail from Gibraltar and Alexandria respectively on 6 May, but departure from the Egyptian port was slow and difficult as the larger ships had to be preceded by minesweepers as a result of mining the previous day. Poor visibility due to a sandstorm also prevented operations by *Formidable*'s aircraft. The following day the Vice-Admiral, Malta, signalled Cunningham to say that the harbour was completely mined, confining his destroyers to port so that they could not escort the convoy since Malta's minesweepers equipped to deal with magnetic mines had all been lost or seriously damaged. Cunningham replied that he must blast a way through the mines using depth charges. As in the Suez Canal, this unorthodox method of clearing mines was a great success, but when the convoy's own minesweeper entered the Grand Harbour on 8 May, she set off nearly a dozen mines!

Their luck was holding. Unusually for the time of year, Cunningham's ships arrived off Malta to find very low cloud, 'almost down to our mast-heads', so although their radar showed enemy aircraft, they were not spotted. One of *Formidable*'s Fulmars found a Ju88 above the clouds and managed to shoot it down. Among the ships bound for Malta, one merchant ship was mined and another torpedoed, although able to continue; overall, the convoy suffered relatively lightly.

Returning to Alexandria, with the reinforcements and the convoy for Egypt, the Mediterranean Fleet came under heavy aerial attack, but the heavy AA fire put up by the cruisers and the carrier drove them off. Despite the dangers of sailing directly across the Mediterranean, Operation Tiger was a great success, and earned the Mediterranean Fleet the warm congratulations of the Admiralty. Yet it could all have been for nothing. Cunningham was astounded and infuriated to learn that the tanks that had been brought to Egypt at such cost and with so much good fortune and courage, had to spend fourteen days after being unloaded being fitted with sand filters for desert conditions, during which time they were vulnerable to enemy air attack. The same happened to the Hurricanes. This all-important item of equipment should surely have been fitted before despatch from the UK.

The extent of the convoy's good fortune may be judged from the loss in Malta of seven Hurricanes, most of them with their pilots, over the islands during a three-day period in mid-May. During the same period, air attacks damaged a further twenty-seven Hurricanes on the ground, as well as four Beaufighters and two Martin Baltimores, with a Blenheim damaged so badly that it was written off.

THE BATTLE FOR CRETE

On 20 May, after four days of bombing, the German airborne attack on Crete began. This was to be followed up by a seaborne invasion. Cunningham's forces attempted to intercept the Germans and engaged them, but they were running short of fuel and ammunition. Air cover was virtually non-existent, with only nine fighters in a mixed Fleet Air Arm and RAF contingent ashore, under naval command, while *Formidable* had been reduced to just four serviceable aircraft by the losses and damage of recent operations. There were no reserves of aircraft or flying personnel. HMS *Gloucester* was crippled and set on fire, with many of her crew killed as they were machine-gunned in the water. The cruiser *Fiji*, out of all but practice ammunition, was crippled by the small bomb dropped by a Messerschmitt Bf109, as it narrowly missed and blew in her hull in the area of the engine room, while half-an-hour later, another aircraft hit the ship with three bombs which exploded in her boiler room, so that shortly afterwards she rolled over and sank.

Worse was to follow. Hastily returned to service on 25 May with a scratch complement of a dozen Fairey Fulmars, many of which were themselves not fully serviceable, *Formidable* was sent to attack Italian-held airfields in the Dodecanese, in a vain attempt to ward off Luftwaffe and Regia Aeronautica attacks and prevent the airlift of enemy troops into the captured airfields on the island. The Royal Navy had by this time lost two cruisers and four destroyers, with many other ships damaged, and all were running dangerously low on ammunition. The carrier also had some Fairey Albacores, hoping to be able to attack enemy shipping, including the invasion barges, or to bomb troop concentrations ashore.

Early on 26 May, *Formidable* arrived with the battleships *Queen Elizabeth*, in which Pridham-Whippell was flying his flag, and *Barham*, at a point a hundred miles south-west of Scarpanto in the Dodecanese, and sent four Albacores and four Fulmars to attack, catching the enemy by surprise and destroying and damaging planes on the airfield. Despite the element of surprise and determined attacks, the carrier had too few aircraft to make any difference to the outcome. Worse, she was exposing herself to danger. As the morning passed, the carrier's radar caught successive waves of enemy aircraft looking for her, and with eight Fulmars operational, sent these on a total of twenty-four sorties during which they engaged Luftwaffe planes on twenty occasions, shooting some of them down. This was an unequal conflict, and at 13.20, Vice-Admiral Pridham-Whippell decided to withdraw, just as twenty Luftwaffe aircraft approached, not from the direction of Greece, but from North Africa. The Germans pressed home their attack, led by Stuka dive-bombers, in a virtual repeat of the raid on her sister carrier, seriously damaging the cruiser *Nubian* and hitting *Formidable* twice. The damage to the carrier proved beyond the capabilities of the stretched and improvised repair organisation at Alexandria, so she was forced to follow *Illustrious* to the United States for repairs.

The following day, the battleship *Barham* was badly damaged, but by that time, the decision had already been taken to evacuate Crete. The battle had cost the Mediterranean Fleet three cruisers and six destroyers, with two battleships, an aircraft carrier and another three cruisers damaged so badly that they could not be repaired at Alexandria. *Formidable* had come close to sharing the fate of *Illustrious*. Having taken troops away from Greece, the Royal Navy now had to repeat the exercise at Crete, saving 17,000 men.

Other British ships also suffered in enemy air attacks during the invasion of Crete as the Royal Navy had struggled to prevent the seaborne element of the landing. On 22 May, as well as sinking the two cruisers *Gloucester* and *Fiji*, the Luftwaffe damaged the heavily armoured battleship *Warspite* and two other cruisers, *Naiad* and *Carlisle*, compared with which the previous night's destruction of a German convoy by three British cruisers and four destroyers was hardly sufficient.

At first the hold of the German paratroops on Crete was tenuous, even when reinforced by troops air-landed by glider and then by the ubiquitous Junkers Ju52/3M transports. Had the British and Greek forces on the island not lost much of their heavy equipment, and especially their communications material, in the retreat from Greece, the situation might have been better. On the other hand, the defenders had expected an attack by sea, not by air, despite the experiences of the German advance into the Low Countries. It is clear that the Mediterranean Fleet was successful in causing much damage to the clumsy barges of the seaborne invasion, but was short of fuel. Worse, at times the pressures forced the fleet to divide its forces, and this was when so many ships fell prey to determined Axis air attack. Had there still been two carriers in the eastern Mediterranean, each with a full complement and right balance of aircraft, the outcome might have been very different.

The situation at the time of the invasion of Crete could have been even worse. After the British success at Matapan, the Italians had suffered such heavy losses that they did not dare intervene in the fighting around Crete. They were not to know that they had missed a rare opportunity, with British ships and their crews worked to the limits, critically short of ammunition, while under heavy aerial attack. Had the remaining Italian heavy fleet units intervened, Cunningham might not have managed to lift 17,000 British, Empire and Greek troops from the island. Pridham-Whippell's bold adventure might have placed his ships in even greater danger than was in fact the case, as a well-coordinated assault by air and sea on the British ships could have been overwhelming.

Another weakness of the Axis assault on Crete was that it was inspired and led by the Luftwaffe, with the German Army simply ordered to follow. A well-coordinated invasion, such as those soon to be mounted by the Allies, with airborne and seaborne troops complementing each other, would again have placed the rescue of British and Greek troops ashore in doubt.

The one benefit of the battle for Crete was that German casualties had been so heavy that Hitler banned any future airborne assaults, and although he reversed this later, by then opportunities had been missed. Meanwhile, this decision proved a turning point in the defence of Malta. The history of World War Two might well have been different had the Germans and Italians attempted to invade Malta first, and especially if Mussolini had managed to capture the Balkans without German support; that would have left Germany free to launch Operation Barbarossa – the invasion of the Soviet Union – a good six weeks earlier, offering the German armies a chance of seizing their key objectives before the onset of the Russian winter.

This good news, however, was far from apparent at the time. Sending convoys to Malta from Gibraltar had by now become all but impossible. Moreover, despatching convoys from Alexandria would also be more diffi-cult, with German aircraft based in Crete able to attack the flanks of any shipping sailing west. The enemy was now closer to the convoy route, and to the Suez Canal.

It is natural when looking at the war in the Mediterranean to concentrate on the almost continuous encounters between opposing forces at sea and in the air; yet a major part of the air and naval operations was in support of British forces fighting in North Africa. Running supply ships through to Tobruk was almost as difficult a task for Cunningham as running supplies to Malta. Shipping was the only realistic method of resupplying the British Army in the desert; overland movement was scarcely an option, given the few roads and the distances. An army lorry could move four or five tons at most, a ship a thousand times more.

While fighting to defend Crete and then to evacuate the island's garrison, from May to July 1941, the Mediterranean Fleet lost four escort vessels and had two more seriously damaged in attempts to maintain supplies to Tobruk. The shallow waters off the North African coast were ideal for one of the Italians' favourite weapons, the magnetic mine. Larger vessels were seldom used, drawing too much water to be safe so close to the coast. Cunningham wanted a chain of airfields along the coastline of Libya to provide protection for shipping, and to maintain offensive operations against the Axis in the eastern Mediterranean and the Aegean; but as always, the wish list of a commander in the field had to weighed against those of other commanders elsewhere.

On the North African battlefront, where the British Army had been driving the Italians back, the diversion of substantial forces for the hopeless battle for Greece had left the forces weakened. This was followed by the appointment of a new German commander, General Erwin Rommel. A British offensive, Operation Battleaxe, started on 15 June, but within two days it had run out of steam, as almost half of the 190 tanks employed were destroyed.

TAKING THE OFFENSIVE IN SYRIA

After the loss of Crete, British naval aircraft were based ashore at Nicosia in Cyprus, within easy reach of Vichy French units in Syria, which was invaded by British and Free French forces on 7 June. It was from Cyprus that 815 Squadron attacked French warships on 16 June 1941, when five Swordfish attacked the flotilla leader, *Chevalier Paul*, and another destroyer, *Guépard*. The *Chevalier Paul* was promptly despatched, but Peter Winter and his pilot were shot down and rescued by the *Guépard*. Subsequent events can only be described as bizarre. Taken prisoners of war, the Vichy French contravened the rules of the Geneva Convention by handing over their own POWs to the Italians in Rhodes. Although Vichy forces managed to hang on until 14 July, prompt action by the British then saved the day for the POWs, as the Vichy High Commissioner and Commander-in-Chief in Syria, General Dentz, was rounded up by the British, together with his staff, and held hostage. Three months later, Winter and another forty-nine British POWs were repatriated in exchange for Dentz and his staff.

The invasion of Syria and Lebanon, with the assistance of Free French forces, ousting a pro-German Vichy administration, was a rare instance at this stage of the war of British forces going on to the offensive and actually gaining territory. It was possibly an operation too far, at a time when the situation in the Western Desert was far from secure, and despite this victory, it was clear that Cyprus could still not be regarded as safe.

SAVING MALTA

Further west, 1941 saw the fortunes of Malta at a low ebb. Two large minelaying submarines, *Cachalot* and *Rorqual,* were pressed into service to run fuel to Malta, and any other essential supplies for which they might have space. On operations known to the crews as the 'Magic Carpet', each submarine managed to carry enough aviation fuel to keep the RAF and Fleet Air Arm aircraft on Malta operational for about three days. Malta's agony was to be prolonged until near breaking point was reached – truly the darkest hour before dawn – the following summer.

Meanwhile, there had been a number of smaller but no less useful operations. One typical of these occurred after a Malta-based reconnaissance aircraft reported five Axis merchant ships near Cap Bon in Tunisia, escorted by three destroyers, at around noon on 15 April. Four destroyers, *Jervis, Nubian, Mohawk* and *Janus,* set sail from Malta at 18.00, using the Kerkennah Islands as cover. Sighting the convoy at 01.58 on the morning of 16 April, they discovered that there were indeed five merchant ships being escorted by a single large destroyer and two smaller destroyers. The British ships opened fire at 02.20, and in little more than five minutes, a skirmish had developed. *Jervis* was showered with shrapnel and pieces of metal when an ammunition ship blew up almost a mile away. In due course, one destroyer was sunk and two others set ablaze, while one merchantman was sunk and the other four set ablaze, but at the cost of the loss of *Mohawk,* although her CO, Commander J. W. Eaton, and most of her crew were saved.

By the autumn of 1941, the Axis was finding it almost impossible to keep ground and air forces in North Africa supplied. Typical of the situation in which the Germans and Italians found themselves was an incident on 9 November, after British aerial reconnaissance aircraft had spotted an Italian convoy heading towards Tripoli. Two cruisers and two destroyers, Force K, were sent from Malta, located the convoy by radar and mounted a surprise attack, sinking all seven merchant ships and one of the six escorting destroyers, without any loss. This again forced the Luftwaffe to intensify its action against the Royal Navy, and especially those units based on Malta.

Reinforcements were sent to Sicily in the form of *Fliegerkorps II*, and both U-boats and E-boats were also deployed.

The German involvement in the Mediterranean was not long in bearing results. On 13 November, *U-81* torpedoed Force H's aircraft carrier, *Ark Royal*, but the ship remained afloat until the next day, when she sank, with many British naval officers blaming her loss on poor damage control. Then on 25 November, *U-331* torpedoed and sank the British battleship *Barham*, which blew up as she rolled over, with heavy loss of life: 862 officers and men died. Cunningham had earlier rejected an Admiralty order that *Barham*, which had not enjoyed the same degree of modernisation as *Warspite* and others of the Queen Elizabeth-class, should be scuttled in Tobruk harbour to stem the Axis advance, preferring to see her continue in an active role with the fleet. Despite such setbacks, the Mediterranean Fleet continued to have its victories, as on the night of 12–13 December, again off Cap Bon, when three British and a Dutch destroyer, using the dark coastline behind them to make identification difficult, torpedoed and sank two Italian light cruisers. This was a brilliant action, since the enemy guns should have been able to keep the destroyers at bay.

The Axis were forced to take increasingly desperate measures with ever stronger convoy escorts. On 17 December, three Italian battleships, with five cruisers and twenty destroyers, escorting a convoy to Tripoli, met Rear Admiral Philip Vian with five cruisers and twenty destroyers escorting a Malta-bound merchantman. There was a brief gunnery exchange, before the Italian admiral, Iachino again, broke off as darkness fell. Again, the balance of armament rested with the Italians, and again, they failed to make the most of it.

Force K, which had so easily destroyed an Italian convoy in November, found itself in trouble on 18 December, running into an Italian minefield off Tripoli. The cruiser HMS *Neptune* and a destroyer were sunk, while two other cruisers, *Aurora* and *Penelope*, were badly damaged. Worse was to follow. The Italians had shown some spirit in several destroyer actions, but their real forte lay in individual acts of bravery, with small, select teams taking high risks and achieving worthwhile results. They could not mount a Taranto operation of their own against Alexandria and the British Mediterranean Fleet, but they could launch a human torpedo attack. On 19 December 1941, the submarine *Sirte* carried three two-man human torpedoes (*maiales*) to the entrance of the harbour at Alexandria. Clambering into the torpedoes, the six Italian frogmen submerged and headed for the harbour, where they succeeded in placing the explosive charges, effectively the warhead of their torpedoes, under the battleships *Queen Elizabeth* and *Valiant*, and an oil tanker. The charges exploded, damaging all three ships, and the two battleships were effectively sunk, both of them resting on the bed of the harbour. The Italians did not realise the true extent of their success, however, for the ships remained upright in the shallow water, so that emergency repairs could be carried out before they too followed *Illustrious* to the United States for a complete refit, which delayed their return to service until 1943.

This was not the first time that the Italians had tried to mount such an attack. Apart from the motorboat attack on Suda Bay, Crete on 26 July, mentioned earlier, they had attempted an attack on Malta's Grand Harbour, using a combination of human torpedoes and small motorboats filled with explosives. The attack had been unsuccessful.

The Royal Navy was soon able to copy the Italian human torpedoes, and used these to good effect in the Mediterranean, but less successfully in Norway against the *Tirpitz*. After the Italian surrender in September 1943, several officers volunteered to use the *maiales* against their own warships in German-held ports, and at least one Italian frogman was decorated by the British for this action.

March 1942 found the Mediterranean Fleet back in action, in one of many desperate attempts to run a convoy through to Malta. Force K in Malta provided a cruiser and a destroyer, while Rear-Admiral Vian provided an escort for the four merchant vessels of four cruisers and ten destroyers. This led to the Second Battle of Syrte on 22 March, as Admiral Iachino in the battleship *Littorio*, with three cruisers and ten destroyers, ventured out to destroy the convoy. On sighting the Italian force, Vian left the convoy with a light escort and headed towards the enemy, laying a smokescreen, not so much to hide the convoy, but to hide his own ships so that he could press home a torpedo attack. A strong wind from the south-south-east blew the smoke on to the Italians, who were hindered in pressing home an attack for fear of the British torpedoes. Iachino then tried to cut off the British ships in a feint to the west, hoping at least to catch the convoy, but failed, and after several more attempts withdrew after three hours, leaving two British destroyers damaged, with the loss of two of his own, damaged so badly that they sank in a storm on their way back to base.

Despite this gallant defensive action, the convoy was delayed, and as it approached Malta shortly after dawn on 23 March, it was found by the Luftwaffe's *Fliegerkorps II*, which sank two of the cargo vessels, while the other two were sunk in Valetta's Grand Harbour after mooring and before their cargo could be unloaded.

Malta was by this time approaching the nadir of its misfortunes. Heavy aerial attacks by *Fliegerkorps II* continued throughout April, so that three destroyers and three submarines were sunk, as well as a number of other ships, and the Grand Harbour and the other harbour facilities between Valetta and Sliema, the Marsamxett Harbour and the creeks off it at Sliema, Pieta and Msida were virtually unusable. Submarines were forced to submerge in harbour during the day to avoid aerial attack, while a meagre dribble of supplies, and especially the all-important aviation fuel, were carried to the island on fast runs, known as 'club runs', by fast minelaying cruisers supplementing the work of the large minelaying submarines. That the balance of naval power was swinging against the British at this time may be judged by the loss on 11 May of three out of four Royal Navy destroyers as they attempted to attack an Axis convoy to Benghazi; but again, it was the Luftwaffe that scored this success, in a brutal reminder that naval power was only as strong, or as weak, as the air power that surrounded it.

During June 1942, it was decided to fight two convoys through to Malta, one from Gibraltar and the other from Alexandria, known respectively as Operations Harpoon and Vigorous. The aim was to see whether the presence of either convoy, once detected, would draw Axis fire and act as a relief to the other, or if both were detected, the Axis would be forced to divide their fire. Setting off on 12 June, the two convoys steamed towards Malta. The full weight of light surface units, U-boats and aircraft, was concentrated upon the Alexandria convoy, which lost two freighters. Realising that the Italians had their heavy fleet units at sea, the convoy was recalled to Alexandria, and although the Italian battleship and cruisers did not engage the convoy or its escorts, shore-based aircraft managed to attack the Italian ships. Meanwhile, the Gibraltar convoy lost four out of its six cargo ships, but two managed to reach Malta. The total cost of these two operations was the loss of the cruiser *Hermione* and five destroyers, while another three cruisers were damaged, against which British air power sank the cruiser *Trento* and damaged the battleship *Littorio* using bombs and torpedoes.

OPERATION PEDESTAL

The terrible toll on merchant ships and naval vessels at this time can be attributed to the sheer absence of British naval air power. *Formidable* had not been replaced when she left the Mediterranean for repairs. The lessons were not lost, however, for the next convoy would have naval air power in abundance, and what is more, higher-performance aircraft in the shape of the Sea Hurricane and the Martlet.

The Sea Hurricane was the first attempt to give the Fleet Air Arm the high-performance aircraft it needed. That the Hurricane prototype had made its maiden flight in 1935 shows the urgency that had been given to making good the deficiencies of the fleet; but even when it did first enter service with the Fleet Air Arm in July 1941, the aircraft were all basic conversions from RAF standard machines fitted with arrestor hooks, and without folding wings, so that not every carrier could operate these aircraft because of the limitations on wingspan imposed by some carrier lifts. The absence of folding wings also severely restricted the number of planes that could be accommodated, whether when ranged on the flight deck or struck down inside the hangar. The early Sea Hurricanes had eight Browning 0.303 machine guns, but later aircraft had four 20mm cannon. On the early versions, the 1,030hp Rolls-Royce Merlin III gave a maximum speed of 268 knots. The Hurricane had two advantages over the faster Spitfire (of which the Seafire variant had folding wings); it had a tighter turning radius, always an important feature for a fighter, and it was easier to repair, essential given the limited number of aircraft that could be carried aboard ship.

The Seafire was well liked by some pilots, especially those who had good reason to be grateful for its protective armour. But both the Seafire and the Sea Hurricane were short on range, which imposed brief patrol periods; moreover, the Seafire was not strong enough for repeated deck landings, and had a tendency to bounce on to its nose.

Superior in many respects was the Grumman Martlet, as the Fleet Air Arm liked to call its Wildcats early in the war. Both the RAF and Fleet Air Arm provided names for their US-supplied aircraft until American entry into the war led to the original US names and designations being adopted to avoid confusion. The Martlet was a high-performance naval fighter, designed for the rough life of naval operations. First flown in 1937, it entered FAA service in September 1940. Its Pratt & Whitney Twin Wasp produced 1,100hp, but this could be boosted briefly to 1,200hp for take-off. Maximum speed was 278 knots. The aircraft had been designed for the USN and had folding wings. Its retractable undercarriage was mounted under the fuselage, giving a narrow track, so that in rough seas the aircraft appeared to 'dance' from one undercarriage leg to the other.

The next convoy for Malta was code-named Operation Pedestal, although to the Maltese it became the Santa Maria Convoy, set to arrive shortly before the feast day of the Virgin Mary. That this comprised no fewer than fourteen merchant vessels immediately suggests that heavy losses were expected, for Malta's small-scale port facilities could not cope with anything like as many merchantmen at one time. Vice-Admiral Syfret led the escort with the powerful battleships *Nelson* and *Rodney*, sister ships nicknamed 'Rodnol' because of their supposed similarity in appearance to tankers, with a superstructure well aft and all nine 16in guns in three turrets forward. Better still, there were four aircraft carriers. The veteran *Furious*, by now the only survivor of the three converted battlecruisers, carried Supermarine Spitfire fighters to fly-off to reinforce Malta's air defences. The elderly carrier *Eagle* had left the Mediterranean early in 1941. Considered too slow for fleet actions following the appearance of the fast armoured carriers such as *Illustrious* and *Formidable*, she was now reduced to the more suitable and vital tasks of escorting convoys and acting as an aircraft transport. The other two carriers were the new *Victorious*, a true sister of *Illustrious*, and the even newer *Indomitable*, a modified variant of *Illustrious* with a number of changes, including a second half-hangar extending aft halfway along the length of the upper hangar deck to allow a larger air group to be carried. In addition, there were seven cruisers and twenty-seven destroyers.

Victorious had embarked 809 and 884 Naval Air Squadrons with a total of sixteen Fulmars between them, while there were five Sea Hurricanes of 885 and, for anti-submarine and reconnaissance work, twelve Albacores of 832. *Indomitable* had nine Grumman Martlets in 806, as well as twenty-two Sea Hurricanes in 800 and 880. *Eagle* had sixteen Sea Hurricanes in 801 and another four in 813. Although working as an aircraft transport, there were four Albacores of 823 aboard *Furious* as spares.

By this time, the Italian Navy was confined to port as fuel shortages started to bite, but the Germans had E-boats and U-boats, and of course, there was always the Luftwaffe. Sailing from Gibraltar on 10 August, the convoy almost immediately ran up against Axis attack. First to go was *Eagle*, lost to four torpedoes from *U-73* at 13.15 on 11 August. She rapidly began to list to port, and within four minutes she had gone. It seems almost miraculous that in sinking so rapidly, only 160 of her ship's company of 953 died. Many of the survivors had to spend hours in the water before a destroyer could risk stopping to pick them up. The news of her loss was received with sadness in Malta, as she had flown-off 183 fighters to Malta on her return to the Mediterranean.

Later that day, the first air attacks began, as thirty-six Luftwaffe aircraft left their base in Sardinia to find the convoy at 20.45. The following morning started with an attack by twenty Luftwaffe planes at 09.15, before a combined force of seventy Luftwaffe and Regia Aeronautica aircraft attacked at noon. Around 16.00, one of the escort vessels found and sank a U-boat. Three hours later, another combined strike hit the convoy, this time of a hundred aircraft, sinking one of the merchant ships and so damaging *Indomitable* that she was put out of action. Her aircraft had to be recovered on to the crowded decks and hangars of *Victorious*.

The Sea Hurricane could cope easily with the Ju87 Stuka, but was a poor match for the faster Ju88. 'The speed and the height of the Ju88s made the fleet fighters' task a hopeless one,' wrote Syfret. 'It will be a happy day when the fleet is equipped with modern fighter aircraft.' He seemed unaware that the lumbering Fairey Fulmar had managed to shoot down Ju88s the previous year. In fighter operations, as in all else, the contest was not just between aircraft of varying performance, but pilots of varying experience.

An hour later, twenty Luftwaffe planes attacked, sinking the cruiser *Cairo* and two merchant vessels, as well as damaging the cruiser *Nigeria* and three other ships, including the vital tanker *Ohio*. Darkness brought no relief, E-boats attacked, sinking five ships and so damaging the cruiser *Manchester* that she had to be sunk later. Then, at 08.00 on 12 August, twelve Luftwaffe aircraft from Sicily struck at the convoy, sinking another ship and battering the *Ohio* still further. At 11.25, fifteen Regia Aeronautica aircraft found the convoy, and after the tanker took more hits and caught fire, *Ohio*'s master ordered the crew to abandon ship; but they reboarded her before they could be picked up as she remained afloat. By this time, the main body of the convoy was entering Grand Harbour, but the *Ohio* had to be taken alongside a warship and helped into the port two days late, on 15 August. She was lucky, for another straggler was sunk by a U-boat.

All in all, nine merchantmen were sunk, with the loss of an aircraft carrier and two cruisers, as well as a destroyer, and with serious damage to two other carriers and two cruisers. Oddly, the five merchant ships that reached Grand Harbour were spared any further attacks, at a time when they would have been most vulnerable, waiting to unload at Malta's very limited port facilities.

This was the turning point of the war in the Mediterranean. On 5 November the Battle of El Alamein ended in the defeat of the Italian and German armies. At one stage Rommel's forces had reached a point only 80 miles from Alexandria. Now his retreat into Tunisia removed German pressure on the Suez Canal. Three days later, victory at last appeared possible with the successful Allied landings in North Africa. Then followed the invasion of Sicily in July 1943, after which Malta was no longer in the frontline. The substantial quantity of fuel aboard the *Ohio* ensured that the RAF and Fleet Air Arm units on the island no longer lived a hand-to-mouth existence, and it incited an increasing level of offensive operations, once again putting Axis forces in North Africa under pressure.

Cunningham would not be with the Mediterranean Fleet for much longer. The following year he would become General Eisenhower's naval deputy, but in October 1943, yet higher demands were placed on him, as he became First Sea Lord, taking over from the ailing Dudley-Pound. By that time, Allied naval supremacy in the Mediterranean had been re-established.

CHAPTER SIXTEEN

Aftermath

Winning the battle but losing the war is an old saying that holds much truth. In fact, victory belongs to those who win the last battle of any conflict, and that is usually the side that has lost the early battles. There have been few instances of a nation that has been attacked being able to respond immediately, which makes the United States Navy's victory at Midway, just six months after the attack on Pearl Harbor, all the more incredible.

That Taranto was a great victory cannot be in any doubt. Had the Mediterranean Fleet possessed the air resources enjoyed by the Japanese at Pearl Harbor, the victory would have been even more overwhelming, probably destroying the entire Italian battle fleet, while neither *Illustrious* nor Malta would have suffered so badly at the hands of the Luftwaffe and the Regia Aeronautica. Yet, wishing for such a concentrated carrier force would have been unrealistic. The Royal Navy had sufficient aircraft carriers, but was forced to deploy them so widely that they were indeed thinly spread. The Home Fleet had to contain the threat of German battleships and cruisers that menaced the vital merchant shipping on which Britain's survival depended, and this was made more difficult once the fall of France provided the Kriegsmarine with a fresh string of strategically important bases with good access to the open waters of the Atlantic. Elsewhere, the Royal Navy had to look for commerce raiders in the South Atlantic and the Indian Ocean. The invasion of the Soviet Union by German forces under Operation Barbarossa might eventually have led to the destruction of substantial German armies and ultimately the defeat of Germany itself, but the initial effect was to place a still greater strain on the Royal Navy, with no corresponding benefits. Worse was to come when Japan entered the war, and in addition to the loss of major surface units for want of air cover, the Royal Navy soon lost an aircraft carrier, the elderly *Hermes*, to Japanese air attack. The carrier, being too small and too slow, could no longer operate fighters.

Here too was another problem. The Fleet Air Arm in 1940 did not possess any aircraft comparable with those that attacked Pearl Harbor, or those that wiped out a Japanese fleet of four aircraft carriers at Midway. Naval air power rests not on ships alone, and the Royal Navy lacked planes to match those in service with the United States Navy and the Imperial Japanese Navy. In the late twentieth century, three aircraft, the American McDonnell Douglas F-4 Phantom and LTV A-7 Corsair II, and the British Blackburn (later Hawker Siddeley) Buccaneer, finally showed that naval aircraft could match the performance of their shore-based rivals. This was not the case, however, during the early stages of World War Two, and even later in the war and during the early post-war years, such aircraft were rare indeed, with the Grumman Hellcat and Hawker Sea Fury being among the exceptions.

That the Fleet Air Arm pulled off a magnificent victory at Taranto is also underlined by the chilling reminder of what happened at Petsamo and Kirkenes. Had that been the outcome at Taranto, British naval aviation would have suffered a serious setback, indeed, it could even have been terminal. Instead of proving its worth, it would have justified the doubts of the 'big gun' brigade. Naval air power would have been reduced to reconnaissance and reporting the fall of shot, plus anti-submarine operations in support of convoys, as the first auxiliary or escort carriers were already being planned.

Attacking the Italian fleet while lying at anchor was an import element of this success. In the Battle of Midway, where the United States Navy won an overwhelming victory and condemned the Japanese to ultimate defeat, sinking four carriers in one day, the USN suffered its worst losses among the crews of the torpedo-bombers. The Japanese carriers proved themselves to be 'soft' targets, vulnerable to the accurate American dive-bombing. The effectiveness of the dive-bomber against even heavily armoured carriers such as *Illustrious* and then, a little later, her half-sister *Formidable*, could be clearly seen, but these ships survived to fight another day. Had *Ark Royal*, or the trio of converted battlecruisers, been on the receiving end of either of these attacks, the outcome, as Pound noted, might have been different. Even *Eagle*, although a converted battleship, had a flight deck that, as one officer put it, 'seemed to flex under the feet'. As it was, *Illustrious* survived to serve with distinction in the Far East, where she suffered yet another gruelling attack, and after the war had the distinction of being the first aircraft carrier to operate swept-wing aircraft in trials with the Supermarine Swift. The survival in some quarters of the old attitude that carriers could not operate high-performance aircraft may be judged by the fact that the Fleet Air Arm had to operate the straight-winged Sea Hawk, whereas the RAF enjoyed the Hawker Hunter, an aircraft that did on one occasion hold the world air speed record.

Why did they succeed at Taranto? One reason must be the sheer brilliance of the plan and the determination to make it work. Too few thought that a large battle fleet assembled in a well-defended harbour would be at risk, especially given the extensive AA fire that the battleships and cruisers could put up in their own defence. As we know, Pound, while pressing for the operation, was pessimistic as to its outcome.

Yet victories are seldom won by boldness and brilliance alone. They are also lost by the enemy. The Italians lacked radar and night-fighters, let alone a system that would control them. This was compounded by poor reconnaissance that would have kept them aware of the movements of the Mediterranean Fleet. Here too was a comparison with the Battle of Midway, where Japanese problems were exacerbated by their inept reconnaissance first thing in the morning, leaving far too many gaps – genuine blind spots – that were exploited by the enemy.

Among many of the World War Two combatant nations, there was often a lack of coordination and co-operation between the different armed forces, and even between air forces and navies. This certainly applied to the Italian Navy and the Regia Aeronautica. Worse, there also appeared to be an element of stupidity, a refusal to appreciate the obvious. If, given the Fulmar's record in despatching 'shadowers', Italian reconnaissance aircraft were failing to return, surely someone should have queried what was happening. Were Italian aircraft so unreliable that mechanical failure was to blame? Was the weather so bad that aircraft were being lost? The answer to both questions was an emphatic 'no'. In any case, an aircraft in difficulties often has time to transmit a 'Mayday' signal.

Perhaps, most telling of all was the Italian failure to appreciate the value of the aircraft carrier. This alone could have been the single main reason for the success at Taranto. Neither the Germans nor the Italians really understood what naval aviation was all about. The Germans allowed themselves to be side-tracked by a prolonged dispute between the Luftwaffe and the Kriegsmarine over who controlled naval aviation. The Italians would have had a similar problem, but even this pales into insignificance set against the refusal to comprehend just how potent a force an aircraft carrier could be, even with elderly aircraft, capable of travelling the oceans at will and arriving ready for operations.

At Taranto, as at Pearl Harbor, the failure to mount a second attack deprived the operation of its full benefit, although at Taranto, to be fair, bad weather intervened. The attack would have had to take place on the night of 12–13 November before the surviving enemy battleships and cruisers were moved. It is possible that the Italian defences would have been more effective on the second night, although several of the ships that had seen action during the first attack were no longer in contention. On the other hand, lingering in a position from which a second attack could have been mounted, *Illustrious*, her aircraft and her escorts would all have been at risk. It seems highly unlikely that she would have avoided discovery a second time round, in which case the terrible events of the following January might have been brought forward. This was an important consideration. At the time, aircraft carriers were an increasingly scarce and precious commodity, and fast armoured carriers such as *Illustrious* even more so.

One option that was not possible was a further attack by carrier-borne aircraft on the Italian battleships once they were in their new and safer anchorages further north, even though Force H with *Ark Royal* did later mount a hit-and-run attack on Genoa. This was risky in such confined waters with Axis aircraft from Sicily and Sardinia added to those based on the mainland. Certainly, Force H could not have supported the Taranto operation without alerting the Italians, and there would have been problems of coordination and planning with aircraft coming from two carriers and arriving from opposite directions. Later in the war, once the Royal Air Force had the Avro Lancaster heavy bomber, as well as large bombs of 12,000lbs and 22,000lbs, the 'Tall Boy' and 'Grand Slam' respectively, the preferred technique of despatching large ships, and heavily fortified positions ashore, was to drop such bombs next to the target. This technique capsized the German battleship *Tirpitz*, hiding secure in a Norwegian fjord, but such options were not available in 1940, or indeed for most of the war.

Yet, if Taranto came as a nasty shock to the Italians, it must also have been something of a surprise to the British. Cunningham took time to appreciate the value of what had been achieved. Churchill seems to have forgotten it fairly quickly, or perhaps the 'former naval person' was too preoccupied with the war ashore. The suspicion remains that the reason why the bravery of the forty-two men who went to Taranto was treated so lightly was simply that they suffered so few casualties. The Fleet Air Arm's two VCs of World War Two were both awarded to men who died pressing home their attacks. Had half of those at Taranto failed to return, the Victoria Crosses could well have rained down upon them.

APPENDIX I

Comparison of Ranks

OFFICERS

RN	RAF
Admiral of the Fleet	Marshal of the RAF
Admiral	Air Chief Marshal
Vice-Admiral	Air Marshal
Rear-Admiral	Air Vice-Marshal
Commodore 2nd Class	Air Commodore
Captain	Group Captain
Commander	Wing Commander
Lieutenant-Commander	Squadron Leader
Lieutenant	Flight Lieutenant
Sub-Lieutenant	Flying Officer
Temporary Sub-Lieutenant	Pilot Officer
Midshipman	no equivalent
Warrant Officer	Warrant Officer

In the Royal Marines, Captain equalled Lieutenant and Major equalled Lieutenant-Commander.

RATINGS (RN) AND NON-COMMISSIONED RANKS

Chief Petty Officer	Flight Sergeant
Petty Officer	Sergeant
Leading Airman	Corporal

Below this, the Royal Navy, in descending order, has ABs (Able Bodied Seamen) and then Ordinary Seamen, while the RAF has SACs (Senior Aircraftmen), LACs (Leading Aircraftmen) and then Airmen.

APPENDIX II

Honours and Awards

The Supplement to the *London Gazette* on 20 December 1940, announced the award of the DSO to the leaders of the two strikes, Lt-Cdrs N. W. Williamson and J. W. Hale, while the DSC was awarded to their observers, Lts N. J. Scarlett and G. A. Carline respectively, and to Capt O. Patch of the Royal Marines and his observer Lt D. G. Goodwin, RN.

The New Year's Honours List for January 1941 recorded that Rear-Admrial A. L. St G. Lyster became a CB, while Capts D. W. Boyd of *Illustrious* and R. M. Bridge of *Eagle* both received the CBE.

It took some time before those in authority recognised just what had been achieved, and it was not until May 1941 that a further Supplementary List was announced. The DSO was awarded to Lt G. R. M. Going, and the DSC to Lts F. M. A. Torrens-Spence, C. S. C. Lea, L. J. Kiggell, R. W. V. Hamilton, H. R. B. Janvrin, A W. F. Sutton, and to Sub-Lts A. S. P. Macaulay, R A. Bailey, P. D. Jones, A L. O. Neale and J. R. Weekes. Lts H. I. A. Swayne, M. R. Maund, G. W. Bayley, H. J. Slaughter and Sub-Lts W. C. Sarra and A. J. Forde, were Mentioned in Despatches, as were eight members of the ship's company.

APPENDIX III

Fleet Air Arm Training in 1940

By 1940, a system of training had been evolved with the Fleet Air Arm's needs in mind, especially the all-important question of flying aircraft from and back to the deck of an aircraft carrier. This was to be refined throughout the war as the Royal Navy took over more of its own training, helped later by training in the United States, which owed so much to Lumley Lyster and the American Admiral Jack Towers.

PILOTS

The glamour of flying – and perhaps for some the extra pay – meant that there was a steady stream of volunteers. Another incentive was the realisation that the most likely outcome for the majority of those who registered compulsorily for National Service was to join the Army. As in peacetime, the initial step was to visit a recruiting office. At first the system was overwhelmed. One man who wanted to fly and thought first of the Royal Air Force was told that he would have to wait until he could be called up because of delays in training all the volunteers available. The Fleet Air Arm was suggested as a way of jumping the queue, with the Royal Marines as another alternative. He opted for the Fleet Air Arm, only to find that the recruiting office had run out of forms. Another man volunteered for the Fleet Air Arm, thinking that he might become an aircraft mechanic, but again there were no forms and when they were sent to him through the post, he found that they were stamped PILOT OR OBSERVER.

Once the forms were completed and sent off, the successful applicant would be summoned to HMS *St Vincent*, the barracks at Gosport, the small town across the harbour from Portsmouth. It was here, in groups of forty or so, that volunteers were given a thorough medical examination. Those who passed then faced an Admiralty interview board, a triumvirate chaired by a senior officer, up to and including a rear-admiral, supported by an instructor lieutenant-commander and an engineer, usually a lieutenant-commander or commander. The board made its decision immediately and usually told the successful applicant whether he was to become a pilot or observer, although sometimes he could make a personal choice. He was then sent home until a vacancy could be found on a course.

Training began with a return to HMS *St Vincent*, but often this substantial stone frigate was overcrowded, and so the overflow was sent to HMS *Daedalus*, just three or four miles away and otherwise known as RNAS Lee-on-Solent, for a week or so until accommodation was available. Recruits joined in batches of fifty or sixty every four weeks, forming into courses with those for observers given even numbers and those for pilots odd numbers. Although almost all of them were to be commissioned, at the start of their training they were kitted out with standard naval ratings' uniform, as naval airmen second class, including bell bottoms. For security reasons – and doubtless economy too as postings between ships were much more frequent in wartime – wartime ratings' cap ribbons no longer showed the name of their ship, but just the simple 'HMS'. Some found a supplier able to produce ribbons showing 'FLEET AIR ARM', but this was unofficial and could only be swapped for the correct ribbon once away from base.

At first, pay was low, given that a well-paid skilled man could expect to earn around £3.10s (£3.50) a week in pre-war Britain. The new recruits received just 14 shillings (70p) per week, but a cup of tea in the NAAFI cost only a penny, and bed and board was free. Cigarettes were a shilling a hundred as they were duty free for naval personnel.

While wartime training was accelerated, the basics were still not ignored. The old 'scrub deck' Navy was not going to encourage any sloppiness, so recruits spent seven weeks at *St Vincent* learning to march, salute and look after their kit, handle a machine gun and gain the rudiments of navigation, Morse, semaphore and meteorology. At the end of their basic training, they would have to pass an examination and then be handed over to the RAF for their elementary flying training at either Elmdon, now Birmingham International Airport, or Luton, now London Luton Airport.

They graduated from *St Vincent* with anchors on their upper sleeves, showing them to be leading naval airmen, equivalent to a corporal in the RAF or Army. At Luton, basic training was given on Miles Magisters, 'Maggies', streamlined monoplanes, while at Elmdon the training was on de Havilland Tiger Moth biplanes. Either way, RAF instructors believed that they could tell whether or not someone was pilot material within a week. On the Tiger Moth, some went solo after as little as five hours, and few took more than ten hours; on the Magister, with a higher wing loading, it took longer, but anyone taking twelve hours started to worry about his chances. Depending on the weather, elementary flying training took around eight weeks, with the student pilots spending between fifty and sixty hours in the air. Pay at this stage was 6s 6d (32.5p) a day, of which 3s 6d was flying pay. On the debit side, as they were on an RAF station, cigarettes now cost 6d for ten, and a half pint of bitter was also 6d.

Graduating from Luton or Elmdon they were still, in naval terms, rated as Leading Naval Airmen, but wore white cap ribbons to show that they were future officers. During the war, one of the many differences between the Fleet Air Arm and the RAF was that almost all naval pilots and observers – the naval term for navigators – were commissioned, whereas the RAF had large numbers of non-commissioned aircrew. Generally, the only way a pilot or observer would be non-commissioned, usually flying as a petty officer or chief petty officer, equivalent to sergeant and flight sergeant respectively, was if they were guilty of a serious misdemeanour during training, which would also have included a prison sentence. Such cases were rare, and normally telegraphist air gunners (TAGs) were the only rating aircrew.

They were now at the RAF's No.1 Service Flying Training School at Netheravon, where they were streamed to become fighter or bomber pilots. This was a big step forward, especially for the prospective fighter pilot who found himself flying Fairey Battles as a prelude to Skuas and Fulmars. The future bomber pilot had a gentler introduction to heavier and higher performance aircraft, starting on Hawker Hart biplanes, as a useful prelude to the Swordfish or Albacores in service with the Fleet Air Arm.

Students at Netheravon were meant to emerge with well over a hundred flying hours, but during the early years of the war it suffered from a shortage of aircraft. It was not unknown for half-a-dozen keen would-be fliers to arrive at dispersal to find just one aircraft, and sometimes none at all. The uncertainties of the British weather could also cut the hours flown, so that sometimes the new pilot would have as little as eighty-eight hours of solo flying. At Netheravon they learned formation flying and aerobatics, night flying, navigation and instrument flying, with dive-bombing for the bomber pilots and fighter tactics for the rest, including shooting at towed targets. On leaving Netheravon, the new pilots received their wings. The pass rate must have varied, but it seems that on average about half failed, or 'dipped', in naval slang. There were also casualties, from accidents and, occasionally, from enemy action.

Leaving Netheravon, the new pilots received their first leave since joining up, just a week, with their commissions dated from the end of the leave. They were all commissioned into the RNVR. Here age played an important part as those over twenty-one years of age became temporary sub-lieutenants, those under twenty-one, temporary acting sub-lieutenants, and those under twenty temporary midshipmen. The last not only received less money, but were not allowed to buy spirits and were usually confined to the gunroom mess rather than admitted to the wardroom.

Thus far the men had been in the hands of the hard-pressed RAF, and now they returned to the Royal Navy for their operational training. They would learn how to handle naval aircraft, and how to fly from aircraft carriers or from the catapult of a cruiser or other major fleet unit. Here they would come across another FAA/RAF difference. The RAF had operational training units, the Fleet Air Arm treated theirs as naval air squadrons, with numbers in the 700 series, along with squadrons handling a miscellany of other supposedly non-operational tasks.

Carrier-deck landing training was given when needed, with refresher training after any lengthy period spent flying from a naval air station. After using a runway marked out as a carrier deck, the new pilots would have a chance to learn on the real thing. The deck-landing school was at RNAS Arbroath, HMS *Condor*, known to some as Aberbrothock, where there was also an observers' school. The fighter school was initially at RNAS Yeovilton, where the circuit became so congested and overcrowded with inexperienced pilots that an unacceptably high number of accidents occurred before an additional training airfield was established nearby at Zeals. The men received torpedo training at RNAS Crail, in Fife, HMS *Jackdaw*. Advanced instrument training was given at RNAS Hinstock, HMS *Godwit*, which also accommodated the anti-submarine school.

During the evacuation from Dunkirk, as mentioned earlier, a number of Fleet Air Arm squadrons were assigned to the RAF, operating under the control of Coastal Command. Shortly afterwards, during the Battle of Britain, the Fleet Air Arm had sufficient pilots, but too few aircraft, so that many pilots and some maintainers were loaned to the RAF. This did at least

ensure that a number of naval airmen had experience of the higher performance fighter aircraft that were to be introduced to the Fleet Air Arm a
year or two later.

OBSERVERS

Initial training for observers was similar to that for aspiring pilots, including the spell at *St Vincent*. The role of observer entailed more than merely
that of a navigator. He did indeed observe, took photographs and, in the
catapult flights, could be called on to help relay the fall of shot in a naval
gun battle. An observer also had to know how to handle the radio, especially in aircraft without a TAG, or when the latter was replaced by a fuel
tank, as happened often with the Swordfish. In naval aviation at this time,
it was thought that even fighter aircraft needed an observer given the
greater problems of finding a fast-moving carrier at sea. This, of course,
also affected the performance of the aircraft, having two seats instead of
one.

The two main observer schools were at Ford, later transferred during the
Battle of Britain to Yeovilton, and at Arbroath. No. 1 Observer School, at
Ford and then Yeovilton, used a variety of aircraft, including Percival Proc-
tors, Albacores, Barracudas, Walrus and Grumman Goose. No. 2 Observer
School at RNAS Arbroath, HMS *Condor*, consisted of 740, 741, 753 and 754
squadrons, again with a mixture of aircraft, including Proctors, Walruses,
Swordfish and Kingfishers. In the early years some Seafoxes, Sharks and
Seals were also stationed there. At one point, 754 Squadron operated a substantial number of Westland Lysanders, designed as Army co-operation
aircraft but in this case used as target tugs.

DECK-LANDING CONTROL OFFICERS

HMS *Illustrious* introduced the role of deck-landing control officers, or
batsmen, as they were known, to the Royal Navy. As war progressed and
their use became compulsory, a school was established at East Haven, home
of the Deck Landing Training School. They were all experienced naval
pilots, and gave up their flying pay on being selected for the arduous and
dangerous task. Initial training consisted of aircraft from the training
squadron, 731, whose pilots endured the nickname of 'clockwork mice',

flying circuits that involved dummy deck landings.

TELEGRAPHIST AIR GUNNERS

Telegraphist air gunners, TAGS, were naval ratings, generally leading hands or petty officers, with the highest rank on a squadron usually being a chief petty officer. Training took six or seven months, during which they would be expected to accumulate sixty hours' flying time. As with so many Fleet Air Arm tasks, what would now be called 'multi-skilling' was the order of the day, so during initial training at RNAS Worthy Down, home of No. 1 Air Gunners School, three squadrons, 755, 756 and 757, provided the early and advanced elements of their wireless course and air gunnery respectively. The advanced wireless course included cross-country flying and beacon flying, suggesting some overlap with the role of the observer. The advanced element of the air gunners' course was provided by 774 Squadron, with live firing at St Merryn in Cornwall.

MAINTAINERS

Throughout the Royal Navy there was a two-tier system for technical ratings. The fully trained tradesmen were known as 'artificers', with their work supported by the less skilled naval air mechanics and riggers. This system increased the manpower available in the shortest possible time, and made the best use of the more skilled men. The less skilled air mechanics were often at leading rank, but could advance to the senior rates. Artificers were normally petty officers, or chief petty officers, and had either served an extended service apprenticeship, at this stage provided at RAF Halton, or were reservists bringing their civilian skills with them.

Heading the artificers and mechanics on any squadron would be an air engineer officer. During the early part of the war, mechanics and riggers, who looked after the airframe, were assigned a specific aircraft, so that a good rapport often developed between aircrew and maintainers. Later, what amounted to a 'garage system' was introduced, with manpower being concentrated on aircraft in turn.

The maintainers were also dependent on the Royal Air Force for their training. The RAF, accustomed at worst to training relatively raw naval recruits, was faced with experienced men accustomed to their own routines and naval jargon. They were divided up by specialisation, airframes, engineers, electrical and ordnance, with training at RAF Henlow, St Athan, in South Wales, and Eastchurch, on the Isle of Sheppey, respectively. Training took about a year, and for the naval air mechanics (A), was divided between six months at Henlow and then four months at RAF Locking, near Weston-super-Mare.

For the naval air mechanics (A), training embraced the theory of flight as well as aircraft repairs and general maintenance, including work on the fabric covering of many airframes, and the study of aircraft hydraulic and pneumatic systems. There was no automatic promotion to a higher rate on completing the courses. The naval air mechanics of all kinds were posted to HMS *Daedalus* at Lee-on-Solent to await drafting to their squadrons. In contrast to modern practice, where special training is regarded as vital for working on different types of aircraft, no such training was given in most cases, although handbooks were usually available. At lower deck level, the numbers of ratings would be increased by the 'hostilities only', or HO, intake.

Glossary

A Air Branch of the RN or RNVR

AA Anti-aircraft

AB Able-bodied Seaman

ADDL Aerodrome dummy deck landing

ASW Anti-submarine warfare

Capt Captain

CAP Combat air patrol

CB Companion of the Order of the Bath

CCA Carrier controlled approach

Cdr Commander

C-in-C Commander-in-Chief

CO Commanding Officer

CPO Chief Petty Officer

DLCO Deck Landing Control Officer, more usually known as the 'batsman'

DLP Deck landing practice

DLT Deck landing training

DSC Distinguished Service Cross

DSO Distinguished Service Order

Dt detachment

E-boat German MTBs or MGBs

FAA Fleet Air Arm

Flt Flight

HMAS His Majesty's Australian Ship

HMS His Majesty's Ship

JNAF Japanese Naval Air Force

Lt Lieutenant

Lt-Cdr Lieutenant-Commander

MAC Merchant Aircraft Carrier

MGB Motor Gunboat

MTB Motor Torpedo Boat

OBE Officer of (the Order of) the British Empire

PMO Principal Medical Officer

PO Petty Officer

POW Prisoner of war

PR Photo-reconnaissance

RAF Royal Air Force

RCNVR Royal Canadian Naval Volunteer Reserve

RM Royal Marines

RN Royal Navy

RNAS Royal Naval Air Station

RNR Royal Naval Reserve

RNVR Royal Naval Volunteer Reserve

TAG Telegraphist Air Gunner

TBR Torpedo Bomber Reconnaissance

TSR Torpedo Spotter Reconnaissance

U-boat German submarine

USN United States Navy

VC Victoria Cross

Bibliography

Bragadin, M. A., Commander, *The Italian Navy in World War II*, Annapolis, Maryland, US Naval Institute Press.

Bradford, Ernle, *Siege Malta, 1940–43*, London, Hamish Hamilton, 1985.

Cunningham, Admiral of the Fleet Lord, *A Sailor's Odyssey*, London, Hutchinson, 1951.

Jones, A., *No Easy Choices; A Personal Account of Life on the Carrier* HMS *Illustrious, 1940–43*, Worcester, Square One, 1994.

Lamb, Cdr C., *War in a Stringbag*, London, Cassell, 1977.

Newton, D., *Taranto*, London, Kimber, 1959.

Nichols, Cdr J. B. USN (Ret) and Pack, S. W. C., *Cunningham the Commander*, London, Batsford, 1974.

Poolman, K., *Illustrious*, London, Kimber, 1955.

Roskill, Capt S. W., *The Navy at War, 1939–45*, London, HMSO, 1960.

— *The War at Sea, 1939–45*, Vols I & II, London, HMSO, 1976.

Schofield, B., *The Attack on Taranto*, London, Ian Allan, 1973.

Smithers, A., *Taranto 1940 – A Glorious Episode*, London, Leo Cooper, 1995.

Winton, J., *Air Power at Sea, 1939–45*, London, Sidgwick & Jackson, 1976.

— *Carrier Glorious – The Life and Death of an Aircraft Carrier*, Leo Cooper, 1986.

Wragg, D., *The Fleet Air Arm Handbook, 1939–45*, Stroud, Sutton, 2001.

— *Carrier Combat*, Stroud, Sutton, 1997.

— *Wings Over The Sea: A History of Naval Aviation*, Newton Abbot and London, David & Charles, 1979.

Index

Figures in **bold** refer to maps and diagrams.

Nairana, HMS 9
Naples, air raid on 138
naval aviation 2, 169–70, 200
naval warfare 2–5, 62–3
Neale, Sub-Lieutenant (A) J. W. 99, 130
Nelson, HMS 196
Neptune, HMS 192
Netheravon 208–9
Nevada, USS 166–7
Nicholls, Roger 38
Nicola Fabrizi 127
Nigeria, HMS 197
Nordholz, raid on, 1914 4
Norman, Kathleen 155
North Africa 50, 70, 135, 189–90, 191, 198
Norwegian campaign 22, 31, 169
Nubian, HMS 127, 187, 191

observers 40–41, 46, 83, 210
O'Connor, Captain Rory 64
Ohio 197, 198
oil 175
Oklahoma, USS 166
Operation Battleaxe 190
Operation Crack 86
Operation Excess 137–50
Operation Harpoon 194
Operation Hats 71–4
Operation Judgement 86
Operation Pedestal 196–8
Operation Tiger 185–6
Operation Vigorous 194
Opie, Lieutenant-Commander, USN 68, 96, 103
Orion, HMS 126–7
Otranto, Straits of 93, 121, 126–7
Ottoman Empire, collapse of 10

Pack, S. W. C. 179–80, 180
Paine, Sub-Lieutenant (A) S. M. 101, 112, 131
Pantellaria Straits 72
Patch, Captain Oliver 65, 100, 111, 129, 131, 133
Pearl Harbor, attack on 124–5, 164–8
  comparison with Taranto raid 159–61, 164
  planning 161–3
Pegasus, HMS 9
Penelope, HMS 192
Pennsylvania, USS 165, 167
Perkins, Sub-Lieutenant (A) E. A. 103, 132, 146
Perth, HMS 155
Pessagno 123
Petsamo, Finland 170

raid on 171, 172, 200
Phoebe, HMS 182
pilots 40–41, 61, 206–10
Pola 131, 181–2
Pollock, Lieutenant David 88–9, 103
Pound, Admiral Sir Dudley (1877-1943)
  24–6, 66, 176, 198
Pridham-Wippell, Vice Admiral 126, 179–80, 187
Prince of Wales, HMS 53

Queen Elizabeth, HMS 185, 187, 193

radar 79
Ramb III 127
Ramillies, HMS 87, 88, 135
ranks, comparison of 204
Read, Captain Albert 47
recognition 129–34, 203
reconnaissance photographs 88–9, 91, 92–3
Regia Aeronautica 50–2, 59
  attacks on *Illustrious* 71–2, 73, 78–9, 121
  attacks on Pedestal convoy 197
  attacks on the voyage to Taranto 88, 90
  dusk attacks 81
  failure of 125–6
  and the Luftwaffe 136
  raids on *Illustrious* at Malta 154
  raids on Malta 60–1, 155
Regia Navale: see Italian Navy
Renown, HMS 177
Rhodes 73
Riccardi, Admiral 54–5
Riviera, HMS 4
Robertson, Commander Flying J. I.
  'Streamline' 29–30, 34, 36, 69, 96
Rodney, HMS 196
Rommel, General Erwin 190
Rorqual, HMS 191
Royal Air Force ix, 2, 7–8, 10, 16, 40, 41
  air crew 208
  bomber missions 117
  Cunningham's attitude to 184
  large bombs 202
  and Malta 57, 184
  at Matapan 180–81
  ranks 204
  reconnaissance flights 82–3, 85–6, 88–9, 121
Royal Fleet Auxiliary 88
Royal Marines 41, 204
Royal Naval Air Service 2, 4, 7–8
Royal Naval Reserve 40
Royal Naval Volunteer Reserve 40, 41, 46